BrightRED Study Guide

CfE HIGHER

PSYCHOLOGY

Alistair Barclay

BrightRED
PUBLISHING

First published in 2020 by:
Bright Red Publishing Ltd
Mitchelston Drive Business Centre
Kirkcaldy
KY1 3NB

A CIP record for this book is available from the British Library

ISBN 978-1-84948-343-8

With thanks to:
PDQ Digital Media Solutions Ltd (layout) and Jill Broom (edit)

Cover design and series book design by Caleb Rutherford – e i d e t i c

Acknowledgements
Every effort has been made to seek all copyright holders. If any have been overlooked, then Bright Red Publishing will be delighted to make the necessary arrangements.

Permission has been sought from all relevant copyright holders and Bright Red Publishing are grateful for the use of the following:

Images licensed by Ingram Image on pages 6, 8, 9, 10, 11, 12, 13, 14, 15, 16, 17, 20, 22, 23, 25, 26, 44, 61, 62, 64, 67, 70, 72, 81, 83, 87, 88, 94, 95, 97, 98, 104, 106, 120, 122; Public domain images on pages 18, 32, 63, 74, 75, 83; Gary Ullah (CC BY 2.0)[1] (p 19); Alan Light (CC BY 2.0)[1] (p 21); delta_avi_delta (CC BY-SA 2.0)[2] (p 24); petrograd99/iStock.com (p 29); Ales Kladnik (CC BY 2.0)[1] (p 30); Heidi Blanton (CC BY-SA 2.0)[2] (p 31); City.and.Color (CC BY 2.0)[1] (p 32); Ed Uthman (CC BY-SA 2.0)[2] (p 34); SteFou! (CC BY 2.0)[1] (p 35); Ewen Roberts (CC BY 2.0)[1] (p 39); Beta-J (CC BY 2.0)[1] (p 44); Chris Engelstad (CC BY 2.0)[1] (p 45); Vic (CC BY 2.0)[1] (p 46); http://mindmapping.bg (CC BY-SA 2.5)[3] (p 52); Samuel Zeller (p 53); Shuets Udono (CC BY-SA 2.0)[2] (p 55); nesnad (CC BY 3.0)[4] (p 55); Simon Matzinger (p 56); Lee Brimelow (CC BY 2.0)[1] (p 56); Bundesministerium für Europa, Integration und Äußeres (CC BY 2.0)[1] (p 57); Fred the Oyster (CC BY-SA 1.0)[5] (p 58); rawpixel.com (p 59); Judith E. Bell (CC BY-SA 2.0)[2] (p 73); World Trade Organization (CC BY-SA 2.0)[2] (p 74); Martin Kozák (p 75).

A note from the author:
With love to FABDOC.
With thanks to many inspiring relatives, critical friends and supportive in-laws.
Thanks for setting the bar high.
Thanks to all the staff at Bright Red for believing in this book.
Special thanks to John MacPherson for publishing the new edition of this book amid all the uncertainties of a national emergency.

Printed and bound in the UK.

CONTENTS

INTRODUCTION

INDIVIDUAL BEHAVIOUR

Sleep, dreams and sleep disorders

Memory

SOCIAL BEHAVIOUR

Conformity and Obedience

Prejudice

RESEARCH

The Research Process

The Research Assignment

THE HIGHER PSYCHOLOGY EXAM

INDEX

INTRODUCTION

STUDYING CFE HIGHER PSYCHOLOGY

The Higher Psychology course consists of two sections: Social psychology and individual psychology. The research topic is assessed by marking the content of your course assignment, but the research topic can also feature in any part of the exam. The final grade on your certificate is assessed by the question paper and the research assignment. This guide is designed to help you achieve an A grade.

HOW THIS BOOK WILL HELP YOU

You're presented with lots of information in the classroom during your course year at school or college. Your tutor will use handouts, books, photocopies, notes, mind-maps, posters and flashcards. So, what do you revise? What do you need to know and what can you miss out? This is called 'intelligent selection'. But, how do you intelligently select and narrow down what to study? This guide is here to help you.

It includes the key information needed for the whole Higher Psychology course, allowing intelligent selection during your precious revision time. Here, you'll find the essential material for passing the course (the assignment and the exam) in an easy-to-digest and concise form.

Use this book and, the chances are, your Higher Psychology grade will improve.

WHY STUDY HIGHER PSYCHOLOGY?

This will depend on your ambition. You may want to gain some insight into your friends' and family's behaviour. You may want to understand the workings of the human brain, or know why people seem so odd and hard to fit in with. Perhaps you want to go to university to study the social sciences and become a criminologist. Maybe you want to become a Sports Psychologist for the Olympic team, or become a nurse and interpret people's social behaviour. It could be you want to become a primary school teacher and study child development. Alternatively, you may wish to write books or pursue a career in expressive drama.

Studying Higher Psychology will develop the critical skills necessary for pursuing any of these goals. It will help you to analyse different human perspectives, evaluate emerging theories, explain scientific concepts and interpret empirical evidence. Completing the Higher Psychology course is a strong leap onto a springboard to advance your ambition.

My ambition is for there to be fewer conflicts in the world. I want to encourage people to talk together. I want to get rid of the prejudices in society and encourage everybody to get along. Studying Higher Psychology can help us all get closer to this goal.

This course has every chance of improving your quality of life. It has an applied component to health and wellbeing in all topics, so studying Higher Psychology helps promote mental health and wellbeing throughout Scotland and abroad. Not bad for a set of SQA tests!

HIGHER PSYCHOLOGY COURSE ASSESSMENT

This course has an external exam. This is a closed-book question paper and represents most of the total mark. There is also a research assignment to complete for the rest of the total mark and this is usually sent by your centre to the SQA well before the end of the course.

THE EXTERNAL ASSESSMENTS: TWO COMPONENTS TO COMPLETE

Component 1: Question Paper
The question paper will sample your psychological knowledge and analytical skills. You are asked to explain human behaviour from a range of perspectives and for

contd

a range of topics. The quality of your answers, in terms of explanation, evaluation and analysis, are used to determine how many of the total marks you will get.

There are two sections of the question paper. Section 1 tests your knowledge of the research process and research topics. Section 2 samples your knowledge of topics from the psychology of individual behaviour. Section 2 asks questions on topics from the psychology of social behaviour.

Component 2: Research Assignment

Your research assignment takes the form of a report on an investigation carried out by you, first hand. The report is written by you and should document how you planned, carried out, analysed and evaluated a psychological research investigation you did during the course. You need to plan this research assignment with your tutor. The quality of your final report determines how many of the total marks you get.

The research assignment requires you to carry out your own primary research on a topic or brief chosen by you and your tutor. This gives you the chance to use your communication and research skills to generate, select, organise, interpret, analyse and evaluate real psychological data.

DON'T FORGET

The question paper and the research assignment will be marked externally by SQA.

DON'T FORGET

Remember, if you work for a very good mark in your research assignment, you're close to achieving one third of the course marks.

HOW TO EXPLAIN

Good **explanations** come from well supported points linked to what you are explaining. A key skill for Higher is how to explain theories, concepts and psychological factors. Do this by referring to supporting research evidence and relevant examples. Here's a tried and tested way to explain:

Point-Evidence-Explain (The PEE technique of Explaining)

In all sections of the Higher Psychology exam you can approach questions with a technique called 'Point-Evidence-Explain'. The PEE technique will keep your answers relevant to the task and supported by psychological research.

> **The PEE Sandwich – it sounds disgusting, but it works:**
>
> **POINT:** Make an unsupported point about some behaviour or psychology (1 mark)
>
> **EVIDENCE:** Give an example of research or behaviour as evidence to support your point. This evidence will be relevant to your point. (1 mark)
>
> **EXPLAIN LINK:** Explain *how* the example research evidence or everyday behaviour supports the point. Remember to link it back to the question or task. (1 mark)

HOW TO ANALYSE

Good **analysis** comes from explaining the links between one effect and another. You can achieve ANALYSIS by comparing one piece of research with other research. You can also explain the importance of any research.

> A key phrase to use for analysis is '***This matters because...***'

The GRAVES technique

The GRAVES technique uses an analysis mnemonic to help remember relevant **analysis paragraphs**.

You can add the GRAVES technique to extend your analysis of research:

- G = Is the research general?
- R = Is the research reliable?
- A = Is the research applicable and important to everyone?
- V = Is the research valid when taken out of the laboratory?
- E = Is the research ethical?
- S = Is the sample representative for general conclusions?

Analysis paragraphs will include the consequences of research, why the research is useful and how important the research or theory is to society. So, when analysing, explain why this research or theory matters. Remember, GRAVES and *'This matters because...'*.

SLEEP, DREAMS AND SLEEP DISORDERS

WHAT IS SLEEP?

Sleep, dreams and sleep disorders is the name of the mandatory individual topic for Higher Psychology. So, let's get started defining these terms: what is sleep and what are dreams? Sleep disorders will be discussed later.

SLEEPING: WHAT IS SLEEP?

It's hard to define sleep. However, it's seen as a recurring, but altered, state of lowered consciousness with reduced nervous-system activity and relaxed muscles. It is a time when the eyes are closed, but they can be in motion. The sleeper often experiences some muscle paralysis.

Sleep can also be viewed as a state of suspended consciousness, where perceptual awareness and other cognitive functions are greatly reduced in responsiveness. Shakespeare called sleep a 'little death'.

Example:

To define sleep, Carskadon et al (2000) described sleep as a 'reversible behavioural state of perceptual disengagement from, and unresponsiveness to, the environment'.

Why do we sleep?

There are a number of psychological theories about the purpose of sleep. These include the biological-restoration theory of sleep by Oswald (1966) – that sleep refreshes the body – and the information-consolidation theory of sleep and dreaming by Crick and Mitchison (1986) – that we sleep in order to process information we've acquired during the day.

DON'T FORGET

It helps to know that 'et al' is used in Psychology books to shorten lists of authors' names. 'Et al' is a Latin abbreviation for 'and associates'. You can use the phrase when referring to long authors' references to save time and effort.

ONLINE

Try downloading and sleeping with a profiling app for a smartphone. In some of these phone applications, you can see a graph of the quality of your sleep for one night measured by the phone's motion detectors.

DREAMING: WHAT IS A DREAM?

Almost everyone can remember having a dream, but what a dream is remains elusive. Dreams are, certainly, mental experiences – but dream content can be surprising.

Dreams occur beyond our everyday understandings of perception. We experience a dream in a lowered state of consciousness. Dreams appear in the host's mind as apparent perceptions. Only self-report measures, such as asking people, can reveal dream content.

People describe dreams as a series of thoughts, images and sensations that often form an incomplete story. Dreams pass through the sleeper's head, mostly involuntarily.

What turns a dream on?

Classic research by Dement and Kleitman (1957) first provided evidence that the phase of sleep when the eyes move rapidly (REM sleep) is the time for dreaming. However, taking a biological approach to answering this question, Solms (2000) has recently reported neuropsychological evidence for a dopamine mechanism in the forebrain that switches dreaming on – usually, but not exclusively, during REM sleep.

Why do we dream?

What determines dream content? What's going on, both physiologically and psychologically, in dreams, in a typical night's sleep?

There are various psychological theories of the purpose of dreams. These include the biological theory of activation/synthesis by Hobson and McCarley (1977) and the psychoanalytic theory of 'wish-fulfilment' dreaming first proposed by Freud in the early 1900s in his *Interpretation of Dreams*.

Will the dream be a reverie or a nightmare? Few can determine this in advance. Dreaming is generally outwith personal control. However, LaBerge et al (1980) define lucid dreaming as the exception to this rule – a lucid dream is a controllable dream.

THINGS TO DO AND THINK ABOUT

What useful variables can be measured to assess sleep quality and quantity?
Try expanding some of these acronyms for the *Sleep, dreams and sleep disorders* topic:

SOL: Sleep Onset Latency (how long it takes to get to sleep)

NWAK: the Number of aWAKenings during a sleep episode

WASO: the time of Waking After Sleep Onset

TST: Total Sleep Time

REM: Rapid Eye Movement

NREM: Non-Rapid Eye Movement

EOG: Electro Occulo Gram (eye motion detection)

EEG: Electro Encephalo Gram (cortical activity detection)

ECG: Electro Cardio Gram (heartbeat detection)

EMG: Electro Myo Gram (muscle activity detection)

DON'T FORGET

The Higher Psychology course will assess your skills in explaining approaches and evaluating theories.

DON'T FORGET

In Psychology, the answers to learn are rarely black and white. Rather, there are viewpoints to explain and theories to analyse with different pieces of research evidence for and against.

ONLINE TEST

Head to www.brightredbooks.net to test yourself on sleep and dreaming.

THE BIOLOGICAL APPROACH TO SLEEP AND DREAMS

At least three different approaches to psychology can help explain the functions of sleeping and dreaming. You will be encouraged to explore the topic of *Sleep, dreams and sleep disorders* using three different psychological approaches. First, the biological approach will be introduced, then the cognitive approach and, finally, the psychoanalytic approach.

SLEEP – THE BIOLOGICAL APPROACH

The biological approach concentrates on biochemical processes such as genetic inheritance, hormone levels and neurotransmitter activity. It focuses on medical applications to health care and improving wellbeing by using medical techniques such as prescribing medication. The biological approach explores which biological processes rest, and which physiological processes continue, during sleep.

To evaluate the biological approach, one strength is its success in revealing the biological and physiological nature of sleep and dreaming. However, the biological approach misses out analysing the subjective content of dreams and ignores the effects of thinking and beliefs on sleep.

In 1937, Loomis published a paper stating that sleep was ***not*** one homogenous physiological state or condition. There were measurable changes in physiology during sleep. This raises the question – what biological function is sleep performing?

VIDEO LINK

Watch 'Circadian Rhythms' at www.brightredbooks.net and hear Michel Siffre talk about his 70 days underground in a cave without clocks or external timekeepers. How did Siffre know when to stop sleeping and start his day?

DON'T FORGET

Learning research studies off by heart will not be enough to achieve the Higher. You'll need to show explanatory, analytical and evaluative skills for the full breadth of the course.

The Biological Approach – Classic Sleep Research

In 1953, Aserinsky and Kleitman were the researchers who first distinguished between REM sleep and NREM sleep (that is, non-REM) sleep. They specified four stages of NREM sleep based on the typical EEG wave patterns identified as occurring in each phase. Later, Rechtschaffen and Kales (1968) established a wave measurement and categorisation system for establishing the stage of NREM or REM sleep from EEG and EOG waves.

Aserinsky and Kleitman (1953) had observed eye motion during sleep and used the term REM sleep. In defining REM sleep, they wrote about a measurable, recurring sleep state with rapid eye motion (REM).

They observed participants sleeping with an EOG sensor on their eyes. They observed and recorded rapid eye motion occurring again and again in some states of a typical night's sleep. REM sleep was not just at the beginning of a night's sleep or at the end of a night's sleep, but recurring rhythmically and cyclically throughout a period of long sleep.

Thus, the biological approach to sleep has relied on measuring physiological changes such as EEG and EOG changes during sleep and dreaming to build a biological perspective on sleep and dreams.

Biological psychologists refer to rhythms in polysomnograph records to explain and describe how humans sleep. They illustrate these changes in physiology by referring to circadian rhythms and ultradian rhythms.

contd

Aserinsky and Kleitman (1953) proposed sleep consisted of four NREM stages:

- Sleep Onset: NREM Stage 1

- Light Sleep: NREM Stage 2

- Deep Sleep Onset: NREM Stage 3

- Deep Sleep: NREM Stage 4

They also described REM sleep and observed that it occurs as a distinctly paradoxical light sleep (similar to NREM Stage 2) but with associated EOG activity. This is paradoxical because it has characteristics of light sleep (that is, high frequency EEG activity), but there is, generally, strong paralysis of the body (called REM atopia) more often associated with a deep-sleep phase of sleep paralysis (NREM atopia).

In 1957, Dement and Kleitman (1957) went on to make laboratory observations of volunteer sleepers to support the link between periods of EOG activity (during REM sleep) and periods of dreaming during this same time.

Example:

Higher Analysis: When using the biological approach to treat insomnia, melatonin can be used as a prescribed medication in the evening. This acts to advance the circadian rhythm of sleep onset. While it is true this body hormone acts to bring on biologically based circadian rhythms, the mechanism is far from direct. There are problems with the timing of the melatonin supplement as many hormones, not just melatonin, are involved in regulating sleep.

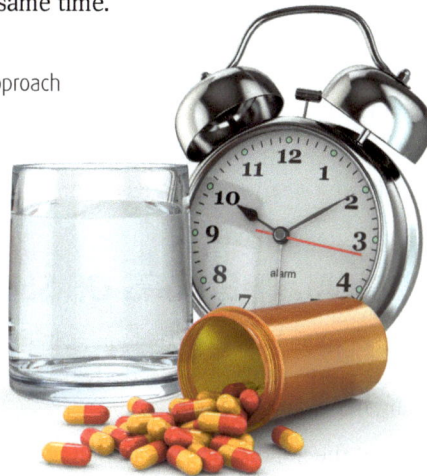

THINGS TO DO AND THINK ABOUT

Extended Question Checklist:

When you come to write extended answers, ask yourself: have I done the following?

- Have I introduced and explained the topic?

- Have I written about two approaches?

- Have I made links between two approaches and relevant research?

- Have I evaluated both the approaches and the relevant research?

- Have I applied the topic to everyday life?

DON'T FORGET

You can show your explanation and evaluation skills in the exam by making links with other factors that affect the topic, comparing alternative theories and referring to different approaches.

VIDEO LINK

Watch the BBC Horizon documentary with Professor Robert Winston called 'Horizon: Secrets of Sleep' at www.brightredbooks.net. This includes a national sleep survey using the Epworth Sleepiness Scale and a test to see if you are a lark or an owl. This is very relevant to studying this topic.

ONLINE TEST

To test yourself on the biological approach to sleep and dreams, head to www.brightredbooks.net

BIOLOGICAL THEORIES OF SLEEP AND DREAMS 1

What are the functions of sleep? Why do we sleep and why do we dream? Is sleep necessary? If so, for what reason and why? Are dreams meaningful or just a random side effect of sleeping? This section aims to help explain and evaluate a few sleeping and dreaming theories.

WHY DO WE SLEEP?

The reasons for sleeping and dreaming can be explained using several different approaches. As already discussed, this text applies three different psychological approaches in turn. First, biological theories, using a biological approach, are explained. Then we'll explore cognitive theories that all adopt an essentially cognitive approach. Finally, the psychoanalytic approach to explaining dreams is analysed, using Freudian theories.

A theory or viewpoint on sleeping and dreaming is a set of assumptions and hypotheses that explain why sleep and dreams occur.

DON'T FORGET ⊕

An approach to psychology is a set of theories that share some feature and can be grouped together as an 'approach'.

BIOLOGICAL THEORIES OF SLEEPING AND DREAMING

A biological explanation can be given as a theory of why we sleep and dream. Generally, biological theories propose an underlying biochemical mechanism, for example, something happening in the brain.

Evidence for the importance of sleep in restoring the biological functions of the body comes from a wide range of sources: neuro-anatomical findings for the role of the brain in controlling sleep (for example, the suprachiasmatic nucleus, SCN) and EEG studies combined with polysomnograph records showing circadian rhythms in sleep.

The biological approach to sleep has resulted in greater understanding of the types and phases of sleeping and dreaming, for example, during REM sleep and NREM sleep. Sleep is so ubiquitous in animals that it must be performing an important function. However, exactly which biological functions sleep performs is still unclear.

DON'T FORGET ⊕

There are many different theories and viewpoints on the functions of sleep and dreaming. The search for why we sleep and why we dream is an active area of current psychological research.

Biological: Oswald's (1966) Restoration Theory of Sleep

The most straightforward biological theory of sleep is Oswald's (1966) restoration theory of sleep. Oswald's (1966) theory might explain the positive effects of gaining more sleep on health and wellbeing.

Oswald (1966) claims that slow wave sleep (SWS) – that is, deep sleep – is reviving because it is restorative. According to this view, time spent in SWS provides the body with a biological rest-break for the physiology of the body and brain to recover.

contd

In this biological restoration theory, sleep helps to maintain and restore the body's internal balance. Evidence for this comes from Kreuger et al (1985), reporting that a lack of SWS sleep reduces the function of the immune system. Thus, restoration theory states that sleep can be explained by declaring it to have a rebalancing role in restoring normal cellular functions.

Some biological theories of sleep suggest other body-maintenance functions. For example, Sassin et al (1960) showed that periods of deep sleep correlate with the time that growth hormone is released.

Biological: The Evolutionary Benefits of Sleeping

Another group of biological theories suggest that sleep is an adaptive behaviour in terms of genetic fitness. According to this view, there may be an evolutionary benefit of staying asleep – such as energy conservation (Webb 1982), protection from predators (Meddis 1975) and regulating food-foraging behaviour (Tobler 2008).

These are all biological, evolutionary theories that share the reliance on Darwin's theory of natural selection and 'survival of the fittest'. Any instinctive behaviour, such as sleep, that promotes survival will be beneficial to the organism's chances of survival. Three evolutionary theories of sleep are presented briefly below:

Example:

Webb (1982) Energy Conservation during Sleep: A Hibernation theory of Sleep

Webb (1982) proposes a hibernation theory of sleep, suggesting that sleep helps conserve energy. Evidence for this comes from Zepelin & Tobler (2008) who present correlations between sleeping and an animal's core body temperature. They note that core body temperature is lowered during mammalian sleep and this must save energy. In addition, they note that small animals with high metabolic rates tend to sleep for longer than larger animals.

Example:

Meddis (1975) Sleep as an Evolutionary Legacy: Protection from Predators

According to Meddis (1975), prey must hide from predators and keep out of harm's way. As a result, sleeping at certain times, out of sight from predators, may have had an evolutionary advantage in the past. Time asleep may have provided protection from predators by avoiding moving about while they hunted. Equally, there may also have been an evolutionary benefit of staying awake during the day such as being alert to dangers.

Example:

Tobler (2008) Sleep as an Evolutionary Legacy: Time-Distance from Starvation

Other biological theories such as those by Tobler (2008) are also based on evolution and propose a genetic legacy in our behaviour. This theory suggests sleep was used to regulate and control hunting rates, eating behaviour or foraging activity. Tobler has, inversely, correlated sleep duration to the amount of time needed to collect food and positively correlated sleep duration for many species with the time-distance from organism starvation.

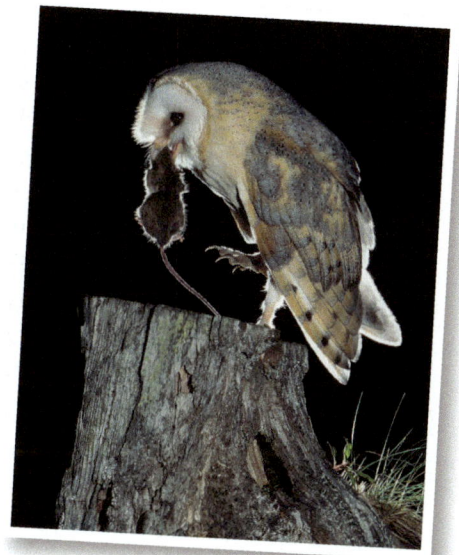

ONLINE

For more zoological papers by Professor Irene Tobler on rodent sleep and mammalian sleep, see www.brightredbooks.net

THINGS TO DO AND THINK ABOUT

Don't mess with my core sleep!

Biological Health Warning! Core Sleep and Optional Sleep – Horne (1988)

Horne proposed there might be multiple reasons for sleep having an evolutionary advantage. As a result, Horne (1988) went on to propose that some sleep is essential (core sleep) while some sleep might be unnecessary (optional sleep).

Can you evaluate the biological approach to sleep?

The biological reasons for sleep are not well established in the literature. Most evolutionary theories lack practical results to confirm or refute the theoretical reasons suggested.

ONLINE TEST

To test your knowledge of the theories of sleep, head to www.brightredbooks.net

BIOLOGICAL THEORIES OF SLEEP AND DREAMS 2

EVALUATION OF THE BIOLOGICAL THEORIES OF SLEEP

The biological reasons for sleep are not well established in the literature. Most evolutionary theories lack practical results to confirm or refute the theoretical reasons suggested. However, there are many evaluative points you can make about biological sleep theories.

Some strengths and weaknesses of the biological theories of sleep are listed here. You might be able to add your own criticisms and your own support for these biological theories – as long you back these up with explanation, analysis or evidence.

Strengths

- Oswald's (1966) restoration theory of sleep appeals, as we do all feel better after a good sleep. Clinical evidence supporting this comes from intensive care units in hospitals. According to Salas & Gamaldo (2008), recovery rates from invasive body surgery and medical operations are better if sleep deprivation is avoided in the post-operative recovery period.

- Clinical research studies are now providing correlational support for Oswald's (1966) restoration theory – that poor quality sleep is less restorative to the body than uninterrupted sleep. For example, Savard et al (2003) found a positive correlation between sleep reduction and the reactivity of the immune system.

- Van Cauter and Plat (1996) correlated deep sleep with the time that growth hormone is released. This gives evidence for Oswald's (1966) theory that cellular restoration, cell development and body repair as well as body growth all occur during sleep.

- Total daily sleep duration has been linked to rates of biological restoration and age. Roffwarg et al (1966) present daily total sleep time percentage data showing that people sleep less per 24 hours as they grow older. During infancy and the early years, when there is rapid growth and high rates of neurogenesis, children sleep for a much higher percentage of the time than adults. Sleep duration decreases when body growth has ceased. The results of Roffwarg et al (1966) link sleeping with body development and age-related growth.

- Restoration theory fits with Marks et al (1995) biological view that sleep patterns are linked to chronological age. With growth and restoration proposed as the function of sleep, the requirement for sleep should reduce with age and maturity. Does sleep follow a genetically controlled pattern of cell growth and body development across the lifespan?

contd

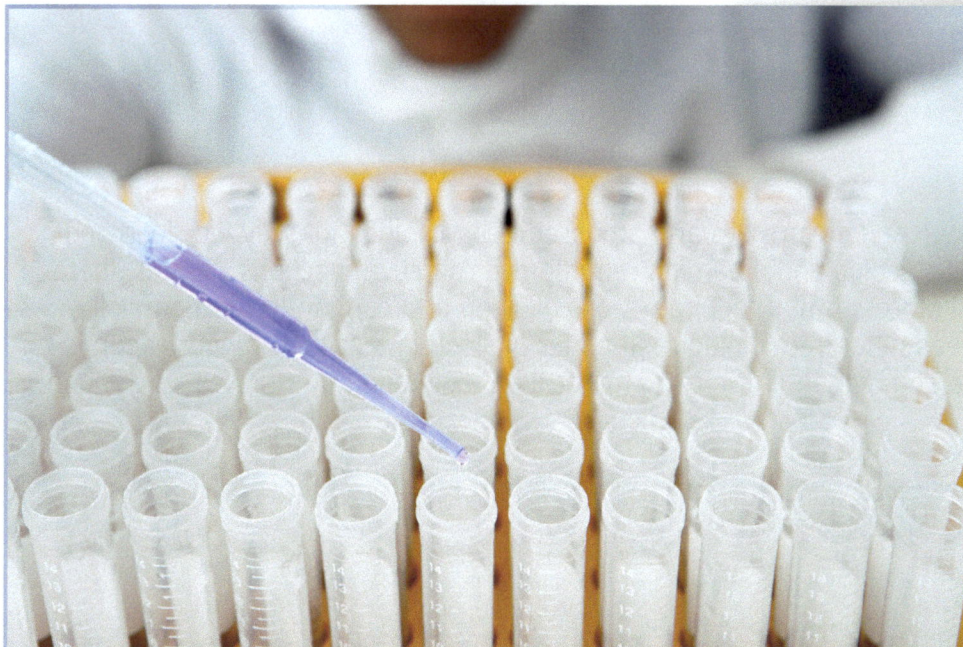

Weaknesses

- Many studies on the effects of sleep are correlational rather than experimental. This means some sleep reports are based on observational work or self-reported, questionnaire data rather than experimental procedures, so no causal relationship can be shown.

- Sleep research studies often test the opposite of the biological restoration hypothesis (that disruption of sleep reduces the effectiveness of the body's cellular processes) rather than directly testing the theory that sleep positively restores the body's cells. Evolutionary theories are in danger of becoming 'Just So' stories, where the effect is used to describe the cause, rather than the cause being fully identified in the theory. In each case, when explaining sleep behaviour, evolutionary theories take the view that 'sleep' exists, therefore it must have some survival advantage. However, in humans, an organ called the appendix exists and it's agreed to be unnecessary.

- Even if sleep was adaptive in our evolutionary history, much of it may now be unneeded. The human environment is now so different from the prehistoric environment that our evolutionary adaptation is fitted to a long-gone environment. Indeed, much of our circadian sleep pattern may now be unnecessary if the original purpose of a night's sleep was to avoid nocturnal predators that are now extinct, for example, the sabre-toothed tiger.

ACTIVITY: EXAM PRACTICE QUESTION:

Explain one psychological theory of the function of sleep and dreams   (8 marks)

ONLINE

Head to www.brightredbooks.net for more revision notes on the biology of sleep. There's a good section on biological rhythms and zeitgebers (external factors that affect sleep).

THINGS TO DO AND THINK ABOUT

Overview of sleep and dream theories – What should you revise?

For this course, as a minimum, you must be able to analyse, explain and evaluate at least three sleep and dream theories. The three mandatory theories for this course are as follows:

1. The biological-restoration theory of sleep by Oswald (1966).

2. The information-consolidation (cognitive reorganisation) theory of dreaming by Crick and Mitchison (1986).

3. The psychoanalytic approach to explaining dreaming including Freud's (1900) wish-fulfilment theory of sleep and dreams.

ONLINE TEST

To test your knowledge of the theories of sleep, head to www.brightredbooks.net

COGNITIVE THEORIES OF SLEEP AND DREAMS 1

Cognitive theories of sleep and dreams are also proposed in psychology for why we sleep and dream. These claim that sleeping and dreaming can improve cognitive functions – that is, there may be internal mental processes that require periods of sleep or dreaming to function well. Cognitive theories of sleep differ from biological theories of sleep in that they suggest sleep is mainly for maintenance and growth of the mind rather than maintenance or growth of the body.

Example:
Sleep and cognition

Cognitive functions that may be improved by sleep are memory, perception-reaction times, attention, language skills and critical thinking abilities. It may also benefit our problem-solving skills.

> **DON'T FORGET**
>
> Cognitive theories of sleep do suggest that gaining more sleep will restore cognitive skills after a sleep debt or sleep deprivation. However, cognitive theories of sleep *do not* suggest we will get cognitive superpowers if we continue to have very long sleeps.

COGNITIVE: CRICK AND MITCHISON'S (1983) REORGANISATION THEORY OF SLEEP

One main cognitive theory of sleeping and dreaming, proposed by Crick and Mitchison (1983), is the reorganisation theory of sleep. According to this consolidation theory, we 'prune' useless memories during REM sleep.

Crick and Mitchison argue that sleep-time allows us 'downtime' to find redundant memories, and dream-time is when this pruning is done (that is, during REM sleep). REM sleep is when we dream, according to Dement & Kleitman (1957), and this is when our mind works through our long-term memories and we forget redundant, useless memories in order to free up space for only what's relevant to us.

Crick and Mitchison (1983) claim that dream sleep (REM sleep) is the time for information consolidation, and this is in line with Stickgold (1998) who sees sleep as an important time for 'offline' memory reprocessing.

> **DON'T FORGET**
>
> The reorganisation theory is also known as the information-consolidation theory.

Axmacher et al (2008) have developed the memory consolidation theory further by proposing an **initial learning phase** in memory formation (for example, during the day, learning something new). Then there is an **information consolidation phase** that may

contd

become saturated during the day, so a period of sleep is needed to allow the second phase of information consolidation to complete. They conclude from monitoring EEG patterns around the hippocampal region (see page 32) during rest that sleep facilitates memory recall. They conclude that memory transfer from the hippocampus to the neocortex is facilitated during the first resting state immediately following encoding.

It may be that different cognitive skills benefit from different types of rest or sleep. For example, REM sleep may be preferentially important for the consolidation of procedural memories, while deep, slow wave sleep might be critical for long-term, episodic memory.

Evidence for this comes from Plihal and Born (1997) who compared sleep intervals (REM and NREM) with waking intervals after participants learned either a verbal, paired list or a procedural, mirror-drawing task. Their results, from a sample of 20 people, showed REM rich sleep improved memory for paired associate words better than SWS did. The word pair association memory task can be described as a **declarative** memory task. They also found that performance on a mirror-drawing task was improved *more* after a similar interval of rest rich in deep sleep rather than rich in REM sleep. The mirror-drawing task is described as a **procedural** memory task.

COGNITIVE: HOBSON AND MCCARLEY (1977) ACTIVATION-SYNTHESIS THEORY

Some theories consider dreams to be meaningful, personal and significant in revealing unconscious wishes, along the lines of Freud's (1900) wish-fulfilment theory. However, Hobson and McCarley's activation-synthesis theory states otherwise.

They explain dreaming as random cognitive events that are triggered by incidental neural firings while asleep. These random activations are synthesized by our cortex into a coherent dream 'story'. According to Hobson (2002), dreams are simply by-products of our sensory system struggling to make sense of meaningless, and apparently random, neural activations in our brains during the sleeping period.

Hobson and McCarley's (1977) activation-synthesis theory fits well with the subjective experience of dreaming. It explains the often-bizarre nature of dreams that can move from one conception to another without the constraints of waking reality, while, at the same time, our dreaming mind tries to maintain a coherent perception of random neural firings.

In Hobson's (2002) view, the side effect of internal, neural activations (such as occasional PGO waves of activation, characteristic of dream sleep, from the limbic system to the cortex) is that our perceptual systems cognitively construct a likely interpretation of all the ongoing neural firing.

VIDEO LINK

Watch the Pixar movie *Inside Out*. This animation gets close to representing Crick and Mitchison's information-consolidation theory in long-term memory with a vacuum cleaner!

DON'T FORGET

It is worth remembering that PGO waves are activation spikes detectable during sleep in the brain that occur while dreaming. PGO waves flow from the pons area in the limbic system to the lateral geniculate nucleus and then to the occipital lobe (the visual processing area of the brain).

ONLINE TEST

To test your knowledge of the theories of sleep, head to www.brightredbooks.net

THINGS TO DO AND THINK ABOUT

Keep a dream diary for seven nights

Hall and Van de Castle (1966) analysed the content of 10 000 dreams by classifying their content into designated categories. They found dream content was related to age, gender and social class.

Why not keep a sleep diary for one week? Choose ten categories of dream **before** you write up a record of your dreams.
Then, look at which category is most frequent. Keep a note of some key sleep variables, like TST, SOL and NWAK for seven nights. This could give you an idea for your research assignment!

COGNITIVE THEORIES OF SLEEP AND DREAMS 2

EVALUATION OF THE COGNITIVE THEORIES OF SLEEP

Like all theories, the cognitive theories of sleeping and dreaming can be evaluated.

Strengths

- Evidence for the cognitive theory of information consolidation during sleep by Crick and Mitchison (1983) can be seen in the paper by Axmacher et al (2008) which relies on interpreting intracranial EEG traces from the hippocampus during periods of sleep in their patients. Their results support the view that long-term, declarative memory encoding is facilitated by memory-trace transfer from hippocampus to cortex (consolidation) in the first period of sleep or rest after learning.

- There is much experimental support for Crick and Mitchison's view that the function of sleep is cognitive reorganisation. For example, according to Huber et al (2004), slow wave sleep can increase some forms of learning by up to 25%.

- There is emerging evidence that learning of procedural skills benefits from a period of sleep before testing. According to Walker et al (2005), finger-tapping exercises were learned better after an interval of sleep rather than being awake. This supports Crick and Mitchison's (1983) information-consolidation theory.

- Primary insomnia sufferers (who can be assumed to be sleep deprived over a long period of time), show marked decreases in cognitive tasks. The specific cognitive tasks affected by insomnia include concentration skills, memory tests and problem-solving. This also supports Crick and Mitchison's (1983) information-consolidation theory.

- Payne and Nadal (2004) have linked Crick and Mitchison's (1983) information-consolidation theory to the activity of cortisol in the brain. They have concluded that cortisol is the main regulator of how much REM and NREM sleep occurs. The sleep deprivation case study of Peter Tripp, who stayed awake for 200 hours, showed serious cognitive decline after a few days without sleep. He was unable to conduct simple memory tests and, towards the end, he started hallucinating. This is consistent with Crick and Mitchison's (1983) view that sleep is necessary for the reorganisation of memories and this case study supports information-consolidation theory.

DON'T FORGET

Don't forget to mention both theories and research in your sleep topic explanations – for example, 'Hobson and McCarley's (1977) random activation–synthesis theory is not supported by Freud's findings from his case studies'.

contd

Weaknesses

- However, sleep deprivation case studies show only short-term effects on the cognitive skills of participants. For example, in the case of maximally sleep-deprived Randy Gardner, after 11 days of no sleep, he was still able to communicate. He only showed a couple of days rebound sleep and reported no *lasting* cognitive side effects. Sleep is not a single event; it has many phases and stages, as the biological approach has revealed. Plihal and Born (1997) found better verbal-learning performance after a deep sleep interval, while they found mirror tracing improved faster after a period of REM-rich sleep, rather than SWS or being awake.

- Axmacher et al (2008) concluded that the length of sleep itself is not the important factor in information consolidation. Any length of sleep helps the reorganisation of memory. Perhaps any period of rest allows information to be reconstructed more efficiently than before.

- Not all animals have the same cognitive skills, yet sleep is almost universal in the animal world. There might be a more basic reason why sleep is needed than only for information consolidation. The cognitive effects of sleeping only explore one level of explanation of the function of sleep (Hobson, 1995): cognitive psychology often misses out the other biological reasons why sleep might be necessary. For example, the immune system recovers during sleep and this might be a more basic reason why sleep is necessary.

- Hobson and McCarley (1977) suggest dreams are incidental and constructed from random neural firings. Yet many psychologists, including Freud (1900), have concluded that dreams are not at all random. The content of dreams often relates to the concerns of the individual; for example, dreams often relate to recent experiences and appear highly meaningful to the sleeper. This goes against Hobson and McCarley's (1977) activation-synthesis hypothesis about dreams.

THINGS TO DO AND THINK ABOUT

Sleep topic practice questions: Theories of dreaming

The focus of debate nowadays on dreams is, what is their function? Are dreams meaningful wish-fulfilment, as Freud (1913) claimed or meaningless activation syntheses as Hobson and McCarley (1977) claimed?

Try these questions:

1. Explain the reorganisational theory of sleep and dreaming.

2. Explain the activation-synthesis theory of dreams.

3. Describe the research evidence for and against two theories of dreaming.

ONLINE

Read the *Psychological Research* paper by Born and Wilhelm (2012) on information consolidation during sleep at www.brightredbooks.net

ONLINE TEST

To test your knowledge of the theories of sleep, head to www.brightredbooks.net

PSYCHOANALYTIC THEORIES OF SLEEP AND DREAMS 1

The psychoanalytic approach to sleep and dreams attempts to explore the role of the unconscious part of the mind in sleep and dreams. The main origin of psychoanalytic theory is from Sigmund Freud's writings on the human psyche. While someone sleeps, it can appear that not much is happening in their mind. However, many unconscious processes may still be active in the psyche. Psychoanalytic theories assume the unconscious mind is in psychodynamic motion rather than fixed, resting or static during sleep.

INTRODUCTION TO PSYCHOANALYSIS

Psychoanalytic theories of sleeping and dreaming claim that your dreams represent your unconscious desires.

Example:

'The pig dreams of acorns and the goose dreams of maize.' A Hungarian saying, recalled by Freud in his book *The Interpretation of Dreams*, 1913.

Freud presents dreams as being wish driven. His theory is that dreams are all expressions of wish-fulfilment.

PSYCHOANALYTIC THEORIES OF SLEEPING AND DREAMING

Most psychoanalytic theories of sleep and dreams rely on Freud's psychosexual wish-fulfilment theory of dream interpretation.

Freud created psychoanalysis as a movement in psychiatry. Famous psychoanalysts who have built on Freudian concepts include Carl Jung, with his theory of the collective unconscious; Alfred Adler, with his theory of the personality; and Karen Horney, with her view on the self-concept.

Many psychoanalytic theories have emerged after Freud. For example, Virginia Axline was a neo-Freudian psychoanalytic therapist. She developed 'play therapy' to help children express their unconscious and hidden motivations through drawing and play, as they were not easily interviewed.

Viktor Frankl promoted his interpretation of suffering in dreams as an applied clinical attempt to find personal meaning in painful memories with post-traumatic stress victims.

Psychoanalysis is now a whole approach to psychology, and it may be defined as any theory or technique of psychological analysis that relies on models or interpretation of the unconscious, or hidden memories of, the mind.

DON'T FORGET ✚

All of Freud's case-study evidence relied on retrospective clinical accounts, poorly remembered childhood memories and highly personalised clinical interpretations.

PSYCHOANALYTIC: FREUD'S (1913) THEORY: THE INTERPRETATION OF DREAMS

Freud noted that, in the retelling of a dream or a story, unadmitted motivations hide behind the often unsatisfactory explanations given by the dreamer. As a result, in his *Interpretation of Dreams*, Freud looked for everyday meanings that revealed unconscious desires, repressed wishes, jealous affections and psychosexual motivations.

Freud was an associationist more than a rationalist; thus, he was looking for the unconscious rules that govern the associations between one thought and the next.

contd

He applied associational rules equally to conscious thoughts and to unconscious dreams. He was looking for the fundamental rules of association between thoughts and dreams.

Why do dreams reveal the unconscious? While asleep, the unconscious can express itself more freely. During the day, the psyche guards itself from emotional upsets, disturbing emotions and sexual desires by employing many subtle, unconscious methods. Freud called these unconscious protection methods 'ego defence mechanisms'. When the dreamer is asleep, the ego defence mechanisms of the psyche are relaxed or altered.

Manifest content and latent content

Freud declares there are two types of dream content that must be considered: manifest content and latent content.

- **Manifest content** is what the dream appears to be about. A dream about a cigar may just be a dream about a cigar. However, while Freud claims some dreams appear to be random nonsense, some dream content may have deeper meaning.

- **Latent Content** is what is symbolic in the dream. The latent content is the disguised wish, desire or urge – the hidden meaning of the dream. So, a dream about a horse may not be just a dream about a horse; it may be that the horse is associated with a parent.

To illustrate interpretation of latent content in dreams, Freud wrote extensively about a few clients' dreams. In one case study called 'Little Hans' (1909), Freud wrote about the interpretation of a small boy's dream. Freud linked the manifest content of Hans' dream to latent content about Hans' fear of his father. (For more about the 'Little Hans' case study, see pages 96–97.)

Further Freudian dream interpretations include Dora's dream of a funeral, his own dream about Irma, and 'Anna O's dream about her mother. Freud used these dream case studies to illustrate his psychosexual theory of child development.

Overall, Freud's theory is that dreams represent unconscious wish-fulfilment in terms of their setting, their characters and the scenes created in the dream. Dreams are not random; they are highly motivated by unconscious associations and Freud concludes they are the 'royal road to the unconscious'.

Freud's Hydraulic Theory of the Human Psyche

Later, Freud presented a hydraulic model of the human psyche. This is his theory of the unconscious and the conscious parts of the human psyche. This shows how latent dream content can influence the manifest dream content of a sleeper. There are three main components in his theory: the action of the id, the ego and the superego all combine to form the personality. These components are further explained on the next page.

ONLINE

Visit the Freud Museum in London online by following the link at www.brightredbooks.net See Freud's original psychoanalytic therapy couch!

THINGS TO DO AND THINK ABOUT

The psychoanalytic approach

Here are five revision questions. After studying psychoanalysis and Freudian theory, try these Freudian 'psychoanalysis' questions on sleep, dreams and sleep disorders:

1. Why are dreams meaningful according to Freudian theory?

2. According to Freud, what forms the content of a dream?

3. Explain how Freud used case-study research evidence to support his dream theory.

4. Describe how psychoanalysis is applied to PTSD (post-traumatic stress disorder).

5. Evaluate psychoanalysis as an approach to explaining sleep and dreams.

ONLINE TEST

Test yourself on the psychoanalytical theories of sleep and dreams at www.brightredbooks.net

PSYCHOANALYTIC THEORIES OF SLEEP AND DREAMS 2

PSYCHOANALYTIC: FREUD'S (1913) THEORY: THE INTERPRETATION OF DREAMS

The id, ego and superego

Freud used the three components of the psyche – the id, ego and superego – to describe the architecture of the human psyche. The chambers of his hydraulic model form a pressure (steam-based) conception of the human mind. Freud felt hydraulic pressure builds up in the psyche, putting it in continual flux (neurosis), and a rebalance of the pressures is needed from within these three active chambers:

- The id –the source of sexual desires, basic pleasures and innate wishes, psychosexual motivations and instinctive drives. It often has an impulsive effect, working on the pleasure principle.
- The ego – the reality principle; the conscious part of the psyche that deals with everyday life. The ego deals with the world in very realistic terms: what can be done, what can be decided and what need not be done. The ego often attempts to achieve a balancing effect between the id's impulses and the superego's inhibitions.
- The superego – this is the source of our moral conscience. The superego follows a 'moral principle' and is created by society, parents, social interactions and experiences during childhood. It often stops us from doing something.

The motive for a dream at night often lies in the daily life of the individual, but during the day, our repressed motivations, our affections and our ambitions remain hidden or guarded very carefully by the 'reality principle' of the conscious 'ego'.

Freud stated that when the ego rests and is asleep, the unconscious desires can emerge 'through the keyhole of dreams'. Freud claimed this was because the ego (that is, the conscious mind) was asleep. Freud's theory of dreams is that wish-fulfilments will be expressed more while dreaming than when awake.

In the early chapters of his book, *The Interpretation of Dreams*, Freud recognises the objection that not all dreams appear as wish-fulfilment. To cope with this, he extends his basic theory to include the theory of the unconscious mind. If the wish-fulfilment is not clear in the dream, then he claims there is some internal resistance to the expression of that wish (that is, ego defence mechanisms at work).

DON'T FORGET

Ego defence mechanisms prevent the unconscious expression of sexual desires. According to Freud, repression causes neurotic symptoms. Unfulfilled wishes are urges repressed by the conscious mind – they remain desired, yet unexpressed.

EVALUATION OF PSYCHOANALYTIC THEORIES OF SLEEP AND DREAMS

A balanced evaluation of the psychoanalytic approach to dream interpretation and evaluations of Freudian theory will, most likely, include an explanation of several strengths and weaknesses of Freud's wish-fulfilment theory, and consider the pros and cons of dream interpretation in general. Here are a few strengths and weaknesses of the psychoanalytic approach to explaining sleep and dreams:

Strengths

- One strength of the Freudian view of dreams is that the characters, settings and stories in our dreams do seem related to our everyday anxieties and our personal concerns. In this way, Freud was probably correct: dreams are not always random.
- There may be positive benefits of allowing wish-fulfilment in dream life. Freud's theory makes wish-fulfilment while dreaming and sleeping have real, survival value.

contd

How? Wish-fulfilment in dreams (for example, punching a parent in a dream) has fewer negative consequences than doing something in real life. Our minds are great simulators of possible futures, so why not spend some time (paralysed!) imagining things in dreams? It's good advice to be careful what you wish for, but REM atopia allows us this freedom in our dreams.

- Freud's ego defence mechanisms are recognised by most people today to be worthwhile descriptions of a few conscious and unconscious coping strategies that we use to alleviate anxiety and handle painful emotions.
- There must be some organising principle to how our dreams are constructed. They are not always random, and Freud was right to look deeper into the unconscious, associational network of our primitive psyche to find out what ultimately causes our dream life.

Weaknesses

- The case-study method, by itself, is a very poor source of evidence to confirm Freud's theories. It is unscientific to generalise the whole population from a handful of case studies.
- Freud's method of dream interpretation is highly subjective. How does anyone know the hidden meaning in a dream if it's hidden?
- Freud's theory is too complex for it to be likely that all of it is correct and accurate. It lacks predictive validity and can be accused of being 'unfalsifiable' (difficult to confirm or reject).

ONLINE

You might like reading the Simply Psychology website for an explanation and an evaluation of Freudian theory. Find the link at www.brightredbooks.net

THINGS TO DO AND THINK ABOUT

Ego defence mechanisms

It's worth knowing how to explain a few of Freud's ego defence mechanisms. Remember, Freud claimed that these work unconsciously in the psyche to manage anxiety.

Here are a few of Freud's ego defence mechanisms, with everyday examples of their use:

- **Repression** – actively keeping something unpleasant out of your conscious mind.

Example:
Forgetting a dentist appointment by pushing it to the back of the mind.

- **Denial** – substituting lies for truth, when a lie is easier to deal with than the truth.

Example:
Not admitting to the truth in order to avoid punishment and guilt.

- **Regression** – deciding to behave like a child at an earlier stage of development.

Example:
An adult crying like a baby in front of their family to get comforted.

- **Projection** – noticing your own feelings in other people and blaming them for the same issues.

Example:
A drug addict telling someone off for being addicted to drugs

- **Displacement** – removing the target for an emotion by swapping the target with another.

Example:
Getting angry with a pillow, or your partner, instead of your boss.

Why not copy out these explanations and supply your own examples of their use in everyday life?

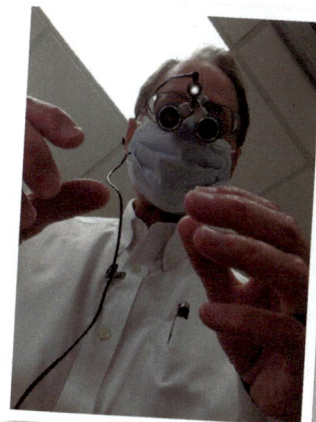

ONLINE TEST

Test yourself on the psychoanalytical theories of sleep and dreams at www.brightredbooks.net

APPLYING KNOWLEDGE: SLEEP DISORDERS

Sleep disorders are a range of health conditions that involve problems with sleeping. You will need to apply your sleep topic knowledge to a few sleep disorders, including circadian rhythm sleep disorders.

INTRODUCING SLEEP DISORDERS

Getting enough sleep can be problematic. Up to one third of the UK population will report insomnia at some stage in their life. Failing to fall asleep, inability to stay asleep or falling asleep unpredictably are all sleep disorders.

A sleep disorder, also known as somnipathy, includes any problem that disrupts a typical sleeping pattern. The International Classification of Diseases (ICD-10) clinically describes sleep disorders as 'disturbance in normal sleeping patterns'– category G47.

Why study sleep disorders?

Sleep disorders are a significant health problem for today's society. According to Mackay (2011) at the Edinburgh Royal Infirmary, Scotland is experiencing a 'tidal wave' of new sleep disorder cases each year.

There are life-threatening health risks associated with having a sleep disorder. Any condition that causes sleep deprivation leads to increased chances of obesity, heart disease, diabetes and cancer. Living with a sleep disorder can cause further accumulating health risks, including a lowered immune system, a higher chance of personal injury, more accidents at work and increased difficulties in social relationships.

The DVLA estimates 20% of road accidents in the UK, per year, are caused by sleepiness. There are also associated memory problems and an increased chance of mental health difficulties.

SLEEP DISORDERS

Insomnia

Insomnia is the condition of those who have a hard time falling or staying asleep. Reports of insomnia increase with age and women are treated more often than men.

There may be secondary causes of insomnia (for example, illness, medication, substance abuse, breathing complications, bladder or bowel difficulties, or pregnancy) but there is a persistent group of insomnia sufferers whose condition cannot be easily explained. This is classed as primary insomnia. Symptoms of insomnia include:

- lying awake in bed for a long time
- sleeping for only short intervals
- staying awake for much of the night
- waking up too early
- feeling tired all the time.

Narcolepsy

Narcolepsy can be defined as sudden-onset daytime sleepiness. This is an uncommon but serious condition. In narcolepsy, recurrent, temporary episodes of sleep (micro-sleeps) occur unpredictably during the day, in surprising places or at socially awkward times. Narcolepsy is also quite intrusive to a person's life – for example, permission to drive a vehicle may be removed.

Temporary sleep paralysis can onset quickly during a sleep attack, with the associated risk of injury from falling. With sleep attacks that can be sudden and uncontrollable, narcolepsy is a serious affliction.

contd

DON'T FORGET

In the biological approach to sleep, getting too little sleep creates a sleep 'debt'. Eventually, the body demands that sleep debt be repaid.

ONLINE

If you are investigating how cognitive behavioural therapy (CBT) works for insomnia, you might enjoy Professor Espie's online sleep improvement programme. Find the link at www.brightredbooks.net and listen to an online avatar of Professor Espie explaining how CBT can be used to treat insomnia.

DON'T FORGET

According to the DVLA, 20% of all car accidents in the UK are caused by driver sleepiness.

Obstructive Sleep Apnea (OSA)

OSA is caused by ineffective breathing for short periods at night during sleep due to airway obstruction. The sleeper awakens each time in order to resume breathing, but deep sleep is repeatedly interrupted and sleep quality is greatly reduced. Untreated, OSA sufferers might attempt to wake up 10 to 50 times during sleep to improve the effectiveness of their breathing.

OSA is a more common condition than narcolepsy, with around 2% of the UK population diagnosed as having it.

When diagnosed, a biological approach to palliative treatment of OSA is taken. Typically, health professionals prescribe a bedside oxygen mask at home to OSA patients. This helps improve their oxygen levels during sleep. This biological intervention immediately improves their quality of life by allowing better sleep. However, oxygen treatment alone does not reduce the blockage, so the mask will continue to be needed.

Restless Leg Syndrome (RLS)

Restless Leg Syndrome describes a syndrome where a recurring sensation compels the resting person to move a leg while sleeping. People diagnosed with RLS report feeling an unpleasant and irresistible urge to keep moving their limbs. Around 5–15% of the population experience this. As yet, there is no agreed treatment.

Circadian Rhythm Sleep Disorders

This includes any condition where the sufferer's internal body clock is out of sync with the external night-and-day cycle. Sometimes, the human body clock fails to keep an appropriate sleep–wake cycle within a fixed day–night pattern of 24 hours. People can struggle with their circadian rhythm for either internal or external reasons. This distinction is used to group the four main types of circadian rhythm disorders and disruption.

When it happens, the regulation of sleeping may become a problem – either causing too much sleep or too little.

Circadian rhythm disorders are thought to be internally caused and there are two basic types – Delayed Sleep Phase Syndrome (DSPS) and Advanced Sleep Phase Syndrome (ASPS). The human body clock can be circadian advanced or delayed.

DSPS is circadian delayed and is exemplified by the night owl; a person who instinctively stays up late and burns the midnight oil. ASPS sufferers are instinctively circadian advanced and go to bed early but rise early, too.

Also within this category, are two other types of circadian rhythm disruption – jetlag and the nightshift. These two categories are thought to be externally caused.

Nightshift workers report circadian disruption because they're working through the night and sleeping during the day. People on nightshift report difficulty sleeping effectively in daylight and experience sleepiness during the night while at work.

Circadian disruption may also occur due to jetlag. Jetlag is caused by travelling between different time zones. This can extend the day, or shorten a night, due to travelling against the local time clock. The circadian disruption occurs because the local day–night cycle has become phase-shifted relative to the traveller's own internal day–night cycle. This is why jetlag causes feelings of daytime sleepiness and night-time wakefulness.

THINGS TO DO AND THINK ABOUT

Why not make a sleep disorder glossary? Here are a few to get started: Insomnia, Bruxism, Cataplexy, Parasomnia, Restless Leg Syndrome (RLS), Obstructive Sleep Apnea (OSA), Narcolepsy, Night Terrors, Advanced Sleep Pattern Syndrome (ASPS), Delayed Sleep Pattern Syndrome (DSPS), Excessive Daytime Somnolence.

Start by naming the sleep disorder and then describing each condition. If you want to take your glossary to the next level, add an approach and a treatment column and then a research evidence column. For example, you might set it out like this:

Sleep disorder name	Disorder description	Approach	Treatment	Treatment research
Insomnia	Inability to sleep effectively	Cognitive	CBT	Espie et al (2007)

ONLINE TEST

Head to www.brightredbooks.net to test yourself on sleep disorders.

STAR STUDY: DEMENT AND KLEITMAN (1957)

Title: *The relation of eye movements during sleep to dream activity: an objective method for the study of dreaming.*

Journal of Experimental Psychology, Volume 53, No. 5, pages 339–346.

Research topic: Do we dream during REM sleep?

ABOUT THE PAPER

In this paper, Dement and Kleitman (1957) were interested in a reliable method of measuring when dreaming occurs – and they wondered if the eyes moving during REM sleep could be associated with dream activity.

The main aim of this laboratory experiment was to observe eye motion during sleep in a number of sleepers, and to record the number of times a clear dream was reported when they were woken up.

The researchers aimed to measure whether a clear dream would be recalled more frequently after an REM sleep awakening than after an NREM sleep awakening.

One main hypothesis of this paper is that dream recall occurs more often after awakening from REM sleep than after awakening from NREM sleep. Dement and Kleitman tested this hypothesis by asking participants to record dreams, if they could be remembered, after being awakened from both types of sleep.

In this way, they aimed to reveal either REM sleep or NREM sleep as the main time of dreaming.

Experimental hypothesis

Participants will more frequently recall dreaming when woken up during REM sleep compared to being woken up during NREM sleep (that is, when no eye motion was detected).

Method

Laboratory Experiment.

Sample

The researchers invited nine participants (seven males and two females). Each participant was asked to have no alcohol or beverages before arriving for a night's sleep in the laboratory. They slept with EEG sensors and EOG sensors attached from their head and eyes to a polysomnograph machine.

Procedure

Participants arrived at the laboratory just before their normal 'bedtime'. Eye motion detectors for an EOG trace were attached to record eye movement potentials, as well as scalp sensors for brainwave (EEG) recordings. Individually, they went to sleep in the laboratory with their EEG and EOG equipment attached for the whole night.

In the room, a voice recorder sat nearby. When awakened, they were to record the content of their dreams into this.

Two conditions were applied – participants were left to sleep, but awakened either during REM sleep or during NREM sleep.

Participants were woken up a number of times per night with a doorbell ringing. The participants were unaware of whether they had just been woken from REM sleep or NREM sleep (it was a single-blind study). They were then to record their dream recollection by describing the content of their dreams into the voice recorder.

contd

Results

Dement and Kleitman (1957) made a number of general observations about their lab sleepers' REM sleep during this study:

- In their nine participants, the REM sleep periods could last between 3 and 50 minutes, but as an overall average, they lasted 20 minutes. In addition, their participants experienced one period of REM sleep, on average, every 92 minutes. REM sleep occurred in all nine participants during every night of sleep, with most REM occurring in the second half of the night.
- In total, for all doorbell awakenings, participants showed a high frequency (80%) of reporting a clear dream following a REM sleep awakening (152 out of 191 REM sleep awakenings). They also reported a low frequency (7%) of dream recall from NREM sleep awakenings (11 out of 149 NREM sleep awakenings).
- Participants often reported feeling bewildered, anxious or confused when awakened from slow wave sleep (deep NREM sleep) but generally could not recall any clear dream from NREM sleep.

Conclusion

These findings lead to the first and main conclusion of the study. Dream recall is more frequent after waking up from REM sleep than NREM sleep. REM sleep is strongly linked with clear and memorable dreaming while NREM sleep is not associated with clear dream recall.

EVALUATION

Strengths

- This is an important study, historically, as it established REM sleep as a time for dreaming in sleep. In this paper, Dement and Kleitman (1957) had found an easily observable physiological correlate to dreaming – eye motion. This firmly established REM sleep as a distinctive, frequent and important phase of sleep.
- This study removed demand characteristics by using a 'single-blind' design for the condition of the awakenings. In other words, the participants did not know – and were not told – whether they had awoken from REM sleep or NREM sleep before recording their dream. This is a strength in the design of the study.

Weaknesses

- Other conclusions from this paper were not so well established. For example, Dement and Kleitman concluded that people dream in real time and their eyes move with whatever they are dreaming about in their dream content. However, this cannot be fully valid, as people often report whole lifetime scenarios being dreamed about within just one short sleep. Also, the eyes may just move rapidly without any perceptual control. The data in the paper is unconvincing.
- The sample size was very small, with just nine participants, and it was gender biased towards males. However, there was a large number of sample points taken with 351 awakenings from sleep monitored overall.
- Laboratory sleep with an EEG cap on, with wires and sensors on the eyes is not necessarily comparable to a typical night's sleep in bed.
- It cannot be said that no dreaming occurs during NREM sleep. It can only be concluded that dreams may still occur, but they are not recalled well.

THINGS TO DO AND THINK ABOUT

Can sleep deprivation be linked to health and wellbeing? Definitely!

For example, Foster (2012) reports links between sleep deprivation and car accidents, plus sleep deprivation as the cause of the Chernobyl nuclear accident. He also makes links between sleepiness and the reason for the Challenger Space Shuttle disaster. Sleep deprivation may also trigger schizophrenia, increased obesity, the onset of diabetes and a reduced immune response to cancer and infections.

DON'T FORGET
When evaluating a theory or an approach for strengths and weaknesses, you can use psychological research studies to help.

DON'T FORGET
When answering an evaluation question, you can mention a research study to support a strength, or show a weakness, of a theory.

VIDEO LINK
TED Talks provide a short presentation by Russell Foster on 'Why do we Sleep?' His talk introduces some of the theories of sleep and dispels some of the myths about it. Watch the clip at www.brightredbooks.net

STAR STUDY: CZEISLER ET AL (1990)

Title: *Exposure to Bright Light and Darkness to Treat Physiologic Maladaptation to Night Work.*

New England Journal of Medicine 322, 1253–1259.

Research topic: This is a laboratory-based sleep experiment that adopts the biological approach to psychology. Czeisler et al (1990) investigate light as an important factor directly affecting sleep regulation. This study supports the view that light is one of the main endogenous factors that influences the circadian entrainment of sleep.

DON'T FORGET ✚

Remember, for this course, you need to develop a critical attitude of mind that can adopt and explain different viewpoints.

INTRODUCTION: APPLYING LIGHT TO THE NIGHTSHIFT

Czeisler et al (1990) investigated whether nightshift workers' alertness and sleeping would improve with light–dark reversal treatment. Most of our body clocks are adapted to the light of daytime when awake and the dark at night-time when asleep in a circadian rhythm. They tested the effect of a reversed exposure to bright light during a nightshift of work and exposure to darkness during the day. Could light–dark reversal improve the alertness of night shift workers by altering the circadian entrainment of their sleep cycle? Would it alter nightshift workers' sleeping patterns?

Aim

The aim of this lab experiment was to test if an exogenous but reversed, light–dark treatment could be used to control the endogenous sleep cycle among nightshift workers. Could the usual circadian maladjustment to nightshift work be treated and reversed with exposure to light at night and dark during the day?

Hypothesis

The experimental hypothesis was that light–dark treatment would improve nightshift-work alertness and reverse circadian adaptation from night-time sleeping to daytime sleeping.

Sample

Eight men were in the sample; their sleep was studied for a few weeks.

Method

Nightshift work was simulated in a laboratory setting at night. There were two conditions for nightshift working – a control condition with low-level lighting and an experimental condition with high-level lighting.

In the control condition, the men were asked to use their home setting for any daytime sleeping they required. For this, sleeping was left unregulated and naturalistic. In the experimental condition, the participants' daytime sleeping at home was treated to having opaque windows and artificial darkness enforced.

Results

Participants in the night light–day dark treatment condition showed more successful adaptation to the nightshift. For example, with the reversed light–dark treatment, the body temperature variable was associated with better adaptation to daytime sleeping. When analysing the variable of body temperature in the control group, without the light reversal treatment, the lowest body temperature of the day happened on average at 03:31 in the night while still on the nightshift.

In the experimental group, after the light reversal treatment was applied, the lowest body temperature occurred at 14:53 in the afternoon while sleeping at home. The men's daytime sleeping pattern more successfully adapted to a daytime circadian rhythm. Indeed, there was a body temperature shift after only four days of intervention.

Results for Biological Variables (and Cognitive Variables)

Other variables showed a similar shift. There was a significant improvement in alertness and nightshift work performance, as measured, at night, by repeated testing on cognitive skills.

contd

Here is a summary of the variables that Czeisler et al (1990) reported showing better nightshift adaptation after this light–dark reversal treatment:

- blood plasma cortisol level
- urinary excretion control
- body temperature
- alertness during night work (self-reported)
- cognitive performance on skills tests

DON'T FORGET

The advice for nightshift workers might be: 'Buy thick curtains with dark linings for your room where you sleep during the day and keep a very bright light on throughout the nightshift!'

CONCLUSION

The conclusion of this experiment was that usual circadian maladjustment to nightshift work can be treated and reversed with exposure to light at night and dark during the day. The human circadian pacemaker can, within just three to four days, be shifted by up to twelve hours by properly timed exposure to bright light. This light–dark intervention can significantly shift the associated decline in alertness, performance and quality of daytime sleeping, in favour of better nightshift working.

Czeisler et al (1990) also claimed that this exogenous intervention in the light–dark cycle has a synchronising effect on the human circadian pacemaker which will directly adapt the awake and sleeping cycle according to the light and the dark.

EVALUATION

Strengths
- Czeisler et al (1990) found evidence for a full 12-hour shift in circadian rhythm adaptation in response to the exogenous factor of light–dark reversal.
- This study can be applied directly to shift-work patterns. It has important implications for improving night-worker productivity. It could also reduce the risk of accidents at work during the night and increase workers' health and safety.
- This study revealed light–dark management as a simple, cheap and practical alteration to nightshift workers' lives that could directly improve their quality of life.
- The light–dark treatment was implemented in an ecologically valid setting – the men's homes. It also had a high degree of laboratory control for its nightshift measurements.

Weaknesses
- This study involved only eight men, possibly limiting generalisation of its conclusions to men and also to the wider population.
- The participants may have shown marked sleep variability and other variables – not all people sleep or work the same way.
- The nightshift work was simulated in a laboratory which may not have reflected typical working conditions. The work involved sitting in a chair for the duration of the night. This may lack ecological validity for some types of nightshift work.
- This study doesn't answer which factor has more influence – light or dark? Does the typical circadian rhythm follow the darkness of the night or is it responding to the lightness of the day? This study does not address the light–dark question.

THINGS TO DO AND THINK ABOUT

In the Higher Psychology course, you'll need to develop the skill of writing long answers to short questions. Each question in the exam has just one **command word** at the beginning to guide you. Try to build up an answer that matches the skill being asked for by the command word. Here's a quick guide as to what response is required:

Describe – outline the main features; make statements on the structure; list distinguishing characteristics.

Explain – reveal causes and effects; clarify influencing factors; describe examples to illustrate linkages and associations.

Evaluate – create a well-balanced list of fully explained strengths and weaknesses; this should allow an overall judgement to be made.

Analyse – isolate the component parts; show the relationship between the parts; break something down into its basic elements in detail; and demonstrate knowledge of their relationship to the whole.

DON'T FORGET

Keep returning to the question to check you're responding correctly to the command word!

EXAMPLE ANSWERS: THE BIOLOGICAL AND THE COGNITIVE APPROACH

Let's look at some worked examples for the biological and the psychological approaches to sleep, dreams and sleep disorders questions.

DON'T FORGET

Use the point, explain, example, research, evaluation (P.E.E.R.E) approach when answering essay questions to keep you on track.

THE BIOLOGICAL APPROACH

Example:

Use the biological approach to analyse the topic of sleep, dreams and sleep disorders.

Point: The biological approach to sleep and dreams considers the physiological and the biochemical aspects of the activity of sleeping and dreaming. Biological psychology is the part of psychology that looks for physical causes of everyday behaviour such as sleeping and dreaming being caused by biochemical changes and events in the body.

Explain: Circadian and ultradian biorhythms have been found by Rechtschaffen and Kales (1968) to affect sleep patterns using a biological approach, with sleep showing a repeating daily rhythm and phases of deep and light sleep within the total sleep time. Sleep control processes, such as alterations in neuro-transmitter levels like serotonin, melatonin and noradrenaline, all work together to maintain the body and the mind in its sleep rhythms. These neurotransmitter changes are proposed as biological causes of sleep. The suprachiasmatic nucleus (SCN) is a brain area within the hypothalamus that has repeatedly been identified as the brain's timekeeper, for example, by Green and Gillette (1982).

Example: Meddis (1975) used the biological approach to suggest evolutionary survival instincts, such as predator avoidance, as a major function of sleep. Further biologists, such as Webb (1982) have proposed sleep patterns follow optimal energy-saving patterns through inherited, genetic predispositions. Regarding dreaming, Hobson and McCarley (1977) suggest a biological explanation for the surreal quality of dreaming; they propose that dreams are meaningless. In this theory, dreams are caused by accidental neural firings; these firings cause random activation of meaningless information – and our brains try to make sense of this – thus forming bizarre but dreamlike stories. Oswald (1966) proposed that the body's cells restore cellular resources and recover during sleep. This is known as the biological restoration theory of sleep and dreaming. In all the explanations above, there are biological causes hypothesised for the patterns observed in everyday sleeping and dreaming.

Research: Recent research by Savard et al (2003) has found a positive correlation between suffering from insomnia and having fewer immune cells in the bloodstream. This provides support for the restoration theory of sleep and dreaming. In addition, when there was a lack of deep, slow wave sleep, Kreuger et al (1985) reported a reduction in the functioning of the immune system.

Evaluation: However, in most cases the biophysical results reported are only associations (that is, correlations) with sleep deprivation or insomnia. Correlations do not always imply causation between variables. As such, the biological processes behind sleep and dreaming remain only partially understood.

DON'T FORGET

Remain evaluative throughout this course. You can evaluate theories and approaches by listing strengths and weaknesses.

Applying the biological approach

You might be asked to explain **applying** the biological approach to sleep, dreams and sleep disorders. To illustrate the application of the biological approach, you could describe hypnotic medication for insomnia as the area of application. For example, hypnotic medication (that is, sleeping pills) might be prescribed to improve the health and wellbeing of people suffering from insomnia. Rosen et al (2000) reported significant improvements in the sleep measures recorded in a group trial over four weeks for those using hypnotic medications over and above their baseline sleep measures.

contd

Hypnotic medication can be prescribed to the insomnia patient to increase total sleep time, speed up sleep onset and allow extended periods of deep sleep. This biological approach provides short-term relief of insomnia by removing the side effects of sleep deprivation; however, patients can become tolerant and addicted to hypnotic medication.

THE COGNITIVE APPROACH

Example:

> Use the cognitive approach to analyse the topic of sleep, dreams and sleep disorders.

Point: The cognitive approach to sleep and dreaming analyses how sleep and dreaming affect cognition and how cognition affects sleep and dreaming. Cognitive psychology is the study of the internal mediating processes of the mind. Cognitive psychologists take an information-processing approach to modelling the internal mental processes of the mind such as perception, attention, language memory and thinking.

Explain: In the topic of sleep, dreams and sleep disorders, cognitive psychologists have studied the effects of sleep deprivation and insomnia on cognitive skills, such as short- and long-term memory, concentration, vigilance and attention skills. Crick and Mitchison (1986) have proposed a cognitive theory of sleep and dreaming where they hypothesise that the time spent asleep and dreaming allows information consolidation in memory – this is a reorganisation theory of sleep and dreaming. Crick and Mitchison (1986) suggested that sleeping and dreaming assists the mind in efficiently processing, reprogramming and remembering the information of the day. This is known as a theory of cognitive reorganisation – like compressing or defragmenting a set of computer files. How is everyday behaviour such as remembering facts or learning and studying for an exam affected by sleep deprivation?

Example: One contemporary study showing the effects of sleep deprivation on memory is by Van der Werf et al (2009). In this test of memory performance, Van der Werf et al found that deprivation of deep sleep (that is, slow wave sleep) was associated with reduced memory test scores.

Research: Further research by Zammit et al (2009) showed that insomnia sufferers exhibited lower scores on tasks involving concentration, memory, attention and problem-solving compared to those in their study not reporting insomnia.

Evaluation: However, while Van der Werf et al (2009) report a measurable effect of a lack of sleep on the hippocampus, these supporting studies do not reveal the exact process to explain why sleeping and dreaming improves memory; why sleep aids cognitive performance; and why concentration is better after sleep.

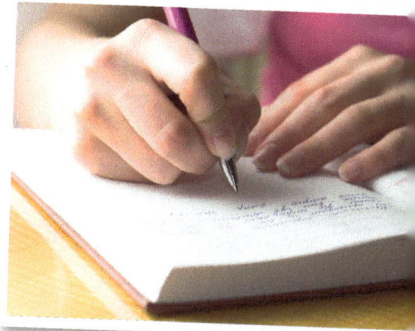

DON'T FORGET

Keep tying back your exam responses to the original question, especially in long-answer questions. After a research study, use 'In this way...', 'This supports...', 'This shows...', etc.

THINGS TO DO AND THINK ABOUT

You might also be asked to explain **applying** the cognitive approach to sleep, dreams and sleep disorders. In this case, you could also use insomnia as an area of application. For example, to treat insomnia, the cognitive approach might be used to help people with insomnia – that is, cognitive behavioural therapy (CBT).

According to Espie et al (2001), CBT has been more successful in clinical trials at improving the wellbeing of people with insomnia when compared to controls. In addition, at follow-up, Espie et al (2001) found that 6–8 weeks of CBT reduced later treatments for insomnia with sleeping pills (hypnotic medication).

ONLINE TEST

Test yourself further on this topic at www.brightredbooks.net

EXAMPLE ANSWER: THE PSYCHOANALYTIC APPROACH

Let's look at a worked example for the psychoanalytic approach to sleep, dreams and sleep disorders questions.

DON'T FORGET ➕

The P.E.E.R.E structure should help you to generate an 'A' quality answer. The SQA are looking for this sort of writing for extended response questions in the Higher Psychology exam.

THE PSYCHOANALYTIC APPROACH

Example:

Use the psychoanalytic approach to analyse the topic of sleep, dreams and sleep disorders.

Point: The psychoanalytic approach to sleep, dreams and sleep disorders explains sleep in terms of the workings of the unconscious mind. Freud proposes the mind has three parts – the id (that part of the psyche driven by the pleasure principle), the superego (that part of the psyche driven by the moral principle) and the ego (the part of the psyche driven by the reality principle). Freud took the view that sleep is for dreaming and dreams are wish-fulfilment. Sleep is when the realm of the unconscious mind is at its most free. For Freud, dreams are the 'royal road to the unconscious mind'. Dreams are dominated by sexual desires and so dreams reveal unrepressed thoughts. In addition, dreams can provide meaningful stories of wish-fulfilment.

Explain: Freud's hydraulic theory of dreaming is mainly explained in his seminal book 'The Interpretation of Dreams'. In this book, Freud states that dreams are condensed wishes or desires expressed in dreams. The scenes in dreams will have hidden (latent) or obvious (manifest) content that may or may not need analysing to reveal repressed thoughts or images of wish-fulfilment.

Example: Freud supports his theory of dreams by describing a number of case studies in his writings. One classic case study, where Freud described applying psychoanalysis and dream interpretation, can be found in his letters to other doctors, written during his practice in Vienna. He wrote to his doctor-friend Josef Breuer about applying psychoanalytic talking therapy with a patient called Bertha Pappenheim. These letters are based on case notes and they are the source of evidence he used to persuade people of the validity of his theory of psychoanalysis. For example, in his famous case study of 'Anna O', now known to be Bertha Pappenheim, he used psychoanalysis to interpret one of her dreams.

Research: Further case notes by Freud describe a case study of a dream by a patient called 'Dora' who seems to be having trouble reaching her father's funeral in a frustrating dream of travelling onwards, running in the woods and losing one's way. Freud interpreted Dora's dream as an anxiety dream motivated by unconscious guilt and regret about missing her father's funeral. If only, in her dreams, could she attend her father's funeral again, he suggested.

Evaluation: To evaluate the psychoanalytic approach, one strength is that each case-study description presented in 'The Interpretation of Dreams' by Freud illustrates his theory of dreams successfully. However, one weakness of the case-study method is that a few case studies are not enough evidence to scientifically support any theory. There is a distinct lack of experimental research later to suggest that Freud's theories of dreams as wish-fulfilment are valid or accurate.

contd

Applying the psychoanalytical approach

You might be asked to **apply** the psychoanalytic approach to sleep, dreams and sleep disorders. At first sight, this might seem hard, however, many practitioners still rely on psychoanalytic techniques to find meaning in dreams during psychotherapy. For example, Victor Frankl (1924) was encouraged by Freud to continue his work on dreams and dream analysis and went on to develop his own 'logotherapy' techniques for finding personal meaning and motivation in his clients' dark dreams of suffering and hurt during war. Frankl's techniques are still applied today, when providing insomnia therapy for those suffering from post-traumatic stress disorder (PTSD).

ACTIVITY:

Try using the P.E.E.R.E structure **three** times to answer this question at the extended Higher level using three different approaches!

> How can biological theories of sleep explain the control of sleep duration?

To answer this, you could include the biological approach – to explain sleep disorders, for example, mentioning insomnia and using individual differences in circadian rhythms (chronotypes: larks and owls) and ultradian rhythms. You could refer to Oswald's (1966) restoration theory and support this with biological research on sleep control centres in the brain, such as the suprachiasmatic nucleus. You could also refer to research on the effectiveness of medication to relieve insomnia, and include an evaluation of biological theories.

Then you could introduce the cognitive approach to controlling sleep duration. An example of a cognitive theory would be Crick and Mitchison's (1986) theory of sleep. This is known as cognitive reorganisation theory. Crick and Mitchison make the point that sleep contributes to cognitive wellbeing by improving memory. You could then present research on memory consolidation. The cognitive approach might use CBT as an applied treatment for insomnia acting to increase sleep duration and relieve insomnia.

How might you use the P.E.E.R.E structure to answer the same question for the psychoanalytic approach? What controls sleep duration? Try structuring this answer yourself!

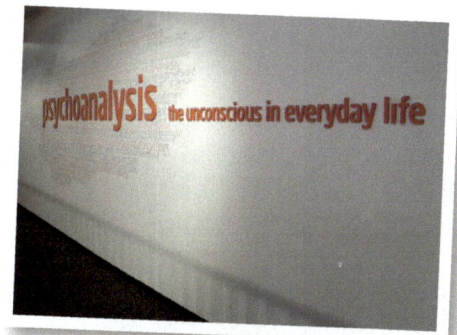

THINGS TO DO AND THINK ABOUT

End-of-topic revision questions

Try answering these for exam revision:

1. What is sleep?

2. Explain the biological approach to sleep.

3. How can **theories** of sleep help explain the function of sleep?

4. Analyse **two** theories of dreaming.

5. Evaluate the cognitive approach to sleep and dreams.

6. How can sleep disorders be treated using the biological approach?

7. How has **research** on sleep explained the purpose of sleep?

8. Evaluate **two** theories of sleep and dreaming.

9. How can sleep disorders help reveal the nature of sleep and dreams?

10. How can psychologists approach insomnia and apply treatments?

DON'T FORGET

Markers dislike finding the word 'proves' in your answer. Avoid it! Try 'suggests'.

DON'T FORGET

Remember to practise consolidating your explaining skills for different approaches and theories. You can practise with past exam papers.

VIDEO LINK

Head to brightredbooks.net and look for the TED talks video of Charles Czeisler speaking in Cambridge about the effect of light on the neurobiology of circadian sleep regulation.

ONLINE TEST

Test yourself further on this topic at www.brightredbooks.net

psychoanalysis the unconscious in everyday life

MEMORY

THE NATURE OF MEMORY

This chapter explores some of the properties of human memory and reviews the evidence for and against three theoretical approaches to memory. Two practical areas are explored: how can memory be improved for exams, and how can the police improve the reliability of eyewitness testimony used in the justice and court system?

When studying memory, there are several approaches to clarifying how human memory works. The Higher Psychology course recommends you learn how to explain, analyse and evaluate at least three of these approaches.

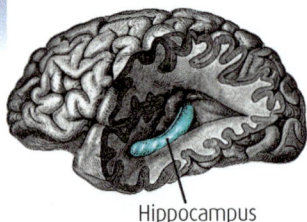

Hippocampus

THE BIOLOGICAL APPROACH TO MEMORY

The **biological approach** suggests memory is physical and can be traced to specific brain areas. The most well known is the hippocampus (a bilateral, connective area in the mid-brain), thought to be involved in the encoding of new memories and laying them down as long-term memories.

In general, Hebb (1949) coined the term 'engram' to refer to the trace of memory (learning) stored in a cell assembly. Engrams are written as a representation within a set of neuron cells in the brain. Biologists often claim there are anatomical areas of the brain devoted to storing certain types of memory.

For example, McGuire (2000) reported structural changes to the hippocampus in London taxi drivers who access their long-term memory of streets daily. In addition, Scoville and Milner (1957) claimed the hippocampus was linked to the encoding of **new** memories into long-term memory. This was based on a case study where the anterograde amnesia experienced by their patient, H. M., after surgical removal of his hippocampal regions. H. M. was unable to remember information he encountered after the onset of the amnesia.

THE COGNITIVE APPROACH TO MEMORY

The **cognitive approach** often adopts an information-processing systems approach to modelling human memory. Cognitive psychologists, such as Atkinson and Shiffrin (1968), tend to worry less about the anatomical basis of memory storage; they build up hypothetical models of what memory stores can do, how storage buffers work and what information-flow processes are needed. The cognitive approach tends to use laboratory experiments to back up these theoretical models (see Miller 1956).

VIDEO LINK

Watch the video reconstruction of Scoville and Milner working with their patient H.M. through the years at www.brightredbooks.net – there's a dramatic twist at the end!

THE PSYCHOANALYTIC APPROACH TO MEMORY

The **psychoanalytic approach** is Freudian. Freud suggested that only our conscious memories are easily reported, but our unconscious memories are hidden and just as important. While the conscious mind is easily viewed, it's just the 'tip of the iceberg' of a much greater system – the unconscious mind is full of repressed and forgotten childhood memories, stored but not recalled.

Freud (1901) claimed, in *Psychopathology of Everyday Life*, that there are many more 'forgotten' memories stored in the unconscious that have been repressed or buried away in trauma or anxiety. If these memories are not dealt with, they can cause neurosis (mild mental illness), neurotic symptoms and anxiety.

Repressed memories can, according to Freud (1901), be used to interpret strange responses to everyday life and events. Freud called some of these neurotic symptoms 'hysterical', for example, uncontrollable laughing or crying in response to a minor incident.

BASIC PROPERTIES OF MEMORY

At a basic level, a memory system involves three processes: encoding, storage and retrieval. Encoding is the taking in of information into memory. Storage is the keeping of the memory trace (a representation). Retrieval is the process of recall, recognition or reconstruction of a stored memory.

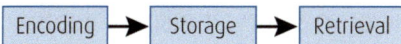

Encoding → Storage → Retrieval

Each process is essential to the functioning memory. If any fail, there will be memory disruption.

Memory capacity

Memory capacity is the **size of the memory store,** and indicates how much information the memory can hold. There's no standard way of measuring organic memory size, leaving us to describe short-term memory (STM) as small and limited, and long-term memory (LTM) as vast and unlimited.

STM: After conducting a range of memory experiments, Miller (1956) described short-term memory as a limited capacity system that, on average, can hold around seven items (plus or minus two). Chunking can increase the number of items stored, if they can be meaningfully linked together.

LTM: Long-term memory represents a vast number of memories over a lifetime. Consider the huge number of cells and neuronal connections in the brain. Few people report their brain being 'full', even after a lifetime of memories. The capacity of LTM is therefore hard to quantify.

Memory duration

Memory duration measures the **time a memory trace lasts** in memory as a representation of the memory. Does a memory fade quickly with time, or does it endure for longer? As the names suggest, this is one of the key differences between STM and LTM. Ebbinghaus (1885) was the first to empirically report a short-term memory store (he called it 'primary memory'). His 'forgetting curves' showed a 'trace decay' pattern over time for forgetting rehearsed lists over a short-term time interval.

In a **short-term memory** situation, Peterson and Peterson (1959) showed that, when rehearsal was prevented by an interference task, recall for list material decreases rapidly with time. See pages 38–39 for a full description.

Long-term memory is long in duration. See pages 38–39 for a description of Bahrick et al's 1975 study. Long-term memory duration is not considered unlimited, but it does, frequently, last a lifetime.

Memory encoding: Memory of what? What is remembered?

Encoding refers to the modality of the information stored in memory. What is codified in the memory representation? For example, if a memory is stored acoustically, sounds will be recalled. Baddeley's results from list-recall studies (1966a, 1966b) concluded that encoding in STM is primarily acoustic while encoding in LTM is primarily semantic.

The coding of the memory trace (the modality of the representation) can be **acoustic** (represents a sound), **semantic** (represents meanings), **iconic** (represents a visual memory), **haptic** (represents a touch), **nosmic** (represents a smell) or **kinaesthetic** (represents a motion).

THINGS TO DO AND THINK ABOUT

Consolidate your learning on the topic of memory through repetition and rehearsal. From these pages and elsewhere, write at least **four key points** for each of the following exam style questions.

1. How can the **cognitive** approach be used to understand human memory?
2. How does the **biological** approach explain the physiological nature of memory?
3. How did Freud explain unconscious memories using the **psychoanalytic** approach?

ONLINE

Look up this optional, individual topic of *Memory* on the 'Psychology4a' link from the Digital Zone. Although it's an A-level site, the topics are covered clearly.

DON'T FORGET

If a **sound** is encoded, stored and remembered, then, the memory store can be called an **acoustic store**.

DON'T FORGET

Procedural Memory – Procedural memory (learning 'how to') consists of memory for how to conduct actions, motions, habits and skilled muscle movements. These procedural memories can't be described as facts, but are used when carrying out a familiar action, for example, riding a bike.

DON'T FORGET

Declarative Memory – Declarative memory (learning 'that') consists of conscious memory for facts and language. It includes all known or reportable knowledge. Declarative memory comprises of everything we can consciously describe, including word meanings and learned facts.

ONLINE TEST

Test yourself on the nature of memory at www.brightredbooks.net

THE BIOLOGICAL APPROACH TO MEMORY: THE HIPPOCAMPUS THEORY

This section analyses how the biological approach explains the topic of memory. It also evaluates research evidence to support the biological theory that the **hippocampus** is the encoding area for long-term **memory**.

THE BIOLOGICAL APPROACH TO MEMORY

The biological approach to memory assumes there are physiological changes in the brain that link with memory. It aims to understand these changes in the formation of memories. Biologists assume that, for every memory stored, there must be physiological changes somewhere in the brain cells, to allow storage of the information.

Hebb (1949) proposed memories were stored in 'cell assemblies'. Cell assemblies, according to Hebb, are changes in the pattern or arrangement of neuron firings and neural connections between adjoining or distant cells. Hebb's theory was the inspiration for computer models of connectionist systems and distributed learning algorithms called 'neural nets'. However, there's much debate on whether memory is distributed across the whole brain or localised in specific parts.

EVIDENCE FOR LOCALISATION OF FUNCTION

Lashley (1929) thought that the more cortical damage in an animal, the fewer memories they would be able to store. The less cortex left, the less learning they would show. This is a generalised, distributed view of brain function, where each part has equivalence, flexibility of application and a generalised contribution to the task of memory.

Brodmann (1909) took the alternative view that the brain is thought to use specific brain locations dedicated to different cognitive tasks, and tried to map the anatomically distinct areas. He used microscope and tissue-staining techniques to map 52 brain areas that have distinct cell structures (cytoarchitecture) and cellular arrangements. His brain area numbering system is still used today.

Brodmann's map promoted the view that the brain has separate, anatomical locations with specialised functions that cannot be performed by other parts of the brain. One theory of the localisation of function is the **hippocampus theory** of memory.

The hippocampus and long-term memory storage

The hippocampus has been identified as a brain area involved in the encoding of long-term memories. This biological theory proposes the hippocampus is **not** the area for long-term memory, but for **encoding** new long-term memories. In other words, the hippocampus is viewed as the 'entry point' for memory consolidation into long-term memory storage.

EVIDENCE FOR THE HIPPOCAMPUS THEORY OF MEMORY

This comes from a range of research studies; including case studies of brain-damaged patients, results from animal memory experiments and monkey brain-lesion studies.

Brain-damaged patients: Case studies involving damage to the hippocampus

Clinical researchers have documented their patients' specific behavioural and cognitive losses after brain damage. Here are some famous case studies:

DON'T FORGET
The hippocampus theory of memory accepts a biologically localised, functional view of memory.

DON'T FORGET
The hippocampus might be a (bilateral) site in the brain where, during memory consolidation, memories are moved from short-term memory to be encoded into long-term memory.

contd

34

CASE STUDY	RESEARCHERS	SUMMARY OF FINDINGS
Clive Wearing	Baddeley (1990)	Wearing suffered from anterograde amnesia. His hippocampus was damaged by an infection of herpes simplex. Procedural skills were still intact, as he could still play the piano.
H. M.	Scoville and Milner (1957)	Exploratory treatment for epilepsy led Dr Scoville to surgically remove H.M's hippocampal regions bilateraly. H. M. had memories from his youth but could not form new long-term memories.
K. F.	Warrington and Shallice (1970)	K. F. showed a grossly reduced digit span indicating severe short-term memory impairment. Long-term memory was still functioning. K. F had a lesion in the Sylvian fissure, but the hippocampus was not damaged. There may be double-dissociation of STM and LTM brain locations.
R. B.	Corkin et al (1997)	Reduced blood flow to R. B.'s brain was shown to cause accidental damage (revealed at post-mortem) to his hippocampus during heart surgery. R. B. woke up from surgery with anterograde amnesia.

Laboratory animal memory experiments involving damage to the hippocampus

Olton et al (1976) used maze-learning tasks with rats that had hippocampal lesions; they failed to learn from their mistakes in the maze. The rats' behaviour seemed to be exploratory, like normal rats. However, the rats didn't store memory for dead-end maze pathways and repeatedly explored the same places – as if without storing long-term memories. Olton et al (1976) concluded that these rats, having no hippocampal regions, further evidenced the hippocampal theory of long-term memory encoding.

ONLINE

Look at studies like McGuire (2000). What happened to the cellular structure of the hippocampus in experienced taxi drivers compared to controls. Why do you think this happened?

ONLINE TEST

Test yourself on this topic at www.brightredbooks.net

EVALUATION OF THE HIPPOCAMPUS THEORY OF MEMORY

Strengths

- The specific anterograde amnesia shown by H. M. supported the view that H. M. could not form new memories in long-term memory after his surgery, even though his short-term memory was still intact. Scoville and Milner (1957) noted that H. M. still had access to long-term memories from before the operation. These symptoms are in line with the theory that the hippocampus performs the function of laying down new long-term memories.
- A wide range of animal research findings support the important role of the hippocampus in long-term memory formation. Mishkin and Appenzeller (1987) observed medial temporal lobe lesions in macaque monkeys would affect standard macaque performance on food recognition tasks. They concluded the destroyed regions of hippocampus were necessary for the long-term memory component of the food recognition task.

Weaknesses

- Long-term memories are not thought to be localised in any specific area of the brain; rather, more widely distributed across the cortex during storage. Penfield's (1958) study of direct electrical stimulation of the temporal cortex suggested the temporal lobe was important for storage of long-term memories, but found the same childhood memory could be reported after stimulation in multiple brain locations. Different regions of the temporal cortex could be stimulated (and even removed!) and yet the same patient recollections could be reported.
- Research evidence from O'Keefe (1979) suggests an alternative function for the hippocampus. O'Keefe's (1979) research on maze exploration in rats hypothesised the hippocampus is full of 'place' cells. O'Keefe describes these 'place' cells as neurons which can be traced as only firing on recognition or recall of a stored place. Might the hippocampus be more of a 'cognitive map' for places rather than an encoding area for long-term memory?

THINGS TO DO AND THINK ABOUT

Evaluate the hippocampus theory of memory

- Bear et al (2001) claim persuasive results for other areas having an important role in long-term memory. They list the 'diencephalon', the 'Mammiliary Bodies' and the 'Papez Circuit' as three other brain areas that might be involved in creating long-term memories.
- According to Scoville and Milner (1957), H. M. had more than his hippocampal regions removed. Temporal lobe surgery also removed H. M.'s fornix, amygdala, perirhinal cortex and entorhinal cortex. All of these could have had a role in forming his long-term memories.

Modelling the hippocampus

In 1909 Brodmann mapped the cellular anatomy of the brain on a piece of paper and numbered the regions. What new tools do we have today to map the topology of the brain? Before you get the modelling clay out, watch *The hippocampal formation: a short overview* at www.brightredbook.net

Now respond to this exam style prompt: **Explain the hippocampus theory of memory.**

STAR STUDY: THE CASE OF CLIVE WEARING

Clive Wearing is a famous neurological case-study of a music historian with brain damage causing him profound amnesia of his life. Clive Wearing's case study is documented by Wilson and Wearing (1995) with details from Clive's scan reports and clinical tests. These help to reveal the effects of his brain damage on everyday memory.

CLIVE WEARING – A PRISONER OF CONSCIOUSNESS – WILSON AND WEARING (1995)

Reference: Wilson, Barbara and Wearing, Deborah (1995) "Prisoner of Consciousness: a state of just awakening following herpes simplex encephalitis." In: Campbell and Conway (Eds) "Broken Memories: Case Studies in Memory Impairment", Blackwell, Oxford, UK.

INTRODUCTION

Clive Wearing suddenly had headaches in 1985 when he was in his mid-40's as a result of a rare herpes simplex infection of the brain (herpes simplex encephalitis).

In the first half of Clive Wearing's life he worked as a music producer on BBC Radio 3. He was a choir master, acknowledged as a music authority on composition in early music. He arranged opera score and conducted choral recitals. Yet, in the second half of his life, he could not remember a single thing from his past or store any episode of life that happened to him.

According to Wilson and Wearing (1995), when engaged in discussion, Clive would provide answers to questions but soon become frustrated with any continued line of questioning. He would often become distracted onto another topic and spent much time upset.

In many cases, brain damaged patients suffer memory loss. This may be restricted to either anterograde amnesia (AA) or retrograde amnesia (RA). Clive Wearing suffered **both.**

Anterograde Amnesia (AA) – the clinical term 'anterograde amnesia' describes a memory deficit where patients cannot encode, store, create or use *new* memories. This may occur after brain damage.

Retrograde Amnesia (RA) – the term 'retrograde amnesia' denotes patients who cannot retrieve *old* memories. This may also occur after brain damage.

Clive had profound amnesia caused by almost complete degradation of the hippocampus (this brain damage causes *anterograde amnesia* and prevents him from creating new episodic memories). He also had lost memory for his life before the infection (i.e. *retrograde amnesia*).

DON'T FORGET ✚

The effects on Clive Wearing's memory were reported in a case study paper by Wilson & Wearing (1995).

CASE RESULTS – CLIVE'S AMNESIA SYMPTOMS

Clive Wearing still recognises his wife and shows joy at her arrival. Yet, he walked past his own house but he did not recognise it as his own. He cannot remember details on the members of his family. According to his wife, Deborah Wearing, Clive lives in a 'time vacuum' and cannot remember his past or make new memories. Clive has lost memory for virtually his whole life (RA) before the infection and he has lost the ability to create new episodic memories (AA).

Wilson and Wearing (1995) report Clive had significant semantic memory loss for the recognition and production of verbal and visual material. For example, he made *frequent category errors* (confabulation) for everyday objects in speech (e.g. mistaking 'jam' for butter, honey or marmalade).

IQ Test Results for Clive Wearing were reduced but *largely unaffected* before and after infection:

Estimated IQ score **before** infection (in 1982) = **122** (the NAR Test)

Estimated IQ score **after** infection (in 1995) = **105** (WAIS Test)

However, anterograde amnesia was profound along with retrograde amnesia for most of his life and childhood. His semantic memory loss was marked and he coped with this using verbal confabulation.

Wilson and Wearing (1995) report that Clive could still play the piano after infection with some improvisation skill and he could sight-read short passages. Some musical skill therefore remains in his procedural memory, though nothing like his previous (pre-infection) abilities. He has lost much technical ability.

BRAIN DAMAGE

Extensive structural changes in Clive's brain were present on scanning his brain. His temporal lobes were damaged, especially the left temporal lobe. His hippocampi on both sides were invisible to detect on scanning and his left-brain ventricles were enlarged.

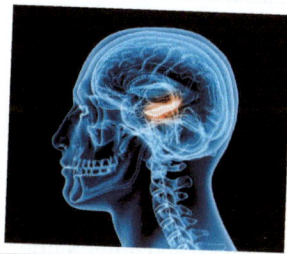

A normal image of the brain with hippocampi highlighted.

CASE STUDY CONCLUSION

It is concluded by Wilson and Wearing (1995) that Clive's *retrograde amnesia* was caused by extensive diencephalon damage while his *semantic memory impairment* comes from frontal lobe damage. It is also concluded that Clive's *anterograde amnesia* is caused by complete 'disappearance of the anatomy' of the hippocampus in both hemispheres.

THINGS TO DO AND THINK ABOUT

ANALYSIS: Compare two Case Studies of Amnesia

Try comparing the case of Henry Molliason (HM) with Clive Wearing:

Look for similarities and differences:

- For example, one *difference* is that there are no reports of HM having semantic impairment as his frontal lobes were left intact whereas Clive Wearing showed confabulation, category errors and semantic confusion.
- Another *difference* is that HM's sense of time and his historical time-line remained unaffected. However, Clive shows no conception of time, except 'right now'. Clive Wearing has no idea what day it is or what just happened a few minutes ago.

➕ DON'T FORGET

For eight years after infection, Clive kept a diary and was convinced he had just 'woken up' for the 'very first time'.

➕ DON'T FORGET

In a moment of self-awareness, Clive Wearing concluded "Now, I am completely incapable of thinking".

➕ DON'T FORGET

Deborah Wearing concluded 'Clive's world now consists of a moment with no past to anchor it and no future to look ahead to'. Yet, he remembered his wife and loved her.

✔ ONLINE TEST

Test yourself on this topic at our online Digital Zone, www.brightredbooks.net/subjects

THE COGNITIVE APPROACH TO MEMORY: THE MULTI-STORE MODEL OF MEMORY

Cognitive theories of memory are often presented as cognitive models that propose structural elements of memory such as 'short-term memory' and 'long-term memory'. These are hypothetical memory stores that may, or may not, exist.

DON'T FORGET

In a cognitive model of memory, sensory data is thought to flow between the memory stores and buffers – usually, in the directions suggested by arrows in the model.

COGNITIVE MODELS OF MEMORY

Cognitive models of memory suggest internal mediating processes for memory and are frequently illustrated in the form of information-processing diagrams. Theoretical stores and buffers for information storage and memory-control processes are proposed.

THE MULTI-STORE MODEL (MSM) OF MEMORY: ATKINSON AND SHIFFRIN (1968)

The Multi-Store Model (MSM) of Memory, Atkinson and Shiffrin (1968), has dominated the topic of memory for decades. It suggests three memory stores with very different properties. Combined, it was suggested these stores could explain the action of human memory.

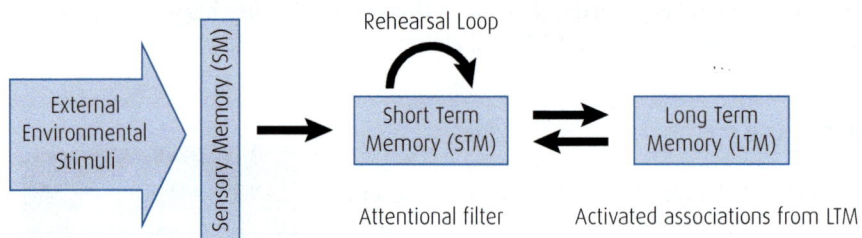

The components of the Multi-Store Model of memory

Components of the MSM

Atkinson and Shiffrin (1968) proposed that external environmental stimuli impinge on our senses and enter a brief but sizeable sensory register, called 'Sensory Memory', with a duration of milliseconds. The model suggests the raw sensory data then enters the STM and can either be forgotten, after 3–18 seconds, or is rehearsed by entering the, primarily 'acoustic', rehearsal loop.

While information is in the STM, it can activate older memories and associations stored in the LTM. In this way, the MSM explains that new incoming material can be stored within LTM or forgotten forever.

DON'T FORGET

Remember, the MSM may be too simplistic for human memory! It doesn't account for other sensory modalities in STM such as visual memories and smells.

ENCODING IN THE MSM

Atkinson and Shiffrin (1968) describe STM as primarily **acoustic**, while LTM is described as primarily **semantic**.

Capacity in the MSM

In the MSM, STM is a limited-capacity short-term system. The capacity proposed by Atkinson and Shiffrin (1968) follows Miller (1956) with seven items plus or minus two. It is also consistent with Jacobs' (1887) digit span results, with a hypothetical limited capacity of around nine numbers. LTM is proposed to be vast in capacity and virtually unlimited in its storage.

Duration in the MSM

STM in the MSM is a short-term store. This is supported by empirical research evidence from Peterson and Peterson (1959) who found smooth, time-based, trace decay in STM,

contd

within the duration of between 3–18 seconds. Peterson and Peterson listed 80% accuracy of recall from STM after three seconds, 60% after six seconds and approximately 40% after nine seconds, but only 10% after 18 seconds delay; these were the results when STM was tested with an interference task, preventing rehearsal.

The duration of LTM is thought, generally, to last a lifetime, but it can be prone to retrieval failure, memory interference, trace-decay and cue-dependent forgetting. In an ingenious field study, Bahrick et al (1975) tested participants' memories 47 years after they had left high school for the names and recognition of the photographs of classmates in their own high-school leavers' yearbook. Even after 47 years, classmate-name recognition was still at around 80% (highest in accuracy), picture recognition was closer to 70% and free recall of classmate names was at 30% accuracy.

EVALUATION OF THE MSM

Strengths

- It has formed a widely used framework of understanding: quickly and clearly establishing the basic characteristics of memory processes that humans must use.

- Its simplicity, with one STM and one LTM, reduces the complexity of brain processing into an easily testable set of hypotheses, about these two stores' capacity, duration and encoding.

- Evidence for the existence of an acoustic rehearsal loop comes from Glanzer and Cunitz (1966). When acoustic rehearsal is prevented by an interference task, they showed removal of the 'recency' effect in the serial position curve. Further, Murdock and Walker (1969) show, from studies of the free recall of 20-word lists, that the 'recency' effect, in the serial position curve, is strongest when the word list is presented acoustically, supporting the primarily acoustic rehearsal loop in the MSM.

Weaknesses

- STM cannot be a unitary store. There must be multiple STM buffers for processing different modalities and organising incoming sensory material of different types. So, it's overly simplistic and reductionist – general criticism of most cognitive theories of memory.

- The STM store cannot act as a general attentional filter if it's primarily acoustic. There are other sensory modalities to consider such as visual memories. This is one of Baddeley and Hitch's (1974) criticisms of the MSM and, in response, they proposed their 'Working Memory' model.

- Is STM active or passive? The control processes of STM are only loosely described by Atkinson and Shiffrin (1968). What information in STM gets rehearsed and what gets forgotten? Does the STM rehearsal loop allow 'maintenance rehearsal' or 'elaborative rehearsal'? As Craik and Lockhart (1972) suggested, deeper interactions with the LTM store would activate associations and elaborate on memories. This type of detail isn't part of the MSM.

THINGS TO DO AND THINK ABOUT

Check you understand the differences between each memory type. Then, try these extended answer questions:

1. Describe one theory of memory that uses the cognitive approach.

2. Explain the components of Atkinson and Shiffrin's (1968) Multi-Store Model of memory.

3. Evaluate the Multi-Store Model, in the light of psychological research on memory.

4. Analyse how the cognitive approach to memory can be used to improve exam revision.

DON'T FORGET

Use flashcards, in a 'memory box' to help you remember researchers' names and dates.

DON'T FORGET

Be ready to provide the names of researchers who have investigated each memory property. For example, Peterson and Peterson (1959) claim a 3–18 second duration for short-term memory when rehearsal is prevented.

VIDEO LINK

To revise the MSM of memory, watch the video clip at www.brightredbooks.net. Let the dancing begin!

ONLINE

A table summarising MSM component properties can be found at www.brightredbooks.net

ONLINE TEST

Test yourself on the MSM of memory at www.brightredbooks.net

THE WORKING MEMORY MODEL – BADDELEY AND HITCH (1974)

In 1974, Baddeley and Hitch (1974) wrote a paper on **working memory** that improved our understanding of memory beyond the multi-store model of memory proposed by Atkinson and Shiffrin (1968). This is a second theory of memory that, like any good theory, needs evaluation, analysis and supporting research.

DON'T FORGET ➕

In the working memory model, the Central Executive can be thought of as a *memory manager*.

WORKING MEMORY AND THE CENTRAL EXECUTIVE

After much clinical research on brain damaged patients Baddeley and Hitch (1974) revealed STM had many discrete components. Each memory component provided different *cognitive memory resources* to a **central executive** memory controller. They claimed human memory functions like a **working memory** system with the central executive system managing what is to be stored or recalled next from its various memory stores.

Here is Baddeley's (2000) model in diagram form:

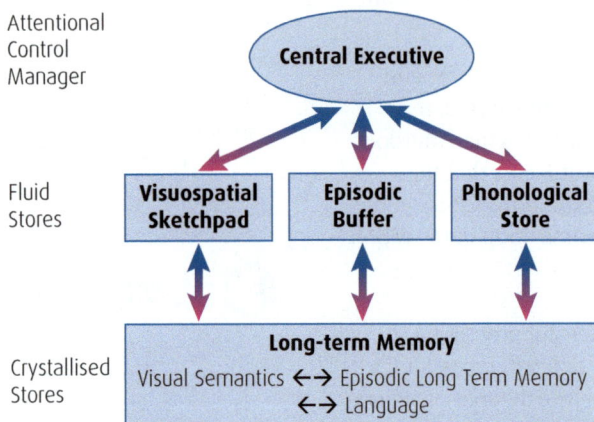

Attentional Control Manager

Central Executive

Fluid Stores

| Visuospatial Sketchpad | Episodic Buffer | Phonological Store |

Long-term Memory
Visual Semantics ←→ Episodic Long Term Memory
←→ Language

Crystallised Stores

Baddeley and Hitch (1974) outlined an alternative cognitive model of human memory called the working memory model. This was to improve our understanding of how human short-term memory operates. Later, Baddeley (2000) added the episodic buffer to this model and this helped clarified how he thought working memory connected with other long-term memory components.

Baddeley (2000) defined **crystallised stores** as long-term unconscious storage systems **capable of learning and accumulating** long-term knowledge (e.g. language knowledge, semantic knowledge).

He defined **fluid stores** as working stores **unchanged** by long-term learning – with only limited capacities and temporary traces or short durations.

THE COMPONENTS OF THE WORKING MEMORY MODEL

Here is a breakdown of the components of the working memory model:

Central Executive – The CE

In working memory, the **central executive** is the memory manager. The central executive is considered an *attentional control system*. It has access to a set of integrated control processes that allow it to manage problem solving activities and memory stores. The Central Executive is most active in complex cognitive tasks *focussing and dividing* attention. Its purpose is goal-directed problem solving and the central executive has a limited attentional capacity.

Visuospatial Sketchpad – The VSS

The **visuospatial sketchpad** stores images, models and mental visualisations for the central executive to use. The allows VSS reconstruction of images and visual 3D models from long-term memory. It acts as an 'inner eye'. The VSS helps with navigation and often represents physical elements of the environment. The VSS uses *visual encoding* includes features such as texture, colour and shape encodings. The VSS allows us to morph, rotate and visualise spatial arrangements, and transformations in 3D space.

Episodic Buffer – The EB

The **episodic buffer** is described as the conscious memory area that the central executive system uses. When handling complex aspects of executive control, the central executive can call on the episodic buffer as a memory area for episodes or events.

contd

This allows *conscious awareness* and retrieval of these events from LTM (which is essentially unconscious until retrieved into the episodic buffer). The episodic buffer is temporary and acts as a working memory slave system between the central executive and the more crystallised LTM. According to Baddeley (2000), the episodic buffer is fluid and temporary in duration and it does not acquire knowledge by learning but has *multi-modal coding* (a common multi-dimensional coding?) which allows cross-binding of information from different working memory sub-systems into recognisable memory 'episodes'.

Phonological Store – The PS

The phonological store plays a role in reasoning but is not essential to reasoning. The phonological store is heavily involved in the acoustic aspect of reading and those with an unusual articulatory store may suffer from dyslexia or reading difficulties, according to Gathercole and Baddeley (1990). The Phonological Store is also assumed to have two sub-components: an auditory part and a verbal part. The auditory part is an *acoustic store* (the phonological loop) and the verbal part is a *sub-vocal articulatory store* for internal verbal rehearsal. In terms of coding, the phonological store is similar to an acoustic loop – like an acoustic sampler – limited in time but not capacity. Peterson and Peterson (1959) suggested there is an acoustic loop with 3-18 seconds duration if rehearsal is prevented and trace decay is allowed to occur.

EVIDENCE FOR THE WORKING MEMORY MODEL

According to Baddeley (2000), sources of support for the *working memory system* comes from five research findings:

1. The Phonological Similarity Effect – "The sad mad lad had a bad Dad" – Reading sentences containing similar sounding phonemes take longer to process than reading sentences with dissimilar sounding phonemes – "The poor crazy man had a sick Mum". Evidence for an acoustic memory store comes from Baddeley (1966a) who found increased *acoustic* confusion in memory for tasks over a short duration.

2. The Word Length Effect – 'university representative constitution devastation' - less long words could be remembered than short words, suggesting an acoustic code for short-term verbal memory tasks. This supports the existence of a *phonological loop* with a limited capacity and short duration – similar to the acoustic rehearsal loop in the multi-store model of Atkinson & Shiffrin (1968).

3. The Effect of Articulatory Expression – Baddeley showed that word recall is greatly reduced by an articulatory suppression task. This supports the existence of an articulatory loop for spoken language.

4. The Effect of Articulatory Expression – the working memory model can explain how information flows from one *coding* to another via the central executive.

5. Neuropsychological evidence – Paulescu et al (1993) brain imaging studies also link another area, Brodmann Area 44 of the left hemisphere, with the phonological store and speech production. They suggest this is the location for an articulatory loop.

THINGS TO DO AND THINK ABOUT

Working Memory – Analysis of the Capacity of the sub-components

Compare the Capacity of the **Phonological Store** and the **Visuospatial Sketchpad**.

Reference: Paivio, A. (1969). Mental imagery in associative learning and memory. *Psychological Review, 76*(3), 241-263.

Compare the *phonological store* with the *visuospatial sketchpad* by direct experimental investigation. Which store has larger capacity? How can we tell? Try comparing memory for a set of 20 words to memory for a set of 20 pictures. Typically, more pictures are recalled correctly than words alone.

Memory capacity for recalling **words** versus **pictures** is a popular choice of research assignment for the Higher Psychology course.

DON'T FORGET

The Visuospatial sketchpad can be thought of as the mind's 'inner eye' and the Phonological Store as the mind's 'inner ear'.

DON'T FORGET

The VSS provides a 'sketchpad' or drawing tool for the working memory system to use.

DON'T FORGET

Evidence for the phonological store comes from studies by Baddeley (1966a) on acoustic confusion over short-durations

DON'T FORGET

Further evidence for a limited duration phonological store comes from research on the word length effect in memory by Baddeley, Thomson and Buchanan (1975).

DON'T FORGET

Articulatory suppression is the repetition of verbal information orally while performing another acoustic task – for example, constantly repeating the word 'bunny' during the learning of a word list.

ONLINE TEST

Test yourself on the working memory model at www.brightredbooks.net/subjects

STAR STUDY: WORD LENGTH EFFECT AND THE STRUCTURE OF SHORT TERM MEMORY

Reference: Baddeley, Thomson and Buchanan (1975) "Word Length Effect and the Structure of Short Term Memory" *Journal of Verbal Learning and Verbal Behaviour*, **14**, pp 575–589.

THE WORD LENGTH EFFECT – BACKGROUND

This paper describes a series of eight experiments, all based on factors that influence short term recall of word lists. Baddeley et al's (1975) paper claims that **trace decay** in *working memory* is the main reason for forgetting over the short-term. The series of experiments supports the existence of a very short duration (i.e. time-limited) **phonological loop** as part of a working memory system rather than an item based STM as in Atkinson and Shiffrin's (1968) multi-store model of memory.

Aim

The aim was to find **word length factors** that influence acoustic memory over the short-term.

Method – a series of eight laboratory experiments

Baddeley, Thomson and Buchanan (1975) investigated eight word length factors that might lower memory recall over the short term in a simple word list memory task. The table, here below, summarises each of the eight experiments.

A series of Eight Experiments on Word Length and its Effects on Short Term Memory	
Experiment One: Audible words.	**Experiment Two:** Audible country names.
Long *versus* short words	Long *versus* short country names.
Experiment Three: Articulatory time.	**Experiment Four:** Articulatory time.
Words not matched for phonemes but matched for occurrence frequency and matched for word length.	Words matched for phonemes, word length and occurrence frequency.
Long duration words *versus* short duration words	Long duration words *versus* short duration words.
Experiment Five: Visual Presentation of Words.	**Experiment Six:** Does list memory recall *vary* as a function of **reading rate** and the **number of syllables** to be read? Finding: reading rate correlated positively with memory recall.
Words matched for phonemes, word length and occurrence frequency.	
Long duration words presented visually versus short duration words presented visually.	
Experiment Seven: Word length and Articulatory Suppression	**Experiment Eight:** Word length, Presentation mode and Articulatory Suppression
Short or long words presented visually; with or without articulatory suppression.	Short or long words presented visually or acoustically with or without articulatory suppression.

Words in the lists to be remembered were often standardised for length and articulation speed. They were selected to be matched for frequency of occurrence in everyday language use and also matched for word length. Example words from the lists included:

- TWO SYLLABLE LONG DURATION WORDS: Friday- humane – harpoon
- TWO SYLLABLE SHORT DURATION WORDS: decor – tipple - pectin

contd

Results

The **main results** of the eight-word length investigations by Baddeley, Thomson and Buchanan (1975) are summarised below:

1. Memory span was sensitive to a word-length effect in most verbal materials when presented acoustically.

2. Even when phonemes and syllables and word frequency were matched, there was still a word length effect (i.e. a duration effect) based on how long it takes to say the word.

3. Articulation time and memory span correlated closely.

4. Memory span and reading rate correlated across many participants.

5. Articulatory suppression **abolished the word length effect** when material was presented visually.

Conclusions

There are **six** main **conclusions** that emerge from this paper:

1. Memory span is inversely related to **word length**. This means that the longer the words are, the fewer words can be remembered.

2. **Trace decay in time** (rather than displacement by limited item capacity) seems to be the main reason for forgetting in the phonological loop of a working memory system.

3. Long duration words **lowered recall** over short duration words. In other words, slow to pronounce long words were comparatively **harder to remember** than quicker to pronounce long words of equal phoneme length. This was even true when words of longer spoken duration were matched against a control list of similar frequency of occurrence words and matched for a similar the number of phonemes.

4. Phonological Loop span could be predicted by the number of words which participant's could read in around **two** seconds. Reading speed correlated with phonological loop span.

5. Articulatory suppression had *no effect* on **visually presented** long words.

6. The hypothesis that STM capacity is a constant number of items (as Miller (1956) claimed) would predict **no** word length effect, yet there **is** a word length effect as described above (in item three).

Overall, the **word length effect** provides evidence that forgetting **cannot** be because of displacement within a limited capacity acoustic buffer of roughly seven items. This is because displacement theory does **not** account for all the results.

Baddeley, Thomson and Buchanan (1975) suggest short-term memory recall for audible words is from a phoneme-based **articulatory store** of limited temporal duration. The phonological loop may function as an *output buffer for speech production* and it is thought to be a supplementary sub-component under the control of the central executive in a more complex model of short term memory known as the **working memory system**.

💭 THINGS TO DO AND THINK ABOUT

What are the implications?

Was Miller (1956) wrong? Chunks or items are **not** the limiting feature of the phonological loop. Rather, the phonological loop has a **time-limited** duration prone mostly to temporal trace decay. The word length effect paper above suggests that all sounds, across a given time instance, are the same size in terms of memory capacity. Therefore, according to Baddeley, Thomson and Buchanan (1975) **any** sound can fit in the phonological loop for its short duration, with or without chunking.

➕ DON'T FORGET

The Word length effect paper supports the Working Memory model rather than the Multi-Store model of memory

➕ DON'T FORGET

One implication of these word length experiments is that Miller's (1956) magic number for the number of items that can fit in STM (7 plus or minus 2) may be wrong.

✔ ONLINE TEST

Test yourself on this topic online at www.brightredbooks.net/subjects

THE PSYCHOANALYTIC APPROACH TO MEMORY 1

The starting point for Freud's theory of memory is 'motivated forgetting'. Freud claimed that memory is emotionally motivated. Memory involves choosing what to remember and, he claimed, unconsciously selecting what to forget.

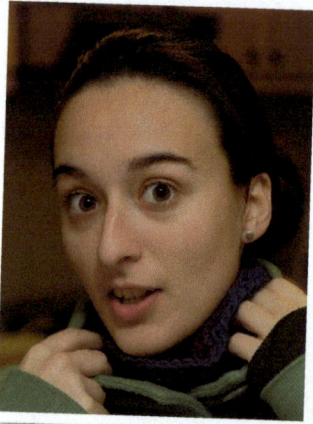

FREUD'S THEORY OF FORGETTING

Freud was curious why something believed forgotten a long time ago, could suddenly be recalled into consciousness. Why is memory so obstinate like that? Does the unconscious defend the psyche from reliving bad experiences?

Motivated remembering and forgetting

Freud's theory of memory is that memories are motivated by instincts and drives. According to the psychoanalytic approach, both the processes of memory and forgetting are driven by unconscious forces. Freud claimed that what we recall and retrieve is very carefully chosen, unconsciously, by the psyche.

Freud argued that what we store of an event is very personal to each individual. Similarly, retrieval from memory is motivated and hardly passive. We are partial to store certain memories, and we select what to remember of events. This biased selection results in unique and personal accounts of the same situations.

MOTIVATED FORGETTING AND REPRESSION

Not only did Freud claim that memory is selective, but forgetting is too. Freud's theory of repression is that forgetting is an ego defence mechanism. The whole psyche actively defends the balance of the ego by using ego defence mechanisms such as repression, displacement, denial and projection from unpleasant memories and sensations.

Motivated encoding

Freud recognised the encoding process of memory is motivated by personal taste, individual selection and unconscious wishes. He also explained that retrieval failure is just as motivated. For example, you might forget an appointment with your dentist. However, you won't forget an appointment with your favourite celebrity.

Freud theorised that behind a misplaced object, such as a lost book, there may be a chilling memory, a dark association or an unpleasant history that, if retrieved from the unconscious, would threaten the balance of the psyche. In many cases, Freud claimed, when the dark association is removed or resolved to a more favourable association, forgetting will cease and the memory will be retrieved. For example, behind mislaid keys, there is likely to be a repressed desire to lose them.

Freud uses many everyday case examples to explain his theory of motivated memory.

Example:

Freud includes a story about Erna, who put some ginger cake in a cupboard, but forgot which cupboard. She lost the ginger cake while a friend was visiting her house. Freud explained that her inability to find the ginger cake in the kitchen when a visitor was arriving was motivated by a desire to keep it for her own eating. Freud depicts this as 'motivated forgetting'.

In every case from his book, *The Psychopathology of Everyday Life*, Freud claimed 'forgetting' was based on a motive of avoiding displeasure. According to Freud, 'distressing memories succumb especially easily to motivated forgetting'.

DON'T FORGET

In Freud's view, the psyche consists of the id, ego and superego. These three components can conflict in motive and cause neurosis and anxiety.

DON'T FORGET

Freud: 'The tendency to forget what is disagreeable seems to me to be quite a universal one.'

ONLINE

Why not visit Freud's Apartment in Vienna, Austria, or plan a trip to the Freud Museum in London? If you can't visit in person, you can find the Freud Museum online using the link at www.brightredbooks.net

SIGNS OF MOTIVATED FORGETTING AND REMEMBERING IN EVERYDAY BEHAVIOUR

Parapraxis (slip of the tongue or 'Freudian slip')

Parapraxis is the term used to describe a type of motivated error in retrieval from memory. One example Freud gives of parapraxis is using the name of a favoured person rather than the person you are dealing with. Parapraxis involves replacing accurate recollections with a preferred alternative.

Example:

Freudian slip: 'Hello Sarah! Oops! I mean, Susan'. If you say the wrong name for your girlfriend, that is parapraxis.

Freud explains slips of the tongue as motivated errors in speech. Word recall errors might disclose the true associations within the speaker for the topic under discussion. Freudian slips are motivated by unconscious forces. For example, saying 'bad to meet you' rather than 'glad to meet you' is a Freudian slip that reveals a hidden displeasure.

Bungled actions

According to Freud, there are few 'innocent' mistakes. Freud claimed action slips and procedural fails do not happen accidentally. They are caused by neurosis, anxiety and motivated drives against success. Bungled actions happen 'on purpose' and in a motivated fashion. Failure to complete an action successfully because of accident or error usually reveals unconscious anxiety and a motivated desire to fail the task.

Forgotten appointments

Freud's explanation for forgotten appointments is deterministic. Losing an invite to a dull party does not occur by chance; forgetting is a deliberate ego defence against attending the event. It's repression. In the same way, ending up at the wrong address may be part of an unconscious desire to avoid an unwanted meeting.

KEY RESEARCH: BREUER AND FREUD (1895), 'STUDIES ON HYSTERIA', THE 'ANNA O' CASE STUDY

One famous case study called 'Anna O', first reported by Breuer and Freud in 1895, supports the Freudian theory of motivated repression of memories.

The patient, 'Anna O', reported that the prescription of a 'talking cure' benefited her feelings and removed some of her anxious and hysterical symptoms. Freud believed that her 'profoundly melancholy fantasies', experienced in her turns of absent-minded daydreaming to Breuer, could be removed with free association and expression.

Freud analysed Anna O's concerns and linked these to the symptoms from Breuer's case history as revealing repressed, hysterical concerns (anxious, neurotic symptoms) from the past that could be recalled, discussed and removed.

Anna O compared the new psychoanalytic 'talking therapy' to 'chimney sweeping' for the psyche. Psychoanalysis aims to remove the repression of difficult memories and resolve unconscious conflicts, thus removing the sources of anxiety in the psyche. (For more about Anna O, see pages 98–99.)

VIDEO LINK

Watch the biographical documentary by NOVA about Freud's life called 'The Father of Psychoanalysis' at www.brightredbooks.net

DON'T FORGET

Nowadays, speech errors that make underlying desires public are known as Freudian slips.

ONLINE TEST

Test yourself on the psychoanalytical approach to memory at www.brightredbooks.net

THINGS TO DO AND THINK ABOUT

Imagine a world without Freud! Whether you like psychoanalytic theory or not, imagine if Freud had repressed his theory of psychoanalysis. How would the world be now? It's fair to conclude that psychiatry, psychology, art and literature would all suffer a loss.

Now, list as many psychoanalytic terms that you can that are a direct result of Freud's work. If you have time, explain these terms by building a Freudian glossary:

unconscious   psyche   denial   repression
libido   id   ego   superego   regression

THE PSYCHOANALYTIC APPROACH TO MEMORY 2

ANALYSING MOTIVATED FORGETTING USING FREUD'S EGO DEFENCE MECHANISMS

In 1923, Freud outlined the psyche with three parts: the id, ego and the superego. He had already adopted a hydraulic model of motivational energy. Freud called the drives in the psyche the pleasure principle, the morality principle and the reality principle. These drives interact dynamically in the unconscious and the ego – in combination, they drive all behaviour.

FREUD'S EGO DEFENCE MECHANISMS

According to Freud, the ego (the conscious part of the psyche) has to defend itself against the impulses of the id's pleasure drive, and balance these with the strict and demanding obligations of the superego's moral principle using what he called ego defence mechanisms.

Here's a list of some of the eleven ego defence mechanisms most relevant to Freud's motivated forgetting theory of memory.

Denial

As an ego defence mechanism, denial involves unconscious refusal of the truth of a memory. Denying a memory might allow an unpleasant truth from the past to be avoided. Note that conscious lying and unconscious denial are very different in causal origin, and only unconscious denial is a defence mechanism, though hard to distinguish in effect.

Repression

Another ego defence mechanism is repression. If someone forgets an event by constantly avoiding recalling it, that's repression. Actively trying to bury a memory describes the process of repression. Repression is Freud's most central ego defence mechanism to psychoanalysis, as unearthing repressed childhood memories became routine during psychotherapy.

Freud claimed repression requires conscious nervous energy to sustain it and, because of this, repression causes anxiety. A central tenet of psychoanalysis is that 'letting off steam', and revealing repressed memories during talking therapy, reduces anxiety.

Displacement

Displacement is listed as a defence mechanism by Freud. Freud explains that displacement onto inanimate objects occurs because it's more acceptable to destroy a door or chair than to destroy your boss, partner or brother, which might be what you feel like doing.

Socially acceptable displacement of aggression and anger may form part of psychotherapy – such as taking up a sport to reduce nervous frustration. Freud acknowledged that displacement of nervous energy into sport or physical activity can act as a 'catharsis' and reduce anxiety.

RESEARCH EVIDENCE FOR FREUD'S PSYCHOANALYTIC THEORY OF MOTIVATED MEMORY

Is there any scientific evidence for Freud's theory of motivated memory and forgetting?

Levinger and Clark (1961) – Emotional words are repressed, thus harder to recall

Evidence for Freud's theory that emotions can be repressed comes from a simple laboratory study comparing the memory recall of word lists by Levinger and Clark (1961). They compared the accuracy of recall for emotionally charged words in a list to recall of neutral words. The accuracy of recall for words like 'tree', 'cow' and 'window' was higher than the accuracy of recall for words like 'fear', 'anger' and 'quarrel', suggesting that these words are too full of negative emotion for the psyche to handle.

While the findings of Levinger and Clark (1961) appear, on the surface, to support the theory of Freudian repression, it can be criticised. Abstract terms, such as 'fear', 'anger' and 'quarrel', are – in general – more difficult to visualise and remember than concrete nouns like 'tree', 'cow' and 'table', with or without an emotional association.

Glucksberg and King (1967) – Memories associated with shocks are repressed

In 1967, Glucksberg and King presented laboratory results from human participants that gave support to Freud's theory of repression of unpleasant associations. After training participants to expect shocks after certain word-pair associations in a pre-test condition, participants were less likely to remember or report recalling linked word associations in the test condition that indirectly associated with words previously linked to the trained word-shock associations.

> ▶ **VIDEO LINK**
>
> If you have seven minutes and twenty seconds to spare, watch the School of Life's humorously illustrated video on Sigmund Freud's Psychotherapy at www.brightredbook.net

> ➡ **ONLINE**
>
> The website called *Simply Psychology* covers Sigmund Freud and 'Anna O' quite clearly and concisely. Find the link at www.brightredbooks.net

EVALUATION OF THE PSYCHOANALYTIC APPROACH TO MEMORY

Strengths

- Under relaxed conditions, people can often report more from their memory stores than when they are anxious or upset. This is consistent with Freud's theory of unconscious memory storage. In addition, in some states of mind, memories can flood out unexpectedly. This gives evidence of an unconscious psyche with greater storage than is easily recalled.
- Support for the psychoanalytic theory of motivated memory was originally provided by the clinical explanations given by Breuer and Freud in their case studies of patients such as 'Anna O'.
- There is some, limited scientific support for repression. For example, Levinger and Clark (1961) and Glucksberg and King (1967) provide empirical evidence from laboratory studies of memory repression.

Weaknesses

- Freud's theory of motivated forgetting may be unnecessarily complex. It is considered unfalsifiable; this makes the theory hard to confirm or reject.
- Freud's theory makes the rather weak assumption that nearly all repressed memories in the unconscious are sexually motivated by association. In particular, his theory of the 'Oedipus complex' (a child's desire to have sexual relations with the parent of the opposite sex) has very little scientific support.
- Freud relied on the case-study method to support his theories. A few case studies are not sufficient to provide empirical support for universal theories. While case studies are useful for explaining theories, they cannot, alone, confirm the general truth of hypotheses.

🟦 THINGS TO DO AND THINK ABOUT

Have a go at these practice exam questions on the psychoanalytic approach to memory:

1. Explain the Freudian theory of memory.
2. Describe how Freud states that ego defence mechanisms protect the psyche from traumatic memories.
3. Analyse how the psychoanalytic approach treats anxiety using repressed memories.
4. Evaluate the Freudian approach to understanding human memory.

> ✅ **ONLINE TEST**
>
> Test yourself on the psychoanalytic approach to memory at www.brightredbooks.net

THEORIES OF FORGETTING

We all depend on memory. Forgetting things is a common everyday problem. Zolan forgets his bag and leaves it on the bus. Clive can't remember his children's birthdays. Fiona can't remember where she put her shoes. Why do we forget?

HOW CAN WE EXPLAIN FORGETTING?

There are at least *four* explanations of why we forget things: trace decay, interference, cue-dependency and brain damage. Each explanation of forgetting will be presented here and have its research support and limitations analysed.

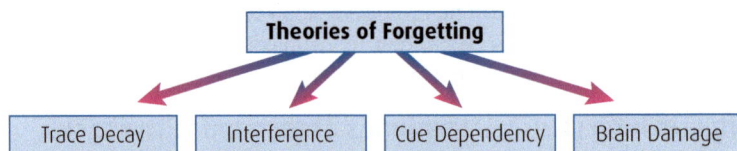

```
                    Theories of Forgetting

   Trace Decay    Interference    Cue Dependency    Brain Damage
```

As shown in the diagram above, we can explain forgetting in at least four ways: trace decay, interference, cue-dependency and brain damage.

THEORIES OF FORGETTING

Forgetting can be due to **trace decay** as the trace representation stored in memory might fade. We can also explain forgetting due to **interference**, as new or old information gets confused with the required memory in storage and interferes with its integrity. Further, we can explain forgetting as cue-dependent with forgetting occurring due to an absence of **retrieval cues**. Finally, we can explain forgetting due to organic causes such as **brain damage**.

DON'T FORGET

Interference works as an explanation of forgetting because when two memories are similar they will be hard to tell apart.

Trace Decay

Trace decay theory suggests that one reason for forgetting (especially in short-term memory) is that the trace representation of the memory is stored successfully but then it fades through time due to trace decay.

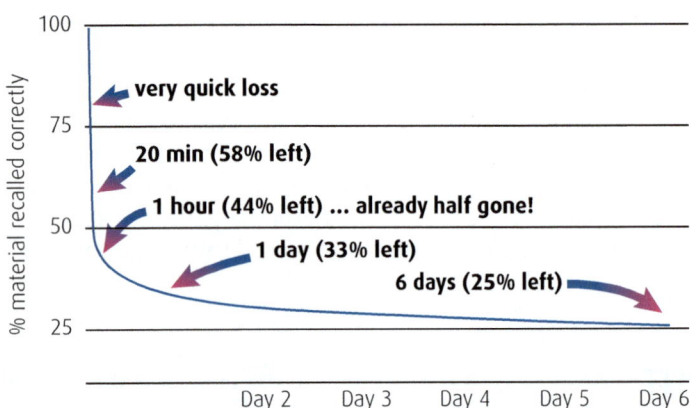

Graph of Ebbinghaus' Forgetting Curve

(labels on graph: 100, 75, 50, 25 — % material recalled correctly; very quick loss; 20 min (58% left); 1 hour (44% left) ... already half gone!; 1 day (33% left); 6 days (25% left); Day 2, Day 3, Day 4, Day 5, Day 6)

In trace decay theory, as time passes, the memory trace decays in strength and the likelihood of recall goes down with time. Trace decay theory is supported by Peterson and Peterson (1959) Short-term retention of individual word items, in the presence of an interference task, show trace decay through time.

Peterson and Peterson (1959) showed that with an interference task, short-term verbal memory decays from high accuracy at 3 seconds to lower accuracy after 18 seconds. This gives evidence for short-term verbal memory being very short (3-18 seconds) and this 'shortness' is due to rapid *trace decay with time*.

DON'T FORGET

Ebbinghaus (1885) studied the properties of LTM and his results demonstrated *trace decay* in long-term memory.

Trace decay in long-term memory is supported by early pioneering research by Ebbinghaus (1885) who created long-term memory forgetting curves for his own memory of nonsense syllables (e.g. FTS, LKQ, MBU).

Ebbinghaus (1885) showed evidence of trace decay theory as his long-term memory

contd

accuracy decreased with time. His forgetting curves showed that recall accuracy from long-term memory went down exponentially as time passed.

Memory for nonsense syllables went down from a high accuracy at 20 minutes, to lower accuracy after one hour, even lower accuracy at 9 hours, through poor accuracy after one day, then very low recall at 2 days and 6 days. Lastly, Ebbinghaus showed lowest accuracy of recall after 31 days.

However, this was a lab experiment with just one participant (i.e. himself) using only meaningless syllables. This means the recall accuracy of the results can be challenged as they lack ecological validity. Even everyday memory has more personal meaning and distinctiveness than nonsense syllables.

Interference

The main idea of interference theory is that two related memories are mixed up during encoding, storage or recall. The interference theory of forgetting states that two similar memories can be confused. Similar memories can be created, they can interfere with each other during storage and they can compete with each other during recall. Thus, memories can interfere with each other and cause forgetting.

McGeoch and MaDonald (1931) presented lab experiments where participants were more likely to recall synonyms confabulated from a *second list* rather than accurately recalling a *first list*. This suggested that prior learning can cause interference with subsequent related learning. This established **interference** as a **theory of forgetting**.

Forgetting can be due to *proactive interference* or *retroactive interference*:

Retro-active Interference: OLD information interferes with and gets confused with NEW information.

This causes confabulation errors. Examples include:

- walking to the wrong street for your car, because you normally park in that street.
- Calling your new pet cat, your old pet cat's name

Schmidt et al (2000) tested participants on their memory for street names from the towns they lived in *during their childhood*. Testing 211 participants from 11-79 years old, they found that former students of a Dutch town school in Molenberg had memories prone to retro-active interference. The more *subsequent addresses* they had lived at since their time as a child in Molenberg, the less easily they remembered the street names from Molenberg. This is taken as evidence of retroactive interference because new learning has made old memories harder to recall. New area street names had acted retroactively to make old Molenberg street names more difficult to recall accurately.

Baddeley and Hitch (1977) provides *further naturalistic evidence* for retroactive interference in their field study on rugby players' memories. Could rugby players remember the names of other rugby players from games played early on in the season?

THINGS TO DO AND THINK ABOUT

Theories of Forgetting – Can you explain why we forget?

Try these revision exercises on **theories of forgetting**. Use different *theories* and *research* in each task.

Start with an easy one:

1. Olivia left her violin on the train. Why did she do this? (4 marks)
2. Analyse one explanation for why we forget. (4 marks)
3. Explain the research evidence for one theory of forgetting. (6 marks)
4. Compare two theories of forgetting and consider which has better research support. (6 marks)

DON'T FORGET

Memories can get confused (retroactive interference) or buried deeper (proactive interference).

DON'T FORGET

Confabulation is the term for reconstructing false or inaccurate memories during recall.

DON'T FORGET

Underwood's (1957) research is support for the theory of forgetting that pro-active interference causes **old** memories to interfere with and prevent accurate recall of **newer** memories.

DON'T FORGET

Pro-active interference: NEW information interferes with OLD information and makes it more difficult to recall.

DON'T FORGET

Underwood (1957) showed pro-active interference in the laboratory when participants were asked to recall *new* lists of nonsense syllables. They kept recalling parts of old lists of nonsense syllables learned 24 hours previously.

ONLINE TEST

Test yourself online on this topic at www.brightredbooks.net/subjects

FORGETTING DUE TO ABSENCE OF CUES

Have you ever had the feeling you know something but can't remember it right now? It is on 'the tip of your tongue'? An absence of memory cues can lead to retrieval failure. This causes cue dependent forgetting.

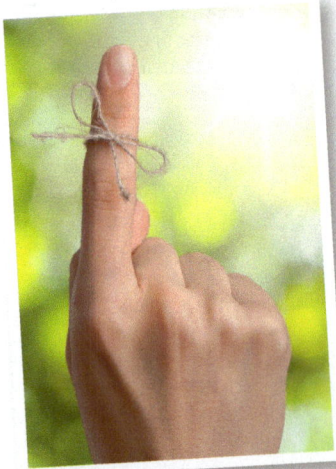

CUE DEPENDENT FORGETTING – CONTEXT AND STATE

Cue dependent forgetting occurs when information already stored in memory feels hard to recall due to a lack of retrieval cues. Cue dependency is when memory storage works, but **retrieval fails**. Cue dependent forgetting is another theory of forgetting because it suggests retrieval failure rather than storage failure is the cause of forgetting.

Cues work in memory to aid retrieval because memory associations can act as connections to other related memories and this helps retrieve associated memories. Therefore, cues can help in the retrieval process.

There are two types of cue dependent forgetting: context and state dependent forgetting. Memory cues can come from the **context** where the memory was encoded or from the **state of mind** of the person trying to do the remembering.

CONTEXT DEPENDENT MEMORY CUES

Context cues have been found to be very important in recall accuracy. **Abernathy (1940)** tested psychology students in the *same room* or a *different classroom* with a test given by either their *own* or a *new* teacher. Those students tested in their usual room with their usual teacher did better in results than those tested in a new room with a new teacher. This supports the theory of context dependent memory.

Godden and Baddeley (1975) carried out a field experiment on underwater divers that supports context dependent memory. Godden and Baddeley (1975) studied 16 deep sea divers and their memory for 40 words learned on land ('dry') or underwater ('wet'). The divers were then tested in each context for memory: either on land ('dry') or ten feet underwater ('wet').

The divers who learned the lists 'dry' recalled more words when tested 'dry' (13.5 words on average) than when tested 'wet' (8.6 words on average). This contrasts with the divers who learned the lists 'wet' recalling more when tested 'wet' (11.4 words on average) than when tested dry on land (8.4 words on average. Therefore, they found a context distinction in recall accuracy based on the learning context being re-instated during testing.

TABLE: Summary of results for the Godden and Baddeley (1975) divers' field experiment on context dependent memory.

LEARNING CONTEXT	RECALL CONTEXT	
	Dry Recall (mean number of words recalled out of 40)	Wet Recall (mean number of words recalled out of 40)
Dry Learning	13.5	8.6
Wet Learning	8.4	11.4

STATE DEPENDENT MEMORY CUES

State dependent forgetting is supported by research on the effects of alcohol. Goodwin et al (1969) tested people when they were either *drunk* or *sober*. Those who learned material when drunk showed better recall for that material when drunk again rather than when sober. This suggests the **brain state** of the individual (drunk or sober) may explain differences in accuracy of recall.

The same *state-dependent effect* has been found for **drugs** (see Bustamante et al (1970) for a study on amphetamines) and **exercise** (see Miles and Hardman (1998) for a study on gym exercising and state-dependent memory).

FORGETTING DUE TO BRAIN DAMAGE – RESEARCH

Specific **brain regions** can be **damaged** and cause memory loss. The effects on memory can be profound. The damage is, often, irreversible. Case studies of patients who suffered brain damage leading to memory loss include **Clive Wearing** and **Henry Moliason**.

Brain damage explains memory loss as a biological process whereby the neurological substrate of memory is disrupted. Brain regions may undergo trauma, become infected by disease, or become inactive after a stroke. In addition, patients may suffer brain lesions or parts of the brain may become tumorous. These *biological causes* can all result in cognitive memory loss. Thus, **brain damage** may be *another* reason why we forget.

RESEARCH ON BRAIN DAMAGE CAUSING FORGETTING: Two famous case studies:

CASE STUDY: Scoville and Milner (1957) - *Henry Moliason* had **psychosurgery** to remove his **hippocampus** and, from then on, he was locked into his old memories unable to form new episodic memories. He suffered from *retrograde amnesia*. Henry Moliason's brain damage was researched and documented by Scoville and Milner (1957).

CASE STUDY: Wilson and Wearing (1995) - *Clive Wearing* contracted a rare form of syphilis encephalitis that infected his brain, especially disrupting the **hippocampus**. Because of his brain damage, he lost the ability to create new memories or recall old memories. Therefore, Clive Wearing suffered from both *retrograde amnesia* and **anterograde amnesia**. Yet, he didn't lose the ability to sing, perform simple piano recitals or conduct a group of singers. Therefore, his procedural memory remained intact. Clive Wearing's brain damage was written about by Wilson and Wearing (1995) in a case study summarising many of his clinical reports.

➕ **DON'T FORGET**

Biological damage to the neurons supporting the *cognitive processes* of memory can cause forgetting in the encoding process, the storage process or the retrieval process.

❓ THINGS TO DO AND THINK ABOUT

Everyday Examples of Cue Dependent Forgetting

Think of everyday examples where forgetting is likely due to a lack of context cues or because state cues are different.

CONTEXT CUES: Example of external Context Dependency: For example, when you get home, forgetting the name of a person you met on holiday. Their name might return to mind if you think about the holiday location (re-instating the context).

STATE CUES: Example of internal State Dependency: Alternatively, you might start feeling in 'holiday mode' again and this state of mind might act as an internal cue. The relaxed *feelings* felt on holiday may be associated with the memory for the name of the person.

Now, create your own example of context-dependent forgetting and state dependent memory.

APPLIED RESEARCH: APPLYING THEORIES TO MEMORY IMPROVEMENT

Applying psychology to everyday life reveals the power of theories to explain and analyse behaviour. Here, memory theories are applied to exams and studying.

DON'T FORGET

Before starting, ask yourself what good is a theory if it fails to predict anything when applied to real life?

APPLIED RESEARCH ON THE TOPIC OF MEMORY IMPROVEMENT

Can the biological approach to memory be applied in everyday life to improve memory and prevent forgetting? Could the cognitive approach to psychology throw light on how to revise better for exams? How can Freudian psychoanalysis improve people's health and wellbeing when it comes to dealing with difficult memories? What do we know about the topic of **memory** in an **applied** setting?

You may need to explain how **to apply** the optional individual topic to everyday life and behaviour. In addition, your analysis and explanation of the application **should be supported by research evidence** to evaluate the effectiveness of the application.

So, how can the individual topic of *Memory* be applied to everyday life?

APPLYING THEORIES OF MEMORY IMPROVEMENT TO REVISION FOR EXAMS

How has research on the topic of memory improved our everyday use of memory? How can we improve our memory for an event? How can we study better for exams?

Baddeley (1997) presents evidence to support the effectiveness of visual memory in revision. Basically, one applied way to improve recall from studying is to use visual learning techniques, acoustic learning techniques and verbal learning techniques in combination to get more out of our human memory storage.

Use visual memory

Since the 1960s, Tony Buzan has promoted the use of **mind-maps** in education around the world. Buzan claims mind-maps match important aspects of the way the mind semantically organises concepts. In mind-maps, meaningful connections and associations are drawn to reflect their linkage in memory.

ONLINE

Learn to mind-map, the Tony Buzan way, at www.brightredbooks.net

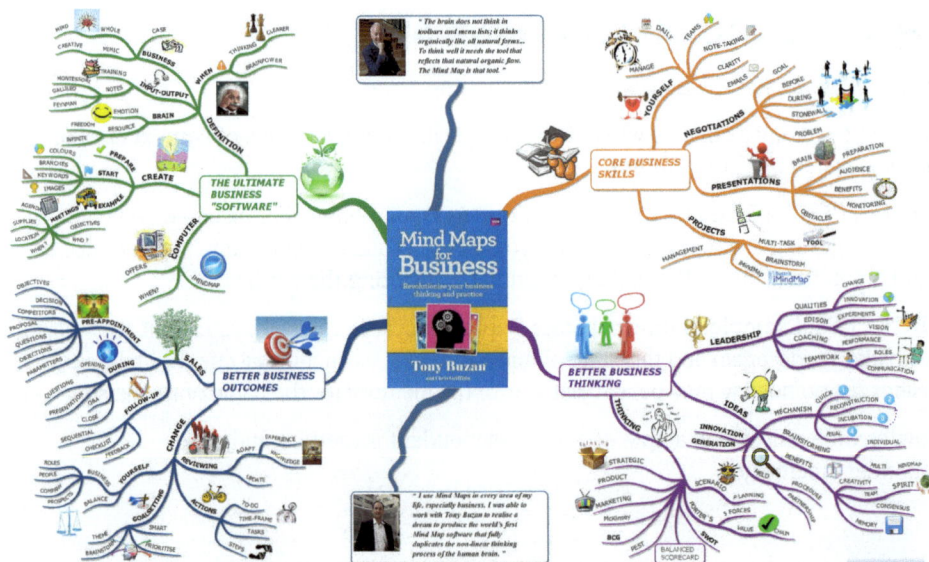

contd

Paivio (1960) supports the view that visual memory has a greater capacity than acoustic memory, as these stores are separate and have relatively independent storage capacities.

Paivio's (1969) 'dual-coding theory' states that visual depictions, combined with words, lead to better recall and improved memory test results because using visual images alongside words engages more of the brain's available storage capacity.

Use all of the working memory (cognitive approach)

Since Atkinson and Shiffrin's (1968) Multi-Store Model of memory, Baddeley and Hitch (1974) have researched and developed a more detailed cognitive theory called the working memory theory.

Baddeley and Hitch (1968) propose a **working memory** model that suggests there are at least three (and possibly four) STM storage components in the mind. In their model of working memory, they claim there is a short-term visual memory store (called the visuo-spatial sketchpad), a phonological loop (for sounds and rhythms) and an articulatory store (for words and language). They suggest these are supervised and controlled by a memory 'manager' component, called the central executive.

In addition, Baddeley (2000) added an 'episodic memory' buffer to the working memory model; its purpose to store the flow of everyday events and sequences of events.

According to the cognitive approach, all the components of working memory should be utilised in turn to assist with encoding and increasing storage capacity limits in order to improve memory retention for exam revision. Effective revision will involve engaging the whole range of verbal, visual and acoustic storage systems.

Use organisation in memory to chunk information

Organising your notes will help you memorise them at each stage – during encoding, storage and retrieval.

Bower et al (1969) showed there was increased free recall of material that could be easily organised into categories. For example, if words in a 20-word list could be grouped together into groups or categories like vehicles and animals, then the material would be more easily recalled in laboratory testing than when using unrelated words in a similar test. Further evidence for the categorical organisation of long-term memory into logical classifications comes from Collins and Quillan (1969).

Chunking together related material will help with exam revision. Semantically related material (that is, linked by similar meaning) can be quickly chunked together by the mind, using some basic principles of organisation. It's easier to remember organised notes than disorganised notes, and reliable evidence supports this view. For example, Bousfield (1953) reported that words in a memory test are often recalled in organised clusters of related words.

Craik and Tulving (1975) distinguish between **two types of memory rehearsal**:

Maintenance rehearsal is the active processing of short-term memory material at a shallow level. It merely keeps the information within short-term storage, without successfully transferring it into longer-term storage.

Elaborative rehearsal (seen as the most effective for improving recall) processes memory at a deeper level and helps transfer the memory from short-term to long-term storage.

💭 THINGS TO DO AND THINK ABOUT

Try these two steps to making a mind-map:

1. Look up a few mind-maps using Google images to inspire you.

2. Create a visually memorable mind-map on A3 paper of one of the Higher Psychology topics.

Remember, research employing mind-maps for revision by Farrand et al (2002) claims a 6% advantage in recall accuracy over typical study skills for the task of learning 600 words of text.

➕ DON'T FORGET

Keep your study notes organised into meaningful chunks, topics, categories and sections.

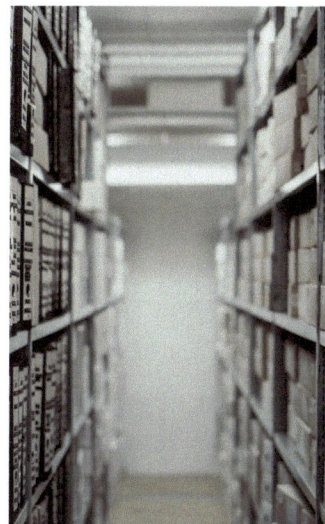

➕ DON'T FORGET

Avoid chunks bigger than seven items. According to Miller (1956), this will assist short-term memory processing in your exam revision.

➕ DON'T FORGET

Go Deep! For improved memory, Craik and Tulving (1975) suggest you should aim for elaborative rehearsal during revision.

➕ DON'T FORGET

Bizarre and **distinctive** material will be remembered better than everyday information because it's unique. This memory improvement is known as the Hedwig von Restorff effect (1933).

APPLIED RESEARCH: APPLYING MEMORY THEORIES TO CRIME – EYEWITNESS TESTIMONY

Loftus and Palmer (1974) carried out **applied research** on reconstructive memory theory and eyewitness testimony. Their applied eyewitness testimony research illustrates how cognitive theories of memory have **helped improve** the reliability of **eyewitness testimony** in criminal justice systems.

WHY IS MEMORY RECONSTRUCTIVE?

Early work on the nature of memory led Bartlett (1932) to conclude memory was **reconstructive**. Bartlett suggested memory retrieval is not accurate. It's not an exact replay of the past. Rather, it's more like the fresh construction of a new perception based on the schemas of the individual.

According to Jean Piaget, a 'schema' is a mental category (or set of ideas) used, personally and cognitively, by an individual to make sense of the world. Piaget's research showed schemas develop with experience, and noted that children's schemas are often inaccurate, naive, simple, developing and incomplete.

Reconstructive memory theory: Bartlett's 'War of the Ghosts' research (1932)

Bartlett (1932) supported the reconstructive theory of memory with his 'War of the Ghosts' study. This research showed long-term memory recall to be **reconstructed** from memory fragments categorised according to the individual and cultural schemas, rather than accurately recalled.

Bartlett demonstrated that when a non-Native American was told a Native American ghost story about fighting dead ancestors and dying of a ghostly sickness, despite being a brave warrior in battle, many culturally significant details were lost in recall.

The non-Native Americans made serious errors in the retelling; they made cultural schema errors in their reconstruction and crafted their recollection of the story into a far shorter and more familiar tale about hunting. Bartlett concluded this provided evidence for the theory that memory is culturally reconstructed, **schema driven** and, therefore, reconstructive in nature.

VIDEO LINK

Watch Mr Martin's explanation of the eyewitness testimony research of Loftus and Palmer (1974) at www.brightredbooks.net

IV = VERB USED IN LEADING QUESTION	DV= AVERAGE SPEED ESTIMATE
Smashed	40.8 mph
Collided	39.3 mph
Bumped	38.1 mph
Hit	34.0 mph
Contacted	31.8 mph

Table showing the average speed estimates for each group in the first experiment from the Loftus and Palmer (1974) study on the reliability of eye witness testimony in response to the verb used in the leading questions.

LOFTUS AND PALMER (1974)

Loftus and Palmer (1974) did some groundbreaking research on reconstructive memory theory and eyewitness testimony. They showed that **leading questions** in eyewitness interviewing (for example, giving information after an event) can alter the memory of events after they've occurred.

AIM: To measure the unreliability of eyewitness accounts and, specifically eyewitness accounts of speed estimates for cars involved in crashes. They realised people were, in general, rather poor at accurately estimating the speed of cars in traffic. Would the strength of the verb used in a leading question change the estimated speed?

HYPOTHESIS: The strength of the verb used in leading questions will distort the estimated speed of the cars witnessed crashing in films of traffic collisions.

METHOD: This was a laboratory experiment, with independent groups design. Forty student participants were used in five groups of eight for their first experimental procedure. Each group saw a range of short films (less than 30-seconds long) of cars colliding. Only the strength of the verb used in the speed estimation question differed between the groups. This made the verb the independent variable. The dependent variable was the average speed estimate for each group.

The critical leading question was always, 'How fast were the cars going when they ******** into each other?'

RESULTS: The results confirmed their hypothesis that the stronger the verb used in the leading question, the higher the participants estimated the speed of the cars when watching the same films. The average speed estimates for each verb used are in the table left:

The highest speed estimate, 40.8 mph, was found in the group who heard the word 'smashed'. The lowest, 31.8 mph, was from the group with the word 'contacted'.

CONCLUSION: There was an association between the strength of the verb used in the leading question and the average estimate of the speed of the cars in the films. The differences between the groups were significant and reliable.

The results of the first of the studies by Loftus and Palmer (1974) support the viewpoint that post-event leading questions can distort the recollection of speed estimates from eyewitness accounts of traffic accidents.

Evaluation

STRENGTH	WEAKNESS
The results are consistent with the theory that the strength of the language used in the leading question caused measurable differences in post-event memory for the crashes. This might have occurred by modification of the memory in reconstruction towards the information contained in the leading questions.	The changes in the speed estimates might have been due to the demand characteristics of the situation.
Laboratory experiment has a high level of control of extraneous variables allowing causality to be more easily inferred.	There is low ecological validity to these laboratory results as they are collected from students witnessing films rather than real accidents and crimes.
The Loftus and Palmer (1974) study is highly replicable as it followed a standardised and well-described procedure.	There is no way of knowing if the memory for the event changes in storage, as Loftus and Palmer (1974) claim, or if the distortion in response is an experiment effect occurring only at the level of the behavioural response.

DON'T FORGET

The Loftus and Palmer (1974) leading-questions study shows how memory theories can be used in crime prosecution and applied to help understand the unreliability of eyewitness testimony.

THINGS TO DO AND THINK ABOUT

Decide who'll be the officer and who'll be the witness. The officer must ask questions while the witness tries to recall as much as they can remember about a real-life event.

Officer: Use the cognitive interview technique, as tested by Geiselman et al (1985), and apply the following five techniques to gather as many notes as you can about the event:

1) Relax the witness and keep them happy to chat.

2) Reconstruct the scene of the event, using recollections from all five senses.

3) Write down any detail mentioned by the witness and zoom in on the detail for more information associated with that detail, however trivial.

4) Reverse the order of recall, if the witness gets stuck retrieving memories.

5) Ask the witness to imagine the event from different points of view, with different priorities and from different person perspectives.

VIDEO LINK

Watch Elizabeth Loftus give a lecture in Edinburgh on her eyewitness testimony research work at www.brightredbooks.net

CONFORMITY AND OBEDIENCE

INTRODUCTION TO CONFORMITY AND OBEDIENCE

In today's society, the pressure to conform and to obey remains strong. We like to think we can resist social pressure and act independently, however, laboratory experiments such as those by Asch (1951) and Milgram (1963) have shown conformity and obedience to be extremely powerful social responses.

OVERVIEW

We tend to believe we're free to make our own decisions and that we don't follow the crowd. But this chapter analyses the powerful social forces influencing conformity and obedience. It aims to provide an exploration of the factors affecting conformity and obedience – individual, situational and cultural. Psychological theories of conformity and obedience are analysed to allow application and evaluation of a range of strategies for resisting social pressure.

TYPES OF CONFORMITY

According to Kelman's (1958) three-process model, there are three steps to true conformity. The first is compliance, the second is identification and the third is internalisation. In Kelman's (1958) theory, the three steps to conformity occur in response to messages from the powerful, the attractive and the credible. He saw this model of conformity as useful in predicting attitude change over time.

Compliance: to the powerful

Kelman (1958) stated that the first level of conformity – compliance – occurs in response to a powerful group. With compliance, there's very little identification or internalisation of the content, attitudes or beliefs of the group, but there is conformity.

Compliance is a yielding to the social power of a group. For example, an individual may internally disagree with a group they're in, however, to avoid an unfavourable reaction from that group, they adopt the group-norm behaviour. Compliance is the most temporary type of conformity and might be called 'false' conformity because it's only at the behavioural level.

Identification: with the attractive

Kelman's (1958) second level of conformity is called identification. With identification, the individual will be willing to accept the influence of the group because they genuinely want to adopt a positive attitude towards it. The individual also finds membership of the group self-defining and satisfying.

According to Kelman (1958), the individual at the relationship level cares about adopting the group's typical behaviours because the group is attractive, important or similar to them; they 'identify' with it.

Identification results in adopting the behaviours and attitudes of the group, although the content of the beliefs of the group might be ignored or glossed over, just for the sake of the social relationship.

Internalisation: of the credible

If the majority group behaviour is maintained, then Kelman (1958) states, the third step of conformity – internalisation – may occur.

Internalisation involves adopting the ideas, content, beliefs, attitudes and behaviours of the group. Internalising the beliefs of a group leads to agreement with the group's values

contd

and this causes both intrinsic and extrinsic rewards for the individual. Rewards from internalisation include group acceptance, continued group membership, reduced anxiety and self-acceptance.

Internalisation results in the truest conformity, is the most resistant to change and the most consistent across a range of situations.

DEUTSCH AND GERARD'S (1955) DUAL-PROCESS THEORY OF CONFORMITY

Both informational social influence and normative social influence might lead to conformity. In their dual-process theory, Deutsch and Gerard (1955) make a distinction between conformity motivated by the desire to be right – informational social influence (ISI) – and conformity motivated by the desire to be liked and accepted by the group – normative social influence (NSI).

Ultimately, conformity occurs by making a distortion of either the individual's independent response (compliance), a distortion of the individual's perception (identification) or a distortion of the person's judgement (internalisation).

Normative social influence (NSI)

According to Deutsch and Gerard (1955), normative social influence (NSI) is a social influence towards conformity to the group norm motivated by the desire to be liked and accepted by the group.

Conformity can be caused by NSI because conformity shows solidarity with the group and holds expectations of positive acceptance by the group (and positive reinforcements from the group) on fulfilment of conformity. If there is non-fulfilment of conformity, there are expectations of alienation by the group and isolation from it.

Informational social influence (ISI)

Deutsch and Gerard (1955) then discuss informational social influence (ISI) as a social influence to conform to the 'social reality' rather than the physical reality.

If a group has been reliable in the past as a source of trustworthy information or judgement, then it will be relied on to some extent in the future. In some cases, conformity is motivated by the desire to be 'right' and the group may provide a source of information for what the correct or appropriate response is.

THINGS TO DO AND THINK ABOUT

Example:

If an army of devils told you there was a fire behind you, you might end up believing there was a fire behind you.

In this fantasy example, the army of devils provide a source of informational social influence (ISI), rather than normative social influence as there's no desire for acceptance or belonging to the group (in other words, no NSI). Yet the group of devils has been useful to you as a source of information, however reliable or unreliable they may be! The conformity to belief in the fire in this example is motivated by ISI – the desire to be right, not liked!

Can you give an example that illustrates the distinction between NSI and ISI?

DON'T FORGET

In evaluation, Deutsch and Gerard (1955) are using the terms NSI and ISI to distinguish between two internal reasons for conformity. However, at the behavioural level, they're hard to tell apart.

VIDEO LINK

There's an entertaining *Candid Camera* clip on the web that shows the power of social conformity in an elevator. Watch it at www.brightredbooks.net

VIDEO LINK

Watch the Philip Zimbardo video documentary at www.brightredbooks.net which includes his Stanford Prison Experiment, an explanation of the Asch (1951,1955) conformity study and the more recent Smoke Filled Room.

ONLINE TEST

Test yourself on conformity and obedience at www.brightredbooks.net

STAR STUDY: ASCH (1951): THE LINE JUDGEMENT EXPERIMENT

Title: 'Effects of group pressure upon the modification and distortion of judgement', Asch, S.E. (1951), in H. Guetzkow (ed.), *Groups, Leadership and Men.* Pittsburgh, PA, Carnegie Press, pp. 177–190.

Research topic: Asch (1951) was interested in what conditions were necessary to allow an individual to rise above group pressure and show independence in their responses. What factors in a situation allow resistance to social pressure? Is submission to group pressure necessary or are there conditions/possibilities for independence?

INTRODUCTION

In a series of laboratory experiments, Asch (1951) demonstrated several factors that promote conformity. Asch showed how these factors influence submission to group pressure. He was interested in what happens to group conformity when the task is easy (unambiguous). Previous studies by Sherif (1935) and Jenness (1932) focused on ambiguous tasks where there was no obviously correct answer for naive participants to stray from, so there was no knowing when conformity was occurring against the desire to be right.

In 1951, Asch developed an experimental lab technique involving a simple line-judgement task; either judged individually and written down, or declared openly to the rest of a test group.

AIM

The experiment aimed to see what factors affect conformity to group pressure in a test group, and to reveal how an individual makes conforming judgements in the presence of an obviously wrong, majority opinion.

Hypotheses

The experimental hypothesis was that, even in conditions of almost complete certainty, a wrong judgement from a group majority will result in some participants yielding to group pressure, and in a distortion or compromise of judgement in some towards the normative influence.

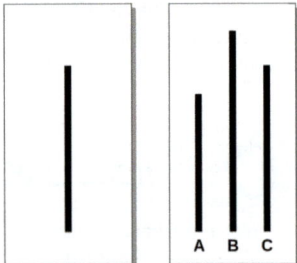

METHOD

This laboratory experiment had an independent groups design. In the presence of actors who were instructed to give wrong answers on certain, critical trials, Asch asked each group member to judge the length of lines and choose either A, B or C as the line with matching length.

Twelve critical trials were used to measure the error rate in the accuracy of the line judgements under the presence or absence of group pressure from a unanimous majority. This formed the independent variable.

On critical conformity trials, in the experimental condition, actors provided an incorrect majority group judgement (for example, B) against the correct answer (C) and the response of one naive participant to the majority influence was recorded. The error rate was the dependent variable.

Sample

In the first instance, there were two groups: 50 males in the experimental condition and 37 males in the control condition.

contd

ONLINE →

Find out more about Asch's factors at www.brightredbooks.net

DON'T FORGET

Conformity and obedience are two types of social influence. In the final exam, you could be set a conformity question, an obedience question or a social influence question. In the latter, remember to refer to both types of social influence: conformity and obedience.

Asch (1951) collected both quantitative and qualitative data on 50 male participants' accuracy of judgement of line lengths in the presence of a group. He compared these results with the number of times a wrong line judgement was made in the control group without the presence of a group majority influence towards a wrong answer. The control group recorded their results in the presence of a group, but in writing and without declaring their answer to the rest of the group.

RESULTS

The main question was would the naive participant act independently from the group or bend their judgement towards the majority answer?

In the 1951 experiment, around one third (32%) of all the estimates in the experimental group made distorted and conforming errors on more than one trial in line with the false answers given by the majority. Surprisingly, 75% of all the participants in the experimental condition conformed at least once to the majority influence, despite the task being easy individually. When answering individually, the control group showed nearly 100% accuracy.

In the presence of a unanimous majority group giving a wrong answer, the average error rate was four out of 12 compared to zero out of 12 in the control group.

CONCLUSION

Asch concluded that, for some people, pressure to conform to the majority influence was strong, while for others it was easier to resist social pressure. To further reveal the factors influencing conformity, Asch went on to report several variations on his original experiment. Asch noted four factors seemed to be influencing conformity rates: group size, unanimity, task difficulty and character confidence.

ONLINE

Look over the Asch's (1951) conformity study online at www.brightredbooks.net a few times. This will familiarise you with the laboratory procedure and allow you to analyse some of Asch's variations.

ONLINE TEST

Test yourself on conformity at www.brightredbooks.net

EVALUATION

STRENGTHS	WEAKNESSES
This laboratory experiment had a high degree of control and replicability. The procedure was standardised and the model allows important social variables to be manipulated to reveal factors affecting conformity.	Asch's (1951) study, while often misinterpreted as showing a high level of conformity, might also support independent behaviour. The headline result of 75% of the sample showing at least one conformity error is often quoted, when only 32% actually showed consistent conformity across a number of trials. Indeed, 24% of the experimental group never conformed on any trial.
A major finding of Asch (1951) is that disturbance of the unanimity of the majority has a larger effect on conformity than group size. Asch reports that a unanimous majority of three has more power than a larger group of disparate opinions has on conformity rates.	Individual differences were masked by average error rates. A large proportion of the participants (13 out of the 50 males) showed no errors at all in their judgement, even under the experimental group pressure. Asch states 'the preponderance of estimates in the critical group was correct despite the presence of the majority'.
Asch debriefed participants and collected qualitative interview data on why they gave wrong answers in the presence of the group. This was to find the reason for any distortion of judgement in response to majority group pressure.	The participants were denied the opportunity to give fully informed consent because the experimenters lied to the participants about the true aim of the laboratory task.

THINGS TO DO AND THINK ABOUT

Conformity questions

These questions require analysis and evaluation of the Asch (1951) Line Judgement Study. Try to write one *paragraph* per mark.

1. Why are the conformity rates in the Asch (1951) experiments high? (4 marks)
2. What factors worked in the Asch (1951) study to create group conformity? (4 marks)
3. When did Asch (1951) report conformity rates going down? (3 marks)
4. Why is this experiment a classic? Explain some of its strengths. (5 marks)
5. Explain **two** weaknesses of the Asch (1951) laboratory experiment. (4 marks)

INDIVIDUAL FACTORS THAT AFFECT CONFORMITY

Since conformity research began, in the twentieth century with researchers such as Sherif (1935) and Asch (1951), later studies have revealed a wide range of factors that affect conformity.

DON'T FORGET

In the Higher Psychology exam you might be asked for factors that affect conformity with examples of supporting evidence to show your skill in analysing the concept of conformity.

DON'T FORGET

One way to remember the headings for these individual factors is to remember the mnemonic 'P.I.N.G.U.'.

INDIVIDUAL, SITUATIONAL AND CULTURAL FACTORS

Factors that affect conformity include **individual factors** that are to do with the characteristics of the person conforming, **situational factors** that are to do with the attributes of the group setting, and **cultural factors** that may explain cross-cultural variations in conformity levels.

INDIVIDUAL FACTORS

Conformity is more likely to occur when certain **individual factors** are favourable to a person yielding and giving way to the majority. Conversely, higher levels of confidence, understanding, self-esteem and expertise all seem to be important factors in reducing conformity. Stang (1973) reports that personal confidence in a situation reduces conformity as does high self-esteem.

Individual factors are the characteristics or attributes of the person who is under pressure to conform. They include **personality**, **identification** with the group, the individual's **need for social approval**, **gender** and **understanding and expertise**.

Personality

There are individual differences in personality and one factor that affects conformity is the degree to which an individual submits to authority and shows conventional behaviour.

Adorno et al (1950) recognised 'Type A' personalities as highly conforming types. They measured the Type A personality using an inventory called the 'F-scale' to measure the 'Authoritarian' personality type. Type A personalities were described by Adorno et al as showing a syndrome of behaviours, including tendencies toward conventionalism, conformity and submission to authority.

Adorno et al (1950) suggested the Type A personality was formed from Freudian projection of internalised hostility and aggression towards parents who have socialised the Type A personality into identification and submission to authority.

Identification

One factor that affects conformity to group pressure is how much a person identifies with the group. This is consistent with Tajfel and Turner's (1979) social identity theory. Identification with a majority in-group increases the pressure to conform to that in-group while non-identification with a majority out-group decreases conformity pressures.

According to Abrams et al's (1990) experiments on similarity to the group, one pressure to conform results from self-categorisation with the group. This flows from wanting to maintain membership of that group, as it's seen as attractive, similar or desirable. As Abrams et al's (1990) group experiments showed, personal identification with a group increased the pressure to conform.

Need for social approval

Another individual factor that may affect conformity is the need for social approval. Crowne and Marlowe (1964) studied this need as an important motive behind social

contd

responses. They created a social desirability scale to measure an individual's need for social approval.

Bornstein (1994) measured people with a high need for social approval and this predicted higher levels of conformity in subsequent tests. However, Loomis and Spilka (1972) did not find support for the need for approval as a factor in conformity.

Gender

According to Eagly (1987) 'Men are more influential, women are more easily influenced'. However, the evidence for this over the years has been mixed.

Glass et al (1981) reviewed conformity findings to conclude there was evidence for a small gender difference with females conforming more.

However, when Eagly reviewed the literature in 1978 it was concluded there was no gender difference in conformity levels. Later, Eagly et al (1981) again reported finding no gender differences in conformity levels. If there is a gender difference in conformity, it's likely to be a role expectation difference that persists due to gender role socialisation, rather than a biological difference.

Understanding and Expertise

Expertise has been listed as a factor that reduces the pressure to conform. Perrin and Spencer (1988) conducted an Asch (1951) type study following the same line-judgement task as part of the procedure. The participants were engineering students who could be assumed to have had some previous expertise in line measurement. Accordingly, the number of conforming errors reported by Perrin and Spencer (1988) for this group dropped to a low level.

THINGS TO DO AND THINK ABOUT

Here are some exam-style formative exercises with marks to help develop your skills.

1. Describe two individual factors that affect conformity levels. (4 marks)

2. Explain how identification with a group increases conformity. (2 marks)

3. Analyse whether gender influences conformity. (3 marks)

4. How do differences in personality explain variations in conformity? (3 marks)

TOTAL MARKS: 12 marks

ONLINE

'SlideShare' is a good resource for PowerPoint presentations on many different topics. You can find one 'SlideShare' PowerPoint resource for Higher Psychology on *Conformity and Obedience* at www.brightredbooks.net

ONLINE TEST

Head to www.brightredbooks.net to test yourself on the individual factors that affect conformity.

SITUATIONAL AND CULTURAL FACTORS THAT AFFECT CONFORMITY

Situational and **cultural factors** have been found to determine the level of conformity and social influence experienced by an individual in a group situation.

DON'T FORGET

One way to remember the headings for these situational factors is to remember the mnemonic 'G.A.T.U'.

DON'T FORGET

Analyse whether *all* errors by participants in the Asch (1951) line-judgement task indicate conformity. Is this a weakness of the dependent variable of this study?

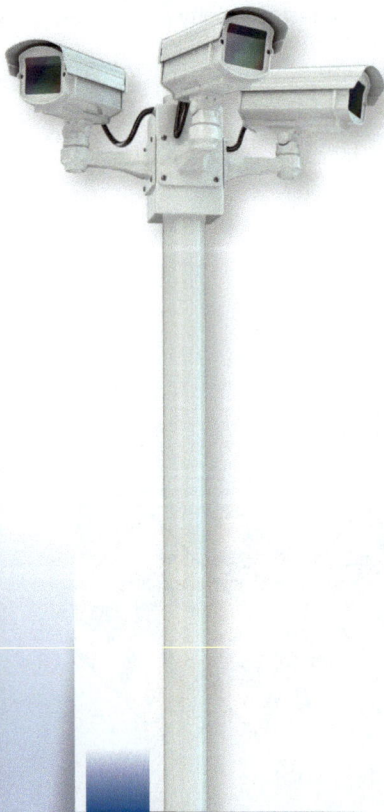

SITUATIONAL FACTORS

Conformity is more likely to occur when certain *situational* factors are favourable to a person moving their responses towards the group norm. Situational factors that affect conformity stem from attributes and characteristics of the group setting.

Situational factors include whether the group is big or small (**group size**), whether the group will see the response of the individual or not (**anonymity**), how difficult or unclear the group task is (**task difficulty**) and whether the group is unanimous or dissenting (**unanimity**).

Group size

In 1952 Asch presented results for how group size affected conformity in his line-judgement task.

Asch (1952) investigated the situational variable of group size by using different group sizes. He investigated conformity rates specifically for zero, one, two, three, four, six and 16 people in the group. The highest conformity rate reported was for four people in the group (35%). This rate compared with a 3% conformity rate for one person in the group, 13% conformity rate for two people in the group and a 33% conformity rate for three people. Larger group sizes of eight and 16 people did not get higher rates: 32% for eight people and 31% for 16.

Anonymity

Anonymity of judgement within a group leads to less conformity to group pressure. However, any perceived social surveillance of one's judgements increases group pressure.

The **public** versus **private** judgement factor (i.e. anonymity) was investigated by Crutchfield (1955). Crutchfield modified the Asch experimental model to be more efficient by replacing the 'actors' in the original study with lights. Crutchfield used lights in a booth to indicate what 'other people' were giving in response to a similar decision-making task.

Six hundred participants were tested in booths, and Crutchfield (1955) noted that conformity increased when the participants thought their judgements were being observed by other people and dropped when they thought they were not. This led to the popular definition of conformity; 'real or **imagined** group pressure', as the participants were not exposed to true social influence, only imagined social influence. However, it may be that some of Crutchfield's participants guessed the lights in the booth were not indicating real judgements.

Anonymity was an important factor in the Asch (1951) lines study, too. In one variation, when Asch asked participants to write their answers down privately (anonymously), instead of declaring their answers to the group, conformity rates decreased greatly – most likely in response to lack of surveillance by the group. The privacy, or anonymity, of their judgement offered them release from the pressure to conform.

Task difficulty

Crutchfield (1955) conducted a conformity study based on a shape-judgement task and varied task difficulty. Crutchfield found that the more difficult the task, the higher the conformity error rate. This supports the view that conformity increases as ambiguity and uncertainty increases.

contd

Barron, Vandello and Brunswick (1996) varied task difficulty and task importance in a conformity experiment. They found that conformity was highest when the task was perceived as difficult and when the task was declared as 'very important'.

Unanimity

In the Asch (1951) experiment, when agreement was not unanimous and there was someone else (an 'ally') in the group who gave a different answer to the rest of the group, the conformity rate dropped from 32% to 5% for the participant sample of 50 men.

Asch reported that unanimity was the most influential variable affecting conformity rates. If there was just one other person not conforming, this dropped participants' conformity rates markedly. The accuracy of the other's view did not seem to matter; as long as there was someone with an alternative view to the majority, the spell of conformity was broken.

CULTURAL FACTORS

Conformity research has been carried out worldwide by researchers such as Berry (1967), who attempted to explain high conformity rates found among the people from Sierra Leone and low conformity rates found from a sample of Canadian Inuits.

Using participant samples from different countries may reveal cultural differences in levels of conformity – there are certainly differences between countries reported – however, other sampling factors may explain these differences too.

Cultural variation

Evidence for cultural differences comes from Bond and Smith (1996) who carried out a meta-analysis of 133 studies using the Asch (1951) procedure from 17 different countries around the world. Bond and Smith (1996) noted that for Indian teachers in Fiji, conformity rates, as measured by Chandra (1973) were high (58%), while for students in Belgium, as measured by Doms (1983), conformity rates on a similar procedure were low (15%). This may arise from differences in cultural socialisation.

Collectivist cultures versus individualistic cultures

Smith, Bond and Kagitcibasi (2006) grouped results of conformity studies together from countries categorised as either individualistic or collectivist. Individualistic cultures encourage citizens to look after themselves and self-fulfilment. In collectivist cultures, the family, community and society are held as more valuable than the individual.

In countries rated as individualistic (for example, North American and European countries), Smith, Bond and Kagitcibasi (2006) found average conformity rates of 25% across a range of studies. They then compared the conformity rates for countries categorised as collectivist cultures (for example, African, Asian, South American countries) and found a higher conformity rate, with an average of 37%.

VIDEO LINK

Watch the 'Explanations of Conformity - Individual Factors' video on factors affecting conformity at www.brightredbooks.net

DON'T FORGET

You can **analyse** with the GRAVES technique to create six paragraphs: Generalisability, Reliability, Applicability, Validity, Evaluation, Sampling.

THINGS TO DO AND THINK ABOUT

Try these four questions on conformity factors for exam practice:

1. Explain how group size and task difficulty can affect conformity. (6 marks)

2. Explain how conformity is affected by situational factors. (4 marks)

3. Explain how culture can affect conformity. (4 marks)

4. Analyse Asch's (1951) experiments on conformity. (6 marks)

TOTAL MARKS: 20 marks

ONLINE TEST

Head to www.brightredbooks. net to test yourself on the situational and cultural factors that affect conformity.

STAR STUDY: MORI AND ARAI (2010): CONFORMITY IN JAPAN

Title: 'No need to fake it: Reproduction of the Asch experiment without confederates'. Mori, K. and Arai, M. (2010), *International Journal of Psychology*, 45 (5), pp.390–397.

INTRODUCTION

Mori and Arai (2010) wondered whether the Asch's (1956) results were still reliable and valid for Japan in 2010. They remembered that Allen and Levine (1960) had doubted the original explanation Asch (1951) gave for the conformity rates in the unanimous majority conditions. Mori and Arai noted that having the experimenter in the room during the Asch (1951) line-judgement task might also have provided demand characteristics towards conformity.

For Mori and Arai (2010), there would be no experimenter present in the room during the line-judgement task.

They conducted a partial replication of the classic Asch conformity study with the aim of testing his original conclusions, but they added a methodological twist. The participants would be given coloured spectacles (similar to 3D goggles) to filter out rival images from the same stimulus. This visual presentation technique (the MORI technique: Manipulation of Rival Images) would remove the need for actors and reduce deception. They focused on the variables of majority versus minority conformity rates and gender.

AIM

The aim of the Mori and Arai (2010) experiment was to confirm the results of Asch (1951) that a unanimous majority influence would increase conformity error rates in an easy line-judgement task, this time, without the effect of acting and deception.

METHOD

This study was a laboratory experiment. Two **independent** variables were examined – gender and majority influence. The **dependent** variable measured was the frequency of conforming errors made on the 12 critical trials where one of the group of four participants in each trial could see different lines.

Sample

A total of 104 participants were tested, with 40 males and 64 females. They were undergraduate university students with an average age of around 20 years old.

Design

This experiment used an independent groups design. Participants were tested in 26 groups of four, with the same gender grouping. Three of the four participants wore identical filter glasses, while the remaining participant wore different glasses. This arrangement filtered the coloured lines to suggest a different right answer to the majority on the critical trials.

Procedure

The room was set up with four seats in front of a projector screen. The same stimulus set of lines as used in Asch (1956) were used to create nine line-judgement tasks with a rival image in green and magenta. The minority viewer in the group of four wore different glasses and would see the lines differently from the rest, suggesting a different correct answer. Each of the four participants was to answer out loud to the group. An instructor issued the instruction to 'make the judgement by yourself'. A background of random visual 'noise' dots was added to the slides.

RESULTS

None of the participants reported noticing the MORI presentation trick in a post-procedural questionnaire. The background error rate for the control condition (with no majority influencing the group) was much higher (with 8% errors) than in the original Asch (1956) study.

Female conformity rates of 29% were shown with 4.41 errors on average out of the 12 critical trials, which were comparable to the male participant results of Asch (1956) with an average of 3.44 out of 12 critical trials. However, male conformity rates were much lower than in the Asch (1956) experiments with around a 5% error rate for both majority and minority conditions.

DISCUSSION

There are many explanations for these results. One may be a cultural difference in conformity rates between the United States and Japan. However, the results do not clearly suggest this. The females in the Mori and Arai (2010) sample showed conformity rates comparable to the males in the Asch (1951) experiment. However, the male results showed little conformity. Gender roles today are very different in Japan from what they were in the 1950s.

The removal of demand characteristics from the procedure (removing the experimenter from the room) may have reduced overall conformity rates.

The task was measurably more difficult than the Asch task with a higher baseline error rate without majority influence.

Some of the Mori and Arai (2010) participants had already studied social psychology and were not necessarily naive, as in Asch (1951). Indeed, a large percentage of the sample had already heard of conformity research. Furthermore, Asch's participants were strangers while many of Mori and Arai's sample knew each other.

CONCLUSION

More research is needed as unanimity in majority influence did not appear to be as important a factor in social conformity as Asch (1951) found. It's possible lower conformity rates may occur with different samples and with the removal of the demand characteristics of the original Asch (1951) study's procedure.

The MORI technique can be used to measure conformity with a diverse range of participants without the need for actors and deception.

EVALUATION

STRENGTHS	WEAKNESSES
The MORI technique requires less acting and deception than the original Asch procedure, so the procedure could be deemed more ethical and efficient.	Some of the participants were not strangers as in the Asch sample; some knew each other before the experiment. A large percentage were not naive to social psychology either, reporting they were aware of conformity studies in social psychology already.
While the overall sample size was quite small, there was a mixed gender balance (40 males, 64 females) and the size was beyond the original Asch study which had only 50 males.	There was still the need for some deception in the procedure as the investigators said the filter glasses were 'to protect your eyes from glare'.
	Background visual 'noise' was added to the task to facilitate the MORI technique. This may have increased the overall difficulty of the task above the easy line-judgement task of Asch (1951).
None of the participants reported suspecting they were seeing different lines and all the participants took the task seriously.	Mori and Arai (2010) claimed their revised procedure was more ecologically valid, however, it's still based in a laboratory and lacking mundane realism.

THINGS TO DO AND THINK ABOUT

Develop a summary of Mori and Arai (2010) in your notes.

Use these four questions to guide you.

1. What was the aim of the Mori and Arai (2010) experiment?

2. How was the Mori and Arai (2010) experiment carried out?

3. What were the main findings of Mori and Arai (2010)?

4. What can be concluded from Mori and Arai (2010)?

Finally, provide a balanced evaluation of the Mori and Arai (2010) laboratory experiment by listing two strengths and two limitations.

DON'T FORGET

You can use the follow-up paper by Arai and Mori (2013) to help analyse the Mori and Arai (2010) findings.

ONLINE

Heriot Watt University has a set of Psychology learning resources for Higher Psychology called *Scholar*, useful for testing, studying and revising. Ask your teacher for a login, then, go to the *Scholar* homepage.

ONLINE TEST

Head to www.brightredbooks.net to test yourself on this topic.

OBEDIENCE THEORIES AND RESEARCH

Why do people obey commands? Are we robots to other people's social choices (**agentic state**) or do we act independently from free will (**autonomous state**)?

MILGRAM'S THEORY OF OBEDIENCE

Milgram's starting point for his theory of obedience was Tinbergen's (1953) observations of dominant hierarchies in birds, amphibians and mammals. According to Milgram (1974), social life has organised social structures that provide survival benefits. Independent social actors can, and frequently do, become submissive in their consciences to the social dominance of a wider, organisational structure.

Milgram's (1974) 'Perils of Authority' Theory

Milgram's research on obedience reveals to us that an individual will easily enter agentic state in response to whoever they perceive as a legitimate authority figure. People are constantly moving from one mode (autonomous) to another (agentic) and back again. This is switching from personal responsibility to social-organisational responsibility.

Milgram presents a two-mode theory of agentic state: one agentic state for obeying external commands and an autonomous state for following your own judgement.

Two modes: agentic state and autonomous state

Agentic state: Agentic state is the suppression of personal control in favour of obedience to an authority. When in agentic mode, individual choice is ignored in favour of acting as an agent 'on behalf of' the social hierarchy.

Example:

An example of agentic shift is acting according to the phrase 'I don't want to do this task, but I must because he asked me to'.

Autonomous state: Autonomous state is the assertion of personal control over the authority of the social situation. When in autonomous mode, the individual is acting from personal judgement and outwith the social hierarchy.

Example:

An example of autonomous state is acting according to the phrase 'I know they asked me to deliver this medicine, but I won't'.

DON'T FORGET

Milgram saw agentic shift as perilous and morally dangerous. His research was done after the shadow of World War Two when Nazi officers obeyed orders to commit war crimes in Europe.

BICKMAN (1974): THE SOCIAL POWER OF A UNIFORM

Bickman (1974) carried out a field experiment on the social power of uniforms in New York. He wanted to see the effect that a uniform had on the perception of legitimate authority and, ultimately, on levels of obedient behaviour. Do uniforms give more social power?

On weekday afternoons in downtown Brooklyn, Bickman used a convenience sample of 153 adult pedestrians in New York. Obedience rates for responses to a range of direct commands from a stranger were measured. The main command analysed for this obedience study was 'Pick up this bag for me!'.

Three uniforms were employed to give three levels of legitimate authority to this command:

Uniform 1. Civilian (sports jacket and tie)

Uniform 2. Milk vendor (milk sales outfit with empty milk bottles being carried)

Uniform 3. Security guard (like a police officer's; with a badge and insignia)

contd

What percentage would obey the command, without further explanation? Here's a summary of Bickman's (1974) results:

- 19% of the observed participants obeyed the civilian
- 14% obeyed the milk vendor
- 38% obeyed the security guard

The sample was roughly gender-balanced with 43% male and 57% female. No gender difference in obedience levels was observed or reported by Bickman (1974). This study has high ecological validity as the obedience behaviour was observed in an everyday New York street environment during a field experiment.

Bickman's (1974) experiment revealed that the type of uniform matters to give legitimacy to an order. The milk vendor's outfit was a uniform but it didn't increase obedience levels. Bickman concludes obedience increases mostly in response to a 'uniform with matching social power', for example, coercive power, legitimate power or reward power. This field experiment supports the social power theory of French and Raven (1959).

HOFLING ET AL (1966) FIELD EXPERIMENT ON NURSES: OBEDIENCE IN HOSPITALS

Hofling et al (1966) investigated nurses' obedience to doctors in a field experiment involving three hospitals in America. The results led to changes in nursing training. Would nurses deliver an unsafe dose of medicine to a patient under unjust instruction from a doctor?

At three hospitals, Hofling and his colleagues arranged for 22 (unwitting participant) nurses to be telephoned in the early evening by a 'Dr Smith' – a stranger claiming to be a doctor. On the phone, Dr Smith required each nurse to give an unfamiliar medicine 'Astroten' to a patient on the ward called 'Mr Jones'.

'Dr Smith' claimed he would sign the authorisation papers for this new drug in ten minutes' time when he would visit the ward. Unknown to the nurses, Astroten was a glucose placebo (a harmless sugar pill). The phone call followed a standard script – finishing only when the nurse obeyed, refused, got advice or became upset.

The Astroten bottle contained 5 mg tablets and was clearly marked with the maximum dose (10 mg) and the phrase 'Do not exceed the maximum dose'. On the phone, 'Dr Smith' asked the nurses to deliver 20 mg to patient Jones.

The results of the experiment were unexpected: 21 out of 22 (that is, 95%) of the nurses obeyed the order without hostility or resistance.

Eleven of the 21 nurses later confirmed they had noticed the dose was over the maximum allowed. They were aware they were breaking three hospital rules:

1. Doctors must prescribe medicines in person.

2. The nurse must check the doctor has legitimate authority.

3. The medication must already be on the list of approved medications.

Nurses reported that doctors often got annoyed if their authority was challenged or if their instructions were not obeyed.

Hofling et al (1966) concluded that doctors can override medical and hospital procedures just by giving unjust orders to nurses. Nurses often work in agentic state. This has the potential to endanger patients' lives if unjust orders are not resisted.

THINGS TO DO AND THINK ABOUT

What would happen today if a nurse was asked by a doctor to go against hospital regulations? Would nurses still obey doctors to the point of putting someone's life in danger?

DON'T FORGET

Hofling et al's field experiment of obedience supports Milgram's (1974) 'agentic state' theory. It uses a more realistic social situation than Milgram's laboratory experiment, yet the obedience results are similarly high.

DON'T FORGET

There was no informed consent by the participant nurses in Hofling et al's field experiment. This led to some anger and concern among the hospital staff afterwards.

DON'T FORGET

All nurses were stopped before administering the dose by another ward doctor. They were all debriefed with an unstructured interview and an offer of counselling.

DON'T FORGET

Rank and Jacobsen (1977) tried this experiment with a more familiar medication 'Valium' at three times the usual dose. Obedience rates dropped to 11% among the nurses (that is, two out of 18).

VIDEO LINK

Watch the quirky animation that analyses and evaluates the obedience experiment by Hofling et al (1966) on nurses at www.brightredbooks.net

ONLINE TEST

Head to www.brightredbooks.net to test yourself on this topic.

STAR STUDY: MILGRAM (1963) OBEDIENCE TO AUTHORITY

Title: 'Behavioral Study of Obedience', Milgram, S. (1963) *The Journal of Abnormal & Social Psychology*, Volume 67, No. 4.

Milgram's (1963) laboratory experiments on obedience to an unjust authority are classic and need to be analysed theoretically, methodologically and ethically for the Higher Psychology course.

BACKGROUND: MILGRAM (1963)

In 1963, at Yale University, Stanley Milgram discovered obedience to authority can be a destructive impulse in all, which 'overrides ethics, sympathy and moral conduct'.

Aim and Hypotheses

The context for Milgram's research was in explaining the Nazi atrocities between 1935 and 1945. The aim was to test a prevailing hypothesis that when it came to obedience 'Germans are different'. It was designed to test whether there might be a personality trait of obedience in the German character that went beyond other people's levels of obedience.

METHOD

Milgram's method was a laboratory experiment. He created a procedure for measuring obedience levels.

IV = laboratory situation with obedience conditions (for example, remote-victim condition)

DV = level of obedience to authority (measured by the highest voltage of shock given). A quantitative value was given to the level of obedience, based on the highest voltage designation on the last switch used before the participant refused to continue.

Design

The original Milgram experiment is known as the 'remote-victim' condition. Milgram's (1963) original paper included a range of experimental conditions, with the first experiment, the 'remote victim' condition, intended for comparison between American and German participants.

However, after witnessing the very high obedience levels with his American participants, he re-focused his research onto a comparison of situational conditions that caused high levels of obedience in anyone. Each of his follow-up experiments, reported in the 1963 paper, vary his original procedure.

Sample

A self-selected sample of 40 American males from a wide range of occupations was recruited. To recruit them, Milgram (1963) placed an advert in a local newspaper around the Newhaven area to take part in an experiment on learning at Yale University. While it could be called a volunteer sample, participants were paid $4.50.

Procedure

Individually, participants entered the laboratory and found an experimenter and what looked like another participant, but who was, in fact, an actor. The participant was selected as the 'teacher' and the actor was always selected, by seeded lot, to be the 'learner'.

Both learner and teacher were led into a room with an electric chair and the 'learner' (actor) was strapped into the chair in front of the 'teacher' (participant) to make them believe the 'learner' would receive real shocks. An example shock of 45 volts was given to the 'teacher' to make them believe the procedure was real.

The participant was then led into an adjoining room and watched closely by an experimenter in a lab coat.

The participants were trained to use a realistic 'Shock Generator' machine with 30 switches on it, ranging in designations from 'slight shock' at 15 volts, through 'extreme intensity shock' at 300 volts to 'Danger XXX' at 450 volts. From here on, no real shocks were given. However, the participant was led to believe they were punishing the 'learner' for mistakes on a word-associate learning task. Each time the learner flashed a wrong answer they were to punish them, moving one level higher on the shock generator from 15 volts with each mistake.

Part of Milgram's 'remote-victim' procedure was for the experimenter to prompt the participant with orders to continue. A series of standardised prompts were used: 'Please continue', 'Please go on'. 'The experiment requires that you continue.' 'It is absolutely essential that you continue'. 'You have no other choice, you must go on'. After the participant refused to continue or delivered the maximum intensity shock of 450 volts, they were debriefed, interviewed and reconciled with the 'learner'.

RESULTS

No participant successfully defied the authority figure before obeying the order to use the 300-volt switch. All 40 participants went over and above the predicted obedience level.

Quantitatively, 26 participants obeyed fully and went to the 450-volt switch. This represents 65% of all the participants obeying completely with the experimenter. Fourteen broke off earlier in the procedure. However, all participants (100%) delivered up to 300 volts.

Qualitatively, the experimenter observed the participants to be under 'extreme levels of nervous tension'. Some exhibited nervous laughter. There was a high incidence of sweating, trembling and stuttering. Just before defiance, comments noted from participants included 'It's a hell of an experiment!', 'I can't do that to a man!', 'This is crazy'.

DISCUSSION

Milgram noted at least two surprising findings. First, the obedience was compliance rather than internalisation as many participants expressed deep disapproval of the harm and hurt they thought they were causing. Second, the tendency to obey in this situation was strong despite the authority figure having no special powers of punishment or penalty.

Conclusion

Milgram concluded the tendency to obey an authority figure is strong. Obedience comes easily and often; it's not rare, it's common. Obedience is observable in a laboratory situation and can be measured. Milgram further concluded that obedience is the 'dispositional cement' that binds people to all systems of authority.

DON'T FORGET

Participants were paid $4.50 even if they didn't complete the experiment. (That's the equivalent of around £30 today.)

DON'T FORGET

When the participants asked if the shocks caused injury, they were told: 'Although the shocks may be painful, there is no permanent tissue damage'.

VIDEO LINK

Analyse the original Milgram (1963) obedience to authority experiment with the short documentary video at www.brightredbooks.net

EVALUATION

METHODOLOGICAL EVALUATION	
STRENGTHS	**WEAKNESSES**
The standardised laboratory procedure was very successful in eliciting obedience and measuring levels of compliance. The dependent variable was effectively measured with the machine's switches – a cleverly designed way of measuring levels of obedience.	The experimental setting and procedure established strong demand characteristics to obey. A preliminary training procedure may have encouraged strong obedience in pre-testing up to 105 volts. The authority figure and the lab coat provided artificial demand characteristics for the participants to continue 'in the name of science'.
Most participants accepted the reality of the situation/the cover story. They were fully convinced they were delivering 'extremely painful' electric shocks and hurting the victim.	The original sample consisted of paid volunteers from America. It was also male biased. Milgram later redressed this gender bias by reporting an exactly comparable set of results for a sample of 40 female participants.

ETHICAL EVALUATION	
STRENGTHS	**WEAKNESSES**
Milgram made sure all participants were fully debriefed after the experiment. They were all reconciled with the actor to assure them no harm was done to the 'learner'.	There was no clear right to withdraw as the experimenter kept using prompts to the contrary, for example, 'You have no other choice, you must go on'. There is qualitative evidence from Milgram that his participants were agitated and angry. He noted them showing nervous tension, lip-biting, groaning, profuse sweating, trembling and stuttering.
The shock generator did not deliver shocks – or nothing more than one 45-volt shock. The cover story and deception allowed less harm to be inflicted than appeared to be the case.	Today's ethical principle of 'protection from harm' was breached by Milgram. Milgram stated that within 20 minutes a poised participant was reduced to a twitching, stuttering wreck, yet they continued obeying. However, this was before the establishment of formal ethical codes of practice.
The purpose of Milgram's obedience experiments was ethical, as it aimed to understand what factors lead to blind and destructive levels of obedience. However, do the ends justify the means?	This experiment required a high level of deception and misdirection. This is now deemed unethical as it denies potential participants the right to give informed consent. The aim of the experiment was kept hidden until the end.

THINGS TO DO AND THINK ABOUT

Should Milgram's experiments be repeated today?

To practice evaluating Milgram's obedience experiments, answer this exam-style prompt:

Evaluate Milgram's (1963) obedience research in terms of **ethics** and **procedure**. (8 marks)

ONLINE TEST

Test yourself on this topic at www.brightredbooks.net

FACTORS THAT REDUCE OBEDIENCE

This section outlines a list of factors that affect obedience. How can we resist the pressure to obey? Here, factors that reduce the tendency to obey are presented. Factors that reduce conformity were presented earlier.

OBEDIENCE AND BUFFERS

It will be clear now, there are situational and individual factors that act as buffers to reduce levels of obedience and similar situational and individual factors that reduce the influence of conformity.

INDIVIDUAL FACTORS THAT REDUCE OBEDIENCE: PERSONAL BUFFERS

Individual factors that affect obedience levels are personality type (see Adorno (1950) and the Type A personality), parenting styles – see Baumrind (1971), gender socialisation, cultural differences and personal locus of control (according to Rotter (1966)), taking autonomous responsibility (Milgram (1974)) and awareness of individual moral values (Kohlberg (1971)).

Obedience Socialisation and Parenting Style: Diana Baumrind (1971)

According to Baumrind (1971), authoritarian parenting creates highly obedient children. According to both Baumrind (1971) and Adorno (1950), authoritarian parenting results in the most obedient and conforming adult personalities.

Adorno noted that children brought up in a highly controlling, authoritarian style repeat the cycle of hostility and become authoritarian-type personalities in adulthood, perhaps through an unconscious Freudian projection of their repressed hostility onto their own children. However, Baumrind's (1971) research recommends and prefers the use of an '**authoritative**' parenting style.

Authoritative parenting is not as demanding or controlling as authoritarian parenting. Authoritative parenting is more democratic; it allows children freedom within limits but prefers the negotiation of these limits with high responsiveness between the parent and the child.

Gender and obedience

Gender is often discussed as an individual factor that affects obedience levels. Milgram (1973) found no difference between males and females in their obedience to authority (both genders showed 65% obedience in the remote-victim condition). However, there is some research supporting a gender difference in obedience levels, for example, see Eagly (1967) or Sheridan and King (1972). A weakness in this gender research is that it could be influenced by cultural changes in the female gender role stereotype.

Retaining autonomous state: take responsibility for actions

Another factor that affects individual obedience is the individual's modal shift between autonomous and agentic state as outlined in Milgram's theory of obedience. According to Kohlberg's (1969) theory of moral development, this can be influenced by the stage of moral development reached in the person's creation of individual values.

In Kohlberg's stage theory, obedience levels will individually vary with age and experience. Someone more experienced at disobedience, with a fully developed 'post-conventional morality' system of values will be less obedient to a situation than a less experienced person with a developing 'conventional morality' system.

Transcripts of disobedient participant's comments during post-experimental interviews can be found in Milgram (1974).

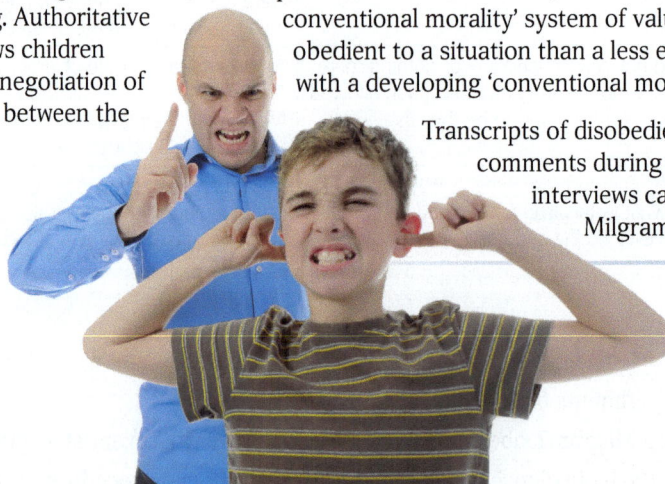

SITUATIONAL FACTORS THAT REDUCE OBEDIENCE: SITUATIONAL BUFFERS

Situational factors can act as buffers to reduce obedience. These factors can include the types of authority giving the orders to obey.

Reduced obedience to illegitimate power

According to French and Raven (1959), obedience levels are in response to the types of power the authority has. These types of power can include reward power, coercive power, legitimate power and referent power. If an authority lacks these types of power, then obedience will be lowered.

Reduced obedience to inappropriate uniforms

In addition, the authority to be obeyed must be perceived as a legitimate authority. Bickman (1974) showed that a uniform can improve the perception of an individual as a legitimate authority, Also, Milgram found more obedience to a man in a lab coat in his laboratory experiments (65%) over a civilian giving orders (20%).

Milgram (1974) continued studying obedience by exploring some of the situational 'binding factors' and individual factors affecting obedience levels. Results from Milgram's follow-up experimental studies have been published in his book *Obedience to Authority: An Experimental View* (1974). A summary of the results can be found in the following table.

Table of Milgram's Experimental Conditions

VARIATION OF CONDITIONS	PARTICIPANTS OBEYING UP TO 450 VOLTS	FULL OBEDIENCE PERCENTAGE
	HIGHEST OBEDIENCE	
Another person flicks the switches	37/40	92.5%
Original remote-victim setup (male participants)	26/40	65%
Original remote-victim setup (female participants)	26/40	65%
Change in experimenter halfway through	20/40	50%
Location in downtown office in Bridgeport	19/40	48%
Teacher and learner in same room (close proximity)	16/40	40%
Touch proximity (hold learner's hand onto shock-plate)	12/40	30%
Orders given by experimenter over the phone	9/40	23%
Civilian gives orders	8/40	20%
Two other teachers rebel	4/40	10%
Teacher chooses shock level	1/40	3%
Arguing experimenters	0/40	0%
	LOWEST OBEDIENCE	

As can be seen from the results in the table, in each of the variations, Milgram (1974) recruited a further 40 (naive) participants for each experiment and went on to obtain different obedience rates for most variations in procedure.

THINGS TO DO AND THINK ABOUT

Obedience questions

'Please, continue. The experiment requires that you continue!' – Milgram (1963)

1. Explain the difference between **conformity** and **obedience**. (4 marks)

2. What **factors reduced** obedience in Milgram's research? (4 marks)

3. How can obedience to authority be studied using **experimental** techniques? (3 marks)

4. Explain two **individual** factors that influence levels of obedience. (4 marks)

5. Describe two **situational** factors that affect levels of obedience to authority. (4 marks)

DON'T FORGET

Obedience occurs in response to a direct and explicit instruction to obey. When there's no direct instruction to obey, the social pressure felt is conformity rather than obedience. In this way, obedience is direct and explicit, while conformity is indirect and implicit.

VIDEO LINK

You might find the full film of the Milgram study interesting. Find it at www.brightredbooks.net

ONLINE TEST

Test yourself on factors that reduce obedience at www.brightredbooks.net

APPLIED STRATEGIES FOR RESISTING SOCIAL PRESSURE 1

How can we resist a command? How can we resist the social pressure to obey? How can we stop conforming to the group? This section of psychology is applied to everyday life. The aim is to explain ways to reduce conformity and to reduce obedience to authority.

STRATEGIES FOR RESISTING SOCIAL PRESSURE

Strategies for resisting social pressure aim to lower the effects of social influence. Each strategy listed below can be used by dissenters to reduce any pressure to obey or conform.

1. Taking responsibility for one's own actions

Milgram's strategy to reduce obedience to unjust authorities is to remain autonomous. Remember that the autonomous state involves remaining individual and taking singular responsibility for one's own actions.

Support for Milgram's (1973) theory of autonomous state shift is both qualitative and quantitative. In conditions where empathy with the victim was increased (learner in the same room) or when there was close proximity to the learner (and in touch proximity), obedience went down. It could be assumed that, in this situation, people felt more empathy and thus more responsible for the pain and the suffering of the victim.

Obedience was higher when the participants were far away from the effects of their own actions (remote proximity). In this way, retaining individual empathy and taking responsibility for one's actions, autonomously, should reduce the social pressure to obey.

2. Developing post-conventional moral reasoning

Kohlberg's (1969) stage model of moral development suggests that the ideal state of morality is post-conventional moral reasoning. This is the last stage in his theory of moral development; the adult stage of morality called 'post-conventional' morality. However, he realised not everyone reaches this stage.

DON'T FORGET

Conventional morality is a system of reasoning about morality that relies on the opinions of other people to inform their own interpretation of the right thing to do. However, what if the majority views are wrong and unjust?

Example:

The tyranny of the majority: a bullying example

In a secondary-school class, if everyone is bullying someone, you might realise the right thing to do is to stop. However, the rest of the class seem to be continuing bullying – and adopting a conventional viewpoint, even though the action is wrong. Your attitude is post-conventional, because you seem to be alone in realising that bullying is wrong here.

Post-conventional morality is known as 'post-conventional' because it comes after the stage of believing that the majority view is usually right. The conventional view is that if everyone else is doing something, it must be the right thing to do. However, according to Kohlberg's research, this is a child-like way of thinking. Hornsey et al (2003) concluded that participants with clear and strong values tend to show less conformity in social conformity experiments.

contd

3. Questioning the motives of other people

Our own motives and other people's motives can be just or unjust and legitimate or not. Personal motives might be to impress people or to be viewed in a favourable light. Obedience might be out of increasing obligation, a social contract of reciprocity, an avoidance of disagreement or a financial incentive.

Wood and Hayes (2012) discuss the social psychology of conformity in advertising and consumer purchasing behaviour. Wood and Quinn (2003) note that fleeting motivations can generate temporary shifts in judgement leading to increased consumer purchasing behaviour.

Example:

Why do politicians visit non-voters in schools? Why do doctors prescribe some medicines rather than others? Why do we get so much junk mail telling us to buy stuff? Why is TV violence deemed as 'harmless' while the advertising industry claims TV advertising is effective? Start questioning the motives!

There's evidence that motives are questioned from Milgram's experiment. When Milgram's experiment was moved to a downtown office location away from the respectable Yale University campus, the experiment had questionable legitimacy. In Milgram's laboratory task, full obedience to the role of 'teacher' went down from 65% to 48%.

In addition, in another variation of Milgram's obedience experiments, when an ordinary civilian in plain clothes gave the orders to continue (as opposed to a man in a science laboratory coat), full obedience dropped to 20%. His legitimate authority to carry out an experiment was more questionable in these conditions.

THINGS TO DO AND THINK ABOUT

Obediently draw a graph of Milgram's results.

Find a graph or a table of Milgram's 1963 percentage rates for each condition. Copy and draw each variation into the chart. This is a useful graphical analysis exercise!

Which conditions had the higher levels of obedience? Which variation had the lowest obedience? To answer this, put Milgram's variations next to each other and compare them. These variations give strong clues as to how to resist social pressure.

DON'T FORGET

Don't forget to ask who's funding a research programme before you sign up as a participant! There may be questionable motives behind the research.

VIDEO LINK

Has obedience behaviour changed since 1963? Watch a contemporary Derren Brown replication of the original Milgram study at www.brightredbooks.net

ONLINE TEST

Test yourself on this topic at www.brightredbooks.net

APPLIED STRATEGIES FOR RESISTING SOCIAL PRESSURE 2

STRATEGIES FOR RESISTING SOCIAL PRESSURE (CONTINUED)

4. Locus of control

In 1966 Rotter created a 20-point scale for measuring the locus of a person's behavioural control. Twenty statements were on the scale with 'True' or 'False' indicated next to them. Participants' responses could be measured by adding up agreement with statements indicating an 'internal' locus of control, or disagreement, indicating an 'external' locus of control.

Example:
What's your locus of control? Are you internal or external?
INTERNAL LOCUS OF CONTROL: I am in control of my own destiny.
EXTERNAL LOCUS OF CONTROL: Others, God or fate control my destiny.

VIDEO LINK

For an inspiring disobedient role model, watch a video-clip of 'Tankman' in Tianamen Square at www.brightredbooks.net One man stopped a line of tanks that were sent to stop student protests in China with just a white flag.

People with a high internal locus of control (High LOC) will believe statements such as 'I control my own destiny'. People with a low level of internal control (Low LOC; external locus) will believe 'They control my destiny'.

Rotter's (1966) locus of control theory is that people with a highly internalised locus of control (High LOC) will be better at resisting social pressure to conform or obey than people with an external locus of control (Low LOC). In support of locus of control, Burger (1992) reported that those with a high control need resisted social pressure to obey better in a replication of Milgram's obedience model.

Rotter's locus of control theory is also supported by an analysis of obedience rates from Elms and Milgram (1974) showing lower obedience in the Milgram obedience model by high-scoring internals (High LOC). In addition, Spector (1983) showed that high internals (High LOC) conformed less in Asch-style conformity experiments than high externals (Low LOC).

DON'T FORGET

According to Singer (1974), disobedience can be used to raise your profile. In *Democracy and Disobedience* Singer states that dissent can be used for gaining publicity and challenging the legitimacy of an authority.

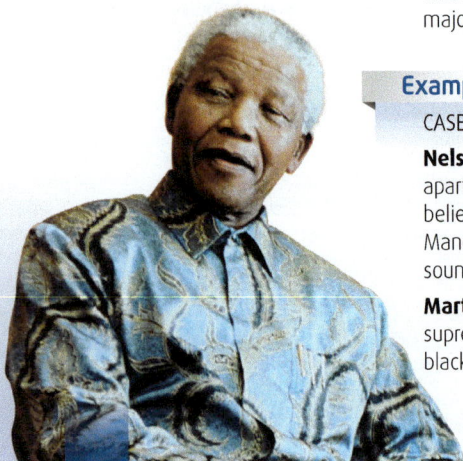

Example:
Education and the enlightenment effect
Social education about social influence has been revealed by Gergen (1973) as an effective way to reduce social influence. Gergen (1973) found there is an 'enlightenment effect' with mere knowledge of social processes such as conformity and obedience reducing overall social influence. So, if you've read this far, you're already enlightened, and so less prone to social influences!

Example:
Imitating disobedient role models
Society has been shaped by many disobedient role models. With historical hindsight, many of these dissidents, dissenters and rebellious individuals are now lauded as more correct than the majority view.

Example:
CASE STUDIES: Remember famous role model dissidents!

Nelson Mandela refused to conform to the white apartheid in his society and went to prison for his beliefs. Much later, after his long prison sentence, Mandela was elected President of South Africa for his sound sense of morality.

Martin Luther King Junior disagreed with white supremacy and imagined a day when there would be a black President of America. He was shot for this belief.

contd

Rosa Parks refused to obey the signs on the bus to give up her seat to a white woman. Parks was arrested for her dissent. She became a role model for black activists in America to reject colour segregation in cafes.

Emmeline Pankhurst, in Britain, refused to be kept out of the democratic voting system and rebelled against the status quo at Westminster by chaining herself to a statue and protesting for women's suffrage. The Suffragette movement was inspired by her protest (and many others). Eventually, women got the vote.

Václav Havel disagreed with the one-party control of Czechoslovakia and became a dissident who went to prison – just for writing against the totalitarian system. Later, after a velvet revolution, Havel was made President of the same country.

Some of these disobedient individuals are now held as positive role models for a just society. Nelson Mandela and Václav Havel were awarded a Nobel Prize for their disobedience.

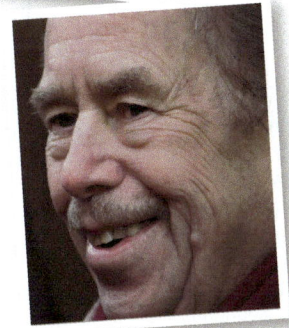

5. Having an ally for social support

A recurring finding in conformity and obedience research is that having an ally for social support within a situation reduces the influence of the social pressure in that situation. So, if you plan to dissent, take a friend!

Evidence for social support as a strategy for reducing social pressure is strong. With just one extra dissenter in the social group, Asch (1951) found conformity rates dropped from 32% to 5%. Having an ally who disagrees with the majority view, or just one dissenting voice against the majority view, is enough to break the spell of unanimity.

In one of Milgram's variations of the obedience experiments, if two teachers were involved who refused to obey, participants also refused much earlier, with only 10% going all the way to 450 volts.

Having an ally or a fellow dissenter does two things. First, it breaks the unanimous position and provides an alternative viewpoint to consider. Second, according to Bandura's (1965) social learning theory, a dissenter provides a role model for social learning, allowing easier imitation of the dissenting response.

Allen and Levine (1971) report that even a dissenter with obviously poor eyesight in the Asch (1951) procedure breaks the unanimous position and lowers the pressure to conform. Allen and Levine (1969) found that the closer the proximity of the dissenter, in the Asch model, the more influence the dissenter had on participants. Conformity was lowest when the dissenting voice was seated next to the participant.

THINGS TO DO AND THINK ABOUT

Applied obedience questions

Try these six short writing tasks on the topic of obedience. In each question, refer to relevant research and, in questions 4 and 6, try to apply the strategies for resisting social pressure.

1. How has Milgram's (1963) research helped reveal factors affecting obedience? (4 marks)

2. Describe one *other* experiment on obedience. (4 marks)

3. According to research evidence, how can social influence be reduced? (4 marks)

4. Explain two strategies for resisting social pressure. (4 marks)

5. How does Rotter's (1966) theory of 'locus of control' affect obedience levels? (2 marks)

6. Explain one application of obedience research to everyday social behaviour. (2 marks)

DON'T FORGET

A diversity of views gives us freedom to express our own conclusions without fear of rejection or exclusion.

DON'T FORGET

Diversity of opinion in a group breaks up social pressure to conform and to obey.

ONLINE TEST

Test yourself on applied strategies for resisting social pressure at www.brightredbooks.net

PREJUDICE

WHAT IS PREJUDICE?

PREJUDICE: INTRODUCTION

All around the world, prejudice leads to discrimination and results in false conclusions about others. If prejudice causes us to see the world in a distorted and biased light, then analysing prejudice, and finding strategies to reduce it, is very relevant to people and society today. In its worst expression, prejudice can lead to extermination and genocide, so society needs methods to reduce it.

DEFINING PREJUDICE

One definition comes from Allport (1954) who stated there are two aspects to prejudice: a definite hostility (or at least negative judgement) about another individual, and an over-generalisation. However, whether positive or negative in attitude, prejudice can be seen as a bias in the judgements we're prone to making when dealing with people we don't know in a group or category.

Prejudice comes from everyday generalisation; it's an error in attitude that results from cognitive over-generalisation.

Example:
In "The Social Animal" Elliot Aronson (1972) defines prejudice as 'a hostile or negative attitude towards a distinguishable group based on generalisations derived from faulty or incomplete information'.

PREJUDICE: OVER-GENERALISATION WITH A BIAS IN FEELING

The 'feeling' component of a prejudice can be understood through Allport's distinction between love-prejudice and hate-prejudice. Here's the love–hate prejudice example.

Example:
LOVE PREJUDICE: At one end of the feeling scale, a 'love-prejudice' feels positive and warm about everything to do with the loved. There's an over-generalisation about everything connected with the loved – the dress, the car, the film, the area, the house, etc., producing positive feelings and warmth. This is (a self-interested) over-exaggeration.
HATE PREJUDICE: At the other end of the scale, a 'hate-prejudice' will over-generalise a hateful feeling and produce a negative association with anything to do with the hated. If love is blind, so is hate ... and so is prejudice.

In this example of its two extremes, prejudice can be viewed as a feeling that's biased towards or against a whole category, be it either positive or negative.

According to Fiske and Taylor (1991) who proposed the **cognitive miser theory** of prejudice, prejudice seems to be the result of a **shortcut** in thinking based on very little information. Prejudice may sometimes lead to a quick conclusion, but at the expense of accuracy or fairness.

Stereotypes are the mental images used to represent categories by perceivers to fill in the gap for missing information about newly perceived members of the category. Thus, categorical stereotyping influences how individuals are perceived.

Example:
Heidi: If the only information you have is that 'Heidi' is Swiss, the Swiss stereotype might tell you immediately that Heidi is female, under 50-years-old, has hair in pigtails, wears leather trousers and seasonally dances up and down mountains to and from her lonely goat-herding house.
However, it's quite possible Heidi is a transgender, bald, 65-year-old, retired motorbike instructor who lives in the urban centre of Geneva and now uses a wheelchair.

DON'T FORGET

The social cognition of prejudice is clearly explained in the classic book by Gordon Allport (1954) *The Nature of Prejudice*. Allport considered prejudice to be an unfortunate side effect of cognition.

DON'T FORGET

By understanding the psychological and cultural origins of prejudice, issues like racism, sexism and ageism can be tackled more effectively.

contd

Prejudice does not see the individual, rather, it involves treating all those categorised together in a similar manner and responding to them as undifferentiated members of a group.

Evaluation of Allport's stereotype theory of prejudice

One weakness of Allport's stereotype theory of prejudice is that stereotypes are not merely static perceptions. Stereotypes are personal interpretations bound up with categories in a person's perceptual system. One strength of Allport's theory of prejudice is that it recognises the normality of prejudice as the result of the many over-generalisations made in everyday cognition.

DON'T FORGET

Tajfel and Turner's (1979) Social Identity Theory of intergroup conflict (SIT) states that we treat individuals as representatives of the groups they belong to rather than just as individuals.

PREJUDICE CAN BE THE RESULT OF ERRORS AND BIASES IN COGNITION

Tversky and Kahneman (1974) itemise some notable biases and errors in cognition that can result in prejudices and unfair discriminations. These include the anchoring bias, the category accentuation error, causal correlation errors, the availability bias and the representativeness bias. Further social prejudices and biases include the halo effect, the self-serving bias and the self-fulfilling prophecy.

The halo effect

Asch (1946) was the first psychologist to identify the halo effect. This is when a 'warm' first impression anchors the person with other centrally positive character traits. This leads to a positive bias in the overall appraisal of a person's character.

Example:

A class will warmly accept a new pupil described as 'kind', but shun a newcomer described as 'cold'. This is true even if they turned out to be the same person.

ONLINE

Read empirical research on the halo effect by Nisbett and Wilson (1977) in the *Journal of Personality and Social Psychology* at www.brightredbooks.net

The halo effect is supported by Nisbett and Wilson's (1977) research on impression formation. For example, if basic biographical information is kept the same, experimentally, attitudes can be formed just by changing one word from 'warm' to 'cold' using the halo effect.

The following table includes a list of more errors and biases in social cognition.

ONLINE TEST

Test yourself on prejudice at www.brightredbooks.net

Prejudice: A Summary of Cognitive Errors and Biases behind Prejudice

NAME OF ERROR OR BIAS (ACRONYM)	EXPLANATION/EXAMPLE	RESEARCH
The Self-Fulfilling Prophecy (SFP)	Teachers' expectations of pupils' performance strongly influences the achievement of their pupils.	Rosenthal and Jacobsen (1968), 'Pygmalion in the Classroom'
The Actor-Observer Bias (AOB)	The actor attributes the cause of a behaviour to external causes, while the observer attributes the cause to internal traits.	Jones and Nisbett (1971), 'The Actor and the Observer: Divergent perceptions of the causes of behaviour'
The Self-Serving Bias (SSB)	To enhance and protect personal self-esteem, failures are attributed to external causes while successes are attributed to internal and stable traits.	Miller and Ross (1975), 'Self-serving biases in the attribution of causality: Fact or Fiction?'
The Fundamental Attribution Error (FAE)	The tendency to over-estimate the influence of personal and dispositional characteristics on peoples' behaviour.	Ross (1977), 'The intuitive psychologist and his shortcomings'
The Anchoring Bias (AB)	The first estimation anchors later estimations. Maths Example: If the first number in a sum is a large number, it will be estimated to be a large sum. If the first number in a sum is a small number, it will be estimated to be a small sum.	Tversky and Kahneman (1974), 'Judgement under uncertainty: heuristics and biases'
The Halo Effect (HE)	The primacy effect of the first impression of a person as 'warm' or 'cold' counts more than later impressions. The initial 'halo' of warmth extends to peripheral traits.	Asch (1946), 'Forming Impressions of Personality'

ANALYSIS: THE LANGUAGE OF PREJUDICE

How do psychologists talk about prejudice? Is prejudice created and sustained in society or is it within the individual? Here's an overview of the terminology needed for analysing the components of prejudice.

THE COMPONENTS OF PREJUDICE

The A-B-C model of prejudice states there are three component responses that make up a prejudice. This is linked to Rosenberg and Hovland's (1960) theory of attitudes. In general, there are three types of psychological response that form three components to any prejudice:

A **Attitude**: attitudinal component includes the feelings that go with the prejudice
B **Behaviour**: behavioural component includes the discriminatory actions linked with the prejudice
C **Cognition**: cognitive component includes the thoughts and beliefs associated with the prejudice

DON'T FORGET

There are many types of prejudice, but the underlying psychological processes causing the prejudices might be universal.

ONLINE

For genuine inspiration on the topic of reducing prejudice, read (or watch) Martin Luther King Junior's 'I have a dream...' speech against racism (1963) at www.brightredbooks.net

VIDEO LINK

Watch Robert F. Kennedy's speech on prejudice reduction in reaction to the shooting of Martin Luther King Jr. at www.brightredbooks.net Is America less racist now than in 1968?

TYPES OF PREJUDICE

Prejudice comes in many forms, but four are sexism, racism, nationalism and ageism. The common feature of these prejudices is the exaggeration of the benefits of an 'in-group' (usually the one you belong to) and the over-generalised stereotypical simplification of the differences with any member of the 'out-group' (usually the one you do not belong to).

- **Sexism** is prejudice and discrimination based on gender groupings. Gender is more diverse than binary (male/female) and it can be the basis for many prejudices.
- **Racism** is prejudice and discrimination based on skin colour or ethnicity. There's no biological definition of race. Yet superficial biological characteristics, such as skin colour, hair colour or parental origin, are often used as an unjust basis for discrimination and prejudice against an individual.
- **Nationalism** is prejudice and discrimination where people prefer people from their own nation to others. Nationalism encourages patriotism at the exclusion of loyalties to other countries or political arrangements.
- **Ageism** is prejudice or discrimination based solely on your year of birth. Whether you feel young or old, ageism excludes certain age groups from activities.

INTRODUCTION TO THEORIES OF PREJUDICE

Several theories of prejudice have emerged from social psychology. Here's an overview of a few.

- **The Authoritarian Personality Theory: Adorno (1950)**
Type A theory predicts that individuals measured with a personality of Type A will, because of their upbringing and beliefs, show more prejudice and discrimination than most. This is an individual theory of prejudice. It suggests parents shape the individual's prejudiced attitudes.

Theories of social cognition: the cognitive approach

- **Social Identity and Minimal Groups Theory: Tajfel (1970)**
According to social psychologists, prejudice can result from an individual's errors and biases in social cognition. For example, in Tajfel's theory of minimal groups, it takes very little to create a prejudice between an 'in-group' and an 'out-group'. This seems to be the result of a competitive motive.

contd

- **Over-generalisation Theory: Allport (1950)**

Allport (1950) went further and claimed prejudice is an inevitable side effect of our 'highly simplifying' **social cognition**. Even in the absence of competition, prejudice will occur. Allport's theory makes clear that 'false generalisations' are often used to fill in our areas of ignorance. For example, all members of a poorly understood group will be treated the same. If this is so, no matter how we organise society, there will always be prejudice.

- **Cognitive Miser Theory: Taylor (1981)**

Cognitive miser theory stated that when the mind has very little information to go on, stereotypes fill the gap. The result of using stereotyping for cognition is a shortcut in judgement, often leading to discriminatory behaviour.

- **Freudian Scapegoat Theories – the Psychoanalytic Approach**

Freud claimed prejudice is created by 'unconscious frustration' and aggression within the individual. Dollard and Miller (1939) outlined the 'scapegoating theory' as the displacement of frustration from one source to creation of feelings of aggression towards another target.

EXPLAINING THE SOCIAL COGNITION OF PREJUDICE

Tajfel's minimal groups experiments reveal that incomplete information about an out-group can lead to a biased and simplistic understanding of everyone outwith the groups you're part of; your in-group.

Stereotyping

Definitions: According to Allport (1954), a stereotype is the image in our heads of a group or category. Stereotypes about in-groups and out-groups are fixed ideas; the result of generalisations, often formed by the media, culture and society.

According to Walter Lippman (1924), a stereotype is an 'oversimplified picture of the world, one that satisfies a need to perceive the world as more understandable and manageable'. Lippman (1924) compares the inaccurate images of stereotypes in our minds to the mere shadow-puppets of reality on the cave wall created by the firelight in the dark cave of ignorance described in Plato's *Republic*.

In ambiguous situations, a stereotype can be used to fill the gap in knowledge and apparently justify the beliefs based on that gap in knowledge.

Stereotypes act both as justification devices for categorical acceptance or rejection of groups and as screening devices to maintain selectively simplified perceptions.

Discrimination

Discrimination is the behavioural expression of prejudice. Prejudiced behaviour can manifest itself subtly or extremely. In his descriptive theory of prejudice, Allport (1954) states there are five levels to prejudiced behaviour. Each level is one step more extreme than the next.

1. Anti-locution: 'I don't like bananas' – subtle prejudice
2. Avoidance: 'Don't go near those bananas!'
3. Discrimination: 'Choose apples instead of bananas'
4. Physical attack: 'Squash those horrible bananas in the bin'
5. Extermination: 'Exterminate all bananas' – the most extreme prejudice

THINGS TO DO AND THINK ABOUT

In preparation for your course exam, try tackling these five prompts:

1. Describe *four* **types** of **prejudice** still common in everyday life. (4 marks)
2. Explain **levels** of **discrimination,** with an example from everyday behaviour. (4 marks)
3. Explain these *three* terms: **prejudice**, **stereotyping** and **discrimination**. (6 marks)
4. Describe the main **A-B-C** components of prejudice. (3 marks)
5. Explain the **negative effects** of stereotyping and discrimination. (3 marks)

DON'T FORGET

If prejudice can be understood and controlled, it would be useful for many societies to reduce all forms of discrimination.

DON'T FORGET

To 'stereotype' is to attribute identical characteristics to every member of a group, regardless of the individual's variation from the stereotype.

DON'T FORGET

Allport (1954) sees stereotypes as an over-generalised image for a group that blocks a full view of the individual.

DON'T FORGET

Good news! Discrimination is now illegal in Scotland. The Equalities Act (2010) of Scotland specifies a law that protects many groups of people against prejudice and discrimination.

ONLINE TEST

Test yourself on the language and terminology of prejudice at www.brightredbooks.net

THEORIES OF PREJUDICE

There are three main explanations for prejudice and discrimination within social psychology. The first theory to be explained here is the **authoritarian personality theory** developed by Adorno (1950). Later pages will examine Tajfel's (1978) cognitive theory of prejudice known as **social identity theory** and **environmental competition theories** by Sherif (1948).

DON'T FORGET

The F-scale was constructed to be maximally indirect and not obviously about prejudice.

DON'T FORGET

How easy would it be to just tick 'True, True, True' or 'False, False, False' in an F-scale test to bias the results?

ONLINE

Try a version of the F-scale online to see how Adorno measured the authoritarian personality. Use the self-report questionnaire method at www.brightredbooks.net

DON'T FORGET

Warning! Some online personality scales are modified versions of certain classics that are not as strongly validated or reliable. You may have to pay for the results!

VIDEO LINK

For a thought-provoking video on Theodor Adorno watch The School of Life's seven-and-a-half minute summary of Adorno's viewpoint on societies, fascism and prejudice at www.brightredbooks.net

ADORNO'S AUTHORITARIAN PERSONALITY – TYPE As

In 1950, Adorno outlined the Type A personality. This 'trait' personality theory describes a measurable source trait in some personalities towards anti-democratic tendencies (for example, tendencies towards intolerance, conformity, obedience, authoritarianism, etc.). These tendencies were later confirmed as correlating with a high degree of prejudice shown in attitudes to others.

According to Adorno (1950), the authoritarian personality expresses anti-democratic tendencies; ethnocentric opinions; anti-humanitarian potential; and deep, general tendencies for prejudice against others within the structure of their personality.

Adorno's psychodynamic explanation of the authoritarian personality

Adorno's justification for the Type A personality theory of anti-democratic prejudice was Freudian. His psychoanalytic explanation relies on the defence mechanisms of repression, identification and projection.

Adorno claimed that during childhood the authoritarian trait would develop as an anti-parental hostility in response to authoritarian parents. The hostility would be repressed into the unconscious. At the same time, identification in childhood with authority power would develop. Later, in adulthood, the childhood hostility would emerge again as aggression towards any available scapegoat group. Prejudice would project outwards in the form of antipathy towards any 'weaker' group.

ADORNO (1950): THE F-SCALE AND THE TYPE A PERSONALITY

Alongside Type A theory, Adorno (1950) developed a new survey instrument called the F-scale to measure the Type A personality. Adorno validated the scale on a diverse sample of over 2000 respondents. It was designed to have a high degree of correlation with existing scales of prejudice and anti-social personality measures. However, unlike other scales, it would be non-specific and indirect in its questions about any specific prejudices and aim to reveal hidden prejudices indirectly.

Adorno hoped the F-scale would universally reveal anti-democratic tendencies and the questions would be applicable to many diverse cultures.

After confirming correlations with other scales, it was concluded that a person scoring highly on the F-scale held the authoritarian personality trait, and this individual could reliably be assumed to be more prejudiced than average.

Nine surface traits were seen to combine to reveal a core anti-democratic source trait: the authoritarian personality trait. The core source trait of the Type A personality is seen as a syndrome of anti-democratic authoritarianism.

The following table shows a description of the structure of the F-scale and its relation to the traits of the authoritarian personality type. The table illustrates how Adorno's (1950) many versions of the F-scale were constructed around the nine surface traits of the authoritarian personality type. Nine prejudiced surface traits were seen to combine to form the Type A syndrome.

contd

The Type A Personality Trait	Surface Trait	Scale Dimension	Non-Type A Personality Trait
Rigid conformist (T)	1	**Conventionalism**	Flexible non-conformist (F)
Example Scale Item:	'It is good hard work that makes life interesting and worthwhile (T/F)'		
Uncritical and submissive (T)	2	**Authoritarian Submission**	Critical and confrontational (F)
Example Scale Item:	'Obedience and respect for authority are the most important virtues children should learn (T/F)'		
Punishes non-conformers (T)	3	**Authoritarian Aggression**	Open to unconventional behaviour (F)
Example Scale Item:	'No insult to honour should ever go unpunished (T/F)'		
Unimaginative (T)	4	**Anti-Intraception**	Subjective and creative (F)
Example Scale Item:	'Some things are too intimate and personal to talk about with friends (T/F)'		
Belief in rigid fate and determinism (T)	5	**Superstition and Stereotypy**	Broad-minded in beliefs (F)
Example Scale Item:	'Everyone should have a deep faith in some higher supernatural force (T/F)'		
Identification with power structures (T)	6	**Power and Toughness**	Non-identification with power (F)
Example Scale Item:	'Our lives are governed by plots hatched in secret by politicians (T/F)'		
Cynical about others (T)	7	**Destructiveness and Cynicism**	Optimistic about others (F)
Example Scale Item:	'There will always be war and conflict (T/F)'		
Believes the world is wild and malign (T)	8	**Projectivity**	Believes the world is benign (F)
Example Scale Item:	'The world will end with a world-destroying earthquake, flood or catastrophe. (T/F)'		
Over-concerned with sex (T)	9	**Sex**	Not obsessed with sexual goings-on (F)
Example Scale Item:	'Men are only interested in women for one reason (T/F)'		

EVALUATION OF AUTHORITARIAN PERSONALITY THEORY

Now, for an evaluation of Adorno's (1950) F-scale, authoritarian personality theory and the concept of the Type A personality as a trait that can measure prejudice indirectly.

STRENGTHS	WEAKNESSES
The F-scale was tested out on a wide range of participants. Adorno (1950) and his colleagues confirmed their scale correlations with a sample size of over 2000 people. This empirical base helped to form the scale and to establish a level of validity behind the concept of the Type A personality.	Some versions of the F-scale are open to response bias. All the items are arranged to point in a similar direction within the scale. This could lead to demand characteristics, the possibility of social desirability bias and acquiescent response set.
The F-scale correlates with other scales measuring specific prejudices when tested on the same people. This cross-test correlation suggests there is validity in the F-scale measurement of the Type A authoritarian trait and that it can validly be linked with a prejudiced personality type.	Adorno's reliance on qualitative case-study data like Freud's is open to claims of biased researcher validation, especially with the use of Freudian-styled projective tests like the Thematic Apperception Test (the TAT).

THINGS TO DO AND THINK ABOUT

Here are some revision questions on the authoritarian personality. Try these for exam practice:

1. What is the authoritarian personality? (2 marks)

2. Why are some people more prejudiced than others? (3 marks)

3. How does Theodor Adorno explain the creation of the authoritarian personality? (3 marks)

4. What does the F-scale measure and how does it do it? (4 marks)

5. What does a high score on the F-scale suggest? (2 marks)

6. Evaluate whether the F-scale is a useful measure of the Type A personality. (6 marks)

ONLINE TEST

Test yourself on the authoritarian personality at www.brightredbooks.net

COGNITIVE THEORIES OF PREJUDICE: SOCIAL IDENTITY THEORY

What are the minimal conditions for the establishing of prejudice between groups? In 1978 Tajfel proposed a **cognitive** theory of **social identity** to explain *prejudice* and *discrimination*.

DON'T FORGET

Tajfel's (1970) 'minimal groups' research suggests that any grouping or categorisation can lead to in-group/out-group prejudice.

DON'T FORGET

The **cognitive approach** to explaining prejudice relies on defining prejudice as an **affective** bias in cognition, with in-group favouritism and out-group discrimination. Tajfel's Social Identity Theory (SIT) presumes no prejudiced type of person and no special environmental conditions that promote prejudice, merely minimal grouping is enough. This occurs in everyday cognition.

DON'T FORGET

Tajfel's main insight in his 'minimal groups' research was that social categorisation alone was enough to produce prejudice and discrimination.

DON'T FORGET

A profound conclusion of Tajfel's minimal group theory and research is that prejudice is **universal** to all societies and is an inevitable cognitive *side-effect* of all in-group/out-group categorisations.

TAJFEL'S (1978) SOCIAL IDENTITY THEORY

Tajfel developed his Social Identity Theory in 1978 which recognised that **self-categorisation** forms part of our personal **identity** and is involved in forming our own social identity. Self-categorisation affects self-definition, interpersonal behaviour, self-perception and self-esteem.

Social categorisation produces prejudice and discrimination because of a cognitive bias in the processes of the mind to accentuate *similarity* within any category and *difference* from other categories.

To support SIT, Turner (1982) reports a simplifying cognitive tendency to *exaggerate differences* between groups and a tendency to *minimise group differences* within. In-group and out-group discrimination was directly created, observed and tested in a Bristol school in 1970 during Tajfel's minimal groups research.

TAJFEL'S (1970) MINIMAL GROUPS RESEARCH: EXPERIMENTS IN INTERGROUP BEHAVIOUR

We are brought up to conform to group affiliations by social learning and we acquire a web of self-categorisations. There's a social identity of 'we' and 'us' that inevitably creates a 'you' and a 'them'. This social construct, known as our social identity, forms then becomes our social reality.

Experiments in intergroup behaviour

Aim: The aim of Tajfel (1970) was to establish the minimal conditions for the creation of prejudice and discrimination in intergroup behaviour. Are there cognitive causes of prejudice rather than social and cultural determinants?

Hypothesis: Is there conformity to a norm of discrimination against the out-group and a preference for the in-group, even if the groupings are minimal, trivial, arbitrary and meaningless?

Sample: Sixty-four Bristol school-boys, aged 14–15 years old

Method

The boys were told they were taking part in a study of visual discrimination and asked to make judgements about arrays of dots on a screen. They were asked to quickly judge how many dots were on the screen for a series of 18 dot pictures. They were then classed into two groups (unknown to them, randomly) as either 'underestimators' or 'overestimators'. This trivial visual discrimination task established the minimal groups.

The boys were then asked to individually fill in a survey of matrices where in-group choices and out-group choices could be made, along with intergroup choices about how much reward each group should get. In a private booth, each boy was asked to judge how much participants in the rest of the groups should be rewarded in 'pennies'. They were told they, personally, would not receive any reward.

A typical matrix in the survey would have two numbered participants, one from each group, and the boy filling the matrix in would have to discriminate how to treat the other boys. They had to decide how much reward to allocate to each participant.

contd

The interesting question was: which strategy would be used to reward the participants? Would the boys choose a strategy of complete fairness (F) or in-group favouritism (MIP: maximum in-group profit)? Would they choose to maximise overall reward (MJP: maximise joint profit) or to maximise out-group discrimination (MID: maximise in-group difference)?

#17 overestimator	1	2	3	4	5	6	7	8	9	10	11	12	13	14
#12 underestimator	13	12	11	10	9	8	7	6	5	4	3	2	1	0

The strategy of fairness (F) is circled here, as the boy has chosen equal rewards for in-group and out-group.

#10 overestimator	1	2	3	4	5	6	7	8	9	10	11	12	13	14
#14 underestimator	13	12	11	10	9	8	7	6	5	4	3	2	1	0

The strategy of maximum in-group difference (MID) is circled here, as the boy has chosen to reward his in-group member (#10 overestimator) and not the out-group member (#14 underestimator).

Results

Fairness or groupness? Two strategies emerged as popular. When the participants in the matrix were from the same group, fairness (F) overall was the most common strategy for resource allocation. This suggests there is resistance to prejudice. However, when an in-group/out-group distinction could be made in the matrix, another popular strategy was to maximise group difference (MID). This is prejudice emerging just from minimal grouping.

Interestingly, in a ranking of more complex matrices, rarely was a strategy of maximising joint profit (MJP) chosen, and a strategy of maximum in-group profit (MIP) was unpopular.

Conclusion

Tajfel (1970) concluded that individuals will choose a strategy of resource allocation that maximises the relative advantage of their own group rather than maximising resource allocation per se. In other words, sometimes group members will refuse resources, if they can maximise advantage to their own group. This is true for the Bristol schoolboys studied and for minimal groups.

Evaluation

STRENGTHS	WEAKNESSES
Follow-up studies give supporting results for Tajfel's minimal grouping theory.	This study was meant to be a baseline study to reveal individual and situational factors that increase or decrease prejudice, much like the Asch's (1951) lines study did for the topic of conformity. However, Tajfel's study did not reveal factors.
In a follow-up study, Tajfel surveyed three groups of 16 boys (a total of 48 participants) who were randomly allocated to each group and minimally categorised as either preferring a painting by Klee versus a group preferring a painting by Kandinsky.	Tajfel's research mostly showed the obvious; that we need **very little basis at all** to establish in-group favouritism and out-group discrimination.
Even on the basis of these minimal groupings, when it came to allocating rewards to participants, in-group prejudice occurred and out-group discrimination followed.	The intergroup experimental tasks lacked mundane realism as children rarely organise the payment of rewards using money.

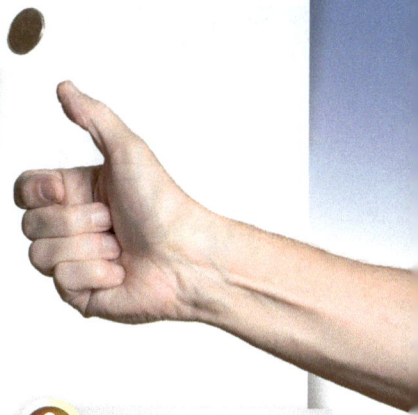

DON'T FORGET

According to this cognitive theory, prejudice is NOT based on specific group characteristics or individual personality traits.

VIDEO LINK

Watch Kevin Durrheim explain Social Identity Theory and Tajfel's minimal group studies in an accessible YouTube lecture at www.brightredbooks.net

ONLINE TEST

Head to www.brightredbooks.net to test yourself on this topic.

THINGS TO DO AND THINK ABOUT

Brown et al (1986) followed up the minimal groups study and found that, with just an openly declared coin toss and the creation of two groups called Group A and Group B, there was sufficient basis for competition and prejudice. Try these questions:

1. What is Tajfel's cognitive explanation of prejudice? (Hint: SIT) (2 marks)
2. Explain why **in-group favouritism** occurs, according to Social Identity Theory, even in minimal groups. (4 marks)
3. How does Tajfel's (1970) study of Bristol schoolboys support a cognitive theory of prejudice? (4 marks)

Which do you prefer?

In Engelshut, Paul Klee

Composition IX, Vassily Kandinsky

REDUCING PREJUDICE – THE MEDIA AND AFFIRMATIVE ACTION

Two important ways to reduce prejudice include using the **power of the media** and through a recruitment strategy of **affirmative action**. Both the media and affirmative action can be used to engineer a future society with more or less prejudice and discrimination.

DON'T FORGET

If the mass media can *increase* prejudice in its audience, surely it can *reduce* prejudice too?

DON'T FORGET

Prejudice and bias in the mass media can increase stereotyping and prejudice. The studies by Kimball (1986), Tan et al (2000) and Frueh and McGhee (1975) all show the power of the mass media over our everyday social behaviour.

ONLINE

Don't forget the relevance of Bandura's (1961) 'Social Learning Theory' to explain the power and influence of the media on behaviour. Watch online Bandura's 'Bobo' doll studies concerning imitative learning.

DON'T FORGET

The BBC's original motto still stands to this day as: 'inform, educate, entertain'.

DON'T FORGET

Does the mass media accurately reflect our own social reality? Does mass media hypnotize or inform?

ONLINE

Equality in Sport: Is it fair to treat people differently in *sport* on the basis of gender? See www.261fearless.org for the full story of Catherine Switzer, the first *female* to enter the all-male marathon in 1967 Boston, USA.

MASS MEDIA

Mass media such as television, social media, radio and newspapers can be used to raise awareness of minority groups in society. This is because the mass media has the *power to inform and educate* its audiences. Therefore, the media can be used to *reduce* discrimination in society by challenging unhelpful stereotypes head on. However, the media can also act to *confirm* stereotypes and maintain prejudices, especially if it persists with only stereotypical representations like echoes in an echo chamber.

Frueh and McGhee (1975) carried out research on the effects of television viewing on stereotyping. They found that the number of hours of TV viewing correlated with the extent and direction of gender stereotyping.

Tan et al (2000) showed that negative group portrayals in the media led directly to increasingly negative stereotypes for those groups in the audience.

This was confirmed by **Kimball (1986)** when they measured gender role stereotyping in a small regional culture. Before television was available to the region, there was less than average gender role stereotyping. However, in a follow-up study, once a television media culture had established itself, there was increased gender role stereotyping. Therefore, the media can *increase* prejudice.

Media Content should Challenge Stereotypes

How **media content** is produced can have a great influence on the existence of stereotypes in society. For example, images that promote diversity and difference should *reduce prejudice* while media content that panders to worn-out stereotypes will only help perpetuate existing inequalities and divisions. Therefore, mass media has an important role to play in reducing prejudice in society.

When the media only includes stereotypical misconceptions of society, then audiences will be mis-educated and mis-informed. Society may come to reflect the media messages like a mirror. According to Gramsci (1971) the mass media is in bed with the ruling elite. The media often confirms the status quo beliefs for its own self-interest. This leads to a **false consciousness** in the audience of untrue stereotypes and established prejudices. This can **distort** our sense of **social reality**.

The media needs to be progressive and idealistic in its construction and selection of content. How the media represents gender, age, ethnicity and other social groups is very important. This is because *unhelpful stereotypes* can be propagated into the future by continued misrepresentation. With misrepresentation, there will be **self-fulfilling biases** created in society.

There are two main ways to remove prejudice from the media. The first is to remove any biases in the formulation and construction of the message – i.e. how it is represented. The second is to check the internal content of the message for bias and prejudice.

DOES AFFIRMATIVE ACTION REDUCE PREJUDICE?

Affirmative action programmes can act to reduce institutional racism and sexism in an organisation.

Affirmative action programmes have been used in many countries. For example, the American government has run affirmative action programmes for many years to encourage diversity in the workplace. Some claim these programmes have helped under-represented groups into American organisations and into work. This can be seen as reducing discrimination across America.

> Affirmative action means setting targets (i.e. quotas) to positively select or recruit under-represented groups into an organisation.

Taylor (1994) studied the effect of affirmative action programmes in America and found its effects to be positively beneficial for the under-represented groups.

Affirmative action programmes can be used to disrupt the status quo and redress the under-representation of groups that causes institutional prejudice and discrimination. Institutional discrimination is a continued momentum towards prejudice that maintains the status quo.

Heilman (2001) studied large organisations and found that institutionalised gender stereotypes can obstruct women's advancement in some organisational hierarchies and these hierarchies are therefore 'institutionally sexist'.

The benefits of Affirmative Action programmes:

- Affirmative action reduces prejudice because it establishes diversity quotas for positive selection during recruitment. Therefore, under-represented groups get opportunities within an organisation just like everyone else.
- Affirmative action encourages diversity in selection and recruitment to an organisation. This reduces the prejudice in an organisation.
- Affirmative action leads to a more diverse demographic of participants within an organisation. In turn, this leads to a more inclusive, successful, creative and robust organisational structure.

However, some people consider positive selection quotas as a form of **reverse discrimination** because affirmative action programmes actively exclude individuals just like prejudice and discrimination. Indeed, in Britain, affirmative action programmes are deemed illegal under the **Equalities Act (2010)** because they discriminate unequally on the basis of *protected categories* such as age, gender, race or class.

THINGS TO DO AND THINK ABOUT

Challenge Media Stereotypes

Cumberbatch and Negrine (1992) analysed the content of six weeks of television and found *zero* representation of disabled, ethnic minority individuals. If the mass media is ideologically loaded with false and simplified stereotypes, how can we disrupt the bias of the mass media?

Remember to challenge the consensus view on social organisation wherever it is discriminatory. Try busting a few worn-out *media stereotypes* that the media should stop using with these *diverse* counter-examples:

- 'All old people are weak and infirm' versus 'Brian, the seventy year old marathon runner'
- 'All mechanics are males' *versus* 'Yani, the female mechanical engineer who repairs planes'
- 'All nurses are women' *versus* 'Pietr, the male nurse at the local hospital'
- 'All politicians are old men' *versus* 'Tanya, the female teenager who became an MSP'

Add your own examples of unhelpful stereotypes and set about finding examples who challenge the stereotype.

DON'T FORGET

If we don't challenge the media establishment to remove its own prejudices then the mass media will promote a false consciousness of our own social reality.

DON'T FORGET

Does the mass media *inject* positive or negative stereotypes and ideology into its audience?

DON'T FORGET

Wasserstrom (1977) talks positively of 'affirmative action' as a desirable instrument of social engineering that helps move social reality towards a better social ideal.

ONLINE TEST

Test yourself on this topic online at www.brightredbooks.net/subjects

APPLIED THEORY: REDUCING PREJUDICE THROUGH EDUCATION

EDUCATION CAN BE USED TO REDUCE PREJUDICE

One educational approach to reducing prejudice is the **melting-pot** approach to encourage integration between groups, ages, genders and cultures. The aim is to produce a global homogeneity. The melting-pot approach is to remove barriers and difference.

Another educational approach to reducing prejudice is **multi-culturalism**. This educates about real cultural and group differences in information programmes emphasising diversity. It does not necessarily encourage integration.

Snowman and Biehler (2000) debate which is best at reducing prejudice in their text *Psychology Applied to Teaching*: is it to use a multi-cultural approach or a melting-pot approach? Perhaps both approaches should be adopted as they are not mutually exclusive.

> **DON'T FORGET**
>
> Jane Elliot was inspired to reduce prejudice in her classroom directly after the civil rights activist, Martin Luther King, was assassinated.

THE 'BLUE-EYES/BROWN-EYES' EXPERIMENT – DIRECT EDUCATION AGAINST PREJUDICE

In 1968 an American primary school teacher, Jane Elliot, devised the 'Blue-Eyes: Brown-Eyes' experiment to provide a memorable and applied way to reduce prejudice. Elliot realised her class needed to directly experience the harmful effects of discrimination for them to be motivated to reduce it.

Jane Elliot quotes a Native American prayer as her inspiration for the 'Blue-Eyes/Brown-Eyes' experiment.

> *'Keep me from judging a man until I have walked a mile in his moccasins.'*

> **DON'T FORGET**
>
> The discriminated-against group quickly lived **down** to other people's lowered expectations. This is confirmation of the 'The Pygmalion Effect' revealed by Rosenthal and Jacobsen (1968).

Example:

Applied research: the 'Blue-Eyes/Brown-Eyes' class demonstration

NAME: Jane Elliot (1968)

AIM: To educate against prejudice by creating reversible prejudice in the classroom and allowing her class of school children to directly experience discrimination through immersive education.

METHOD: This was a classroom-based experiment with eleven young primary school children.

She wanted to test what would happen when the teacher created a divided and stereotypically prejudiced 'superior' group and an 'inferior' group. For the purposes of the demonstration, she based the prejudice on the arbitrary feature of eye colour.

PROCEDURE: How discrimination was implemented in the classroom.

Over three days, Elliot asked her class to treat their classmates differently on the basis of eye colour.

1. Day 1: On the first day, the 'blue-eyes' group were treated with extra privileges (no black collars, longer breaks, better treatment at lunchtime, extra water drinking rights). Overt discrimination was encouraged on the basis that the 'brown-eyed' group were inferior.
2. Day 2: On day two, Elliot announced she had made a mistake and reversed the discrimination – the 'brown-eyes' group were to be seen as 'superior' and given the extra privileges, while the blue-eyes group were to be classed as 'lazy' and 'inferior'.
3. Day 3: On the third day, the prejudice and segregation was removed. Debriefing started and the children were told the eye-colour prejudice was baseless and made up by the teacher. After a full explanation of the reason for the demonstration, both groups were to be treated equally and were to work together without any segregation.

RESULTS: On day one, the (so-called) superior 'blue-eyes' felt self-pride and hatred towards the 'brown-eyes' while the (so-called) inferior 'brown-eyes' group felt depression and exclusion. On day two, the roles reversed and, with it, discrimination reversed. Hostility, aggression and prejudice emerged between the groups. On day three, when the segregated groups were combined again and equal treatment resumed, the children showed real signs of happiness and friendship being restored. Elliot also noted a 'self-fulfilling prophecy' at work in the 'blue-eyes/brown-eyes' demonstration. The 'superior' group showed enhanced school performance during their day of superior treatment and the 'inferior' group showed lowered test scores in response to their lowered expectations.

> **DON'T FORGET**
>
> Elliot's insight was that to reduce prejudice it was not sufficient to talk about it, but necessary to experience it.

contd

In a thirteen-year follow-up to this demonstration, Elliot found that the original participants in her classroom testified in a 1984 documentary that they acted with more tolerance to others later in life. **CONCLUSION:** Elliot believed that empathy-training programmes like her 'Blue-Eyes/Brown-Eyes' demonstration can increase empathy for out-group members, and reduce prejudice and discrimination.

'By removing prejudice, we create instant cousins!' Jane Elliot.

Further support for empathy-training programmes comes from Aboud and Levy (2000) who found this type of education benefited anyone, independent of age or gender.

VIDEO LINK

Head to www.brightredbooks.net to watch the FRONTLINE documentary *A Class Divided* on Jane Elliot's original experiments. The film includes part of Elliot's original 1970's report for ABC News called 'The Eye of the Storm'.

OTHER WAYS TO EDUCATE AGAINST PREJUDICE

Here are some other applied ways to reduce prejudice and discrimination:

The jigsaw technique

Aronson et al (1978) devised 'the jigsaw technique' as a co-operative learning method. The jigsaw technique requires everyone in the class to cooperate for completion of the programme. Everyone takes responsibility for 'teaching' one bit of the course. This is much like Sherif's (1956) 'super-ordinate goal' approach to reducing conflict and discrimination (further explained later), but the super-ordinate goal is applied in education (see page 76).

Boost self-esteem!

Prejudice may be a way of upholding self-esteem when it's low. So, does a boost in self-esteem reduce prejudice? Fein and Spencer (1997) improved participants' self-esteem by encouraging values of self-worth and establishing personal values in a written exercise. They then found scores of participants' self-esteem increased and prejudicial attitudes declined between measures before and after the written exercise. This study by Fein and Spencer (1997) suggests self-esteem may be a linked factor that maintains prejudice.

ONLINE

For a good read about prejudice online, head to www.brightredbooks.net

Cognitive dissonance training

Festinger (1957) coined the term 'cognitive dissonance' and revealed that people often hold inconsistent values and incompatible beliefs which, once they're aware of them, they will be motivated to alter. Cognitive dissonance training can be used in anti-discriminatory training programmes. For example, people can be asked to agree with incompatible statements such as 'I'm all for equality,' and 'I've never signed a petition supporting equal pay'.

DON'T FORGET

If self-esteem is improved, could this act against prejudice?

Lobby for legislation!

Equality and diversity legislation can act to reduce prejudice. Oskamp (2000) found a link between social norms and legislation changes. When civil rights acts are discussed and promoted in a society, Oskamp (2000) reports that discrimination reduces. So, lobbying for the creation of new anti-discrimination legislation should help to reduce prejudice directly and change attitudes in the process, indirectly.

'The opposite of love is not hate, it is indifference.' Elie Weasel

DON'T FORGET

Cognitive dissonance raises the discomfort felt by people holding inconsistent views and should, in turn, motivate action against indifference to discrimination.

THINGS TO DO AND THINK ABOUT

How can prejudice be reduced? Try this Cognitive Dissonance Training:

1. Where is discrimination occurring today (for example, sexism, racism, ageism)?

2. Who is getting hurt by this discrimination? Should this be allowed to continue?

Circle what you have done to stop prejudice and discrimination:

- Designed a Poster
- Written an email
- Talked to a manager
- Lobbied for legislation
- Spoken against prejudice in class
- Bought a badge
- Campaigned or marched
- Worn a protest t-shirt
- Gone to the press

ONLINE TEST

Test your knowledge about reducing prejudice through education at www.brightredbooks.net

APPLIED RESEARCH: SHERIF'S (1956) SUPER-ORDINATE GOAL THEORY

THE ROBBERS CAVE SUMMER CAMP FIELD EXPERIMENTS

How can prejudice be reduced? One of Sherif's studies from 1954 is known as **the Robbers Cave field experiment**. In reality, it's one of three summer-camp studies summarised in a *Scientific American* paper titled 'Experiments in Group Conflict' by Sherif (1956). In all three summer camp studies, Sherif observed the interaction of two competitive groups that formed spontaneously. It was in 1954 that the groups were called the 'Eagles' and 'Rattlers'.

Equal status contact or super-ordinate goals?

Sherif (1956) outlines a theory of prejudice reduction that states that groups working towards a shared **super-ordinate goal** will more effectively reduce conflict and prejudice than merely **equal status contact.** Sherif (1956) supported his super-ordinate goal theory by presenting friendship and sociogram data from three field research studies in intergroup conflict at a number of boys' summer camps in America.

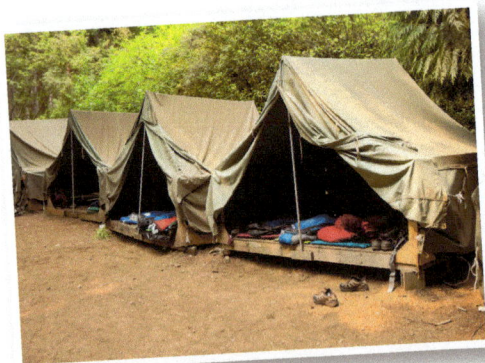

Example:

Sherif – The Robbers Cave Field Experiments
A series of field experiments on **prejudice reduction** were carried out by Sherif at the Robbers Cave national park in America. In 1949, Sherif studied boys forming two groups at the summer camp: the boys formed groups they called the Dogs and the Devils. Then, in 1953, different boys formed two groups at a summer camp, calling themselves the Panthers and the Pythons. Lastly, in 1954, a further sample of boys formed two groups, the Eagles and the Rattlers.
AIM: To test the hypothesis that competition increases conflict and co-operation decreases conflict.
METHOD: The method used was a field experiment with a questionnaire to allow a friendship analysis of the boys' relations. In each camp, two groups of 12-year-old boys were recruited as a naive participant sample.

Stage 1: The Group Formation Stage:

In Stage 1 of Sherif's field experiments on intergroup conflict, the boys were kept within their in-groups, at opposite ends of the camp, naive and unaware of the other group's existence. In-group identity was built up and group cohesion was encouraged.

Stage 2: The Realistic Conflict Stage

In Stage 2, the boys were made aware of the other group by introducing intergroup contact and competition for resources. They were encouraged to enter competitions against the out-group. Sherif arranged tournaments for a single trophy and head-to head activities to earn scarce 'points' off and against the other group.

Stage 3: The Super-ordinate Goal Stage

In Stage 3, co-operative activities were introduced with the boys acting together to achieve super-ordinate goals. Could super-ordinate goal-setting reduce conflict, discrimination and prejudice? Super-ordinate tasks included fixing a water-tank together, pushing a stalled vehicle to jump start it together, and pulling a tow rope co-operatively to move a truck some distance without fuel.

RESULTS: A socio-gram technique (a social network diagram) was used to analyse the social network of the boys' intergroup relations, friendship links and group preferences after each stage of the experiment.

ONLINE

Head to www.brightredbooks.net to view a presentation on the Robbers Cave field experiments.

DON'T FORGET

Sherif defines a super-ordinate goal as something necessary to do but only made possible by intergroup cooperation.

DON'T FORGET

This was an important new concept in conflict reduction being field tested. Could super-ordinate goal-setting reduce discrimination, conflict and prejudice?

RESULTS AFTER PHASE 1 – AFTER FORMATION OF THE GROUPS
After Phase 1 of forming the groups, they made the boys aware of the other group (the out-group). Immediately, the boys showed a biased estimation of ability for the in-group boys' achievements and downgraded the out-group. There was an increase in negative stereotyping of out-group members and a prejudice for in-group friendship choices.

RESULTS AFTER PHASE 2 – AFTER REALISTIC CONFLICT
After Phase 2, there was realistic conflict. The boys planned raids on each other's food supplies. Some boys collected apples for 'ammunition' against the out-group. The boys designed posters to convey messages against the out-group. In at least one case, they started physically fighting and they attempted to burn the out-group's flag.

RESULTS AFTER PHASE 3 – AFTER CO-OPERATION ON SUPER-ORDINATE GOALS
After Phase 3, and the introduction of super-ordinate goals, the boys' friendship networks were mapped and measured again to see if they had changed from Phase 2.
Overall, friendship ratings reversed. Stereotype ratings of the out-group changed from 40% 'unfavourable' before Phase Three to 40% 'favourable' after Phase Three. The percentage of out-group friendship choices increased, with both groups moving in the direction towards the 50:50 'in-group: out-group' friendship ratio.

Sherif (1956) analysed his experimental field data from questionnaires on intergroup and interpersonal friendships among summer-camp boys to conclude that for prejudice to reduce, it's not enough for two competitive groups to meet. Only after working together on a co-operative task that required intergroup dependency, did the boys reduce their hostility, prejudice, conflict and discrimination.

CONCLUSION: Overall, Sherif (1956) concluded that if both groups worked toward a super-ordinate goal, this was the most effective factor in reducing prejudice. Sherif's (1956) research paper also concluded that equal status contact is not enough to reduce prejudice or conflict.

EVALUATION: Here's a table with a list of evaluative points about Sherif (1956).

STRENGTHS	WEAKNESSES
Realistic conflict theory (competition between groups for scarce resources) was directly tested by Sherif in Phase 2 of each field experiment. This was shown to reliably create conflict and increase prejudice and discrimination between the groups.	Sherif (1956) defined the research hypotheses post-event (i.e. after starting the summer camps) which could have resulted in self-fulfilling data interpretation and post-hoc justification.
Equal status contact theory was shown to be ineffective at predicting a reduction in prejudice during Phase 2. Equal status contact is not enough, on its own. During this phase of Sherif's experiments, equal status contact occurred between the groups on apparently equal terms. Yet hostility increased rather than decreased during phase 2.	Like all field experiments, there may be many uncontrolled extraneous variables at work in the summer-camp studies. Although these studies have high ecological validity, how naive were the boys of the experimental hypotheses by the end of each study?
Super-ordinate goals acted quickly in Phase 3 to break down group identities. Co-operative achievement of super-ordinate goals was enough to reduce prejudice and conflict. After Phase 3, Sherif (1956) surveyed the boys to find a measurable increase in out-group friendship relations and an overall more positive attitude rating of the out-group.	Each of Sherif's (1956) three field experiments focus on a single-age group only (12-year-old boys) and just one gender (males). In each case, the boys may have been prone to demand characteristics and shown participant reactivity.

THINGS TO DO AND THINK ABOUT

Work co-operatively with a study buddy on these prompts with exam-style marks:

1. Explain the three phases in the procedure of the field experiments reported by Sherif (1956). (3 marks)

2. Describe the main findings and results from Sherif's (1956) summer-camp studies. (5 marks)

3. Explain one factor that successfully reduces prejudice. (2 marks)

4. Evaluate the field experimental **method** used by Sherif in the summer-camp studies. (4 marks)

5. Analyse how *important* the Robbers Cave studies are to the topic of prejudice (6 marks)

VIDEO LINK

Watch a good video on The Robber's Cave Field Experiments at www.brightredbooks.net

ONLINE TEST

Test your knowledge about prejudice at www.brightredbooks.net

THE RESEARCH PROCESS

OVERVIEW OF THE RESEARCH PROCESS

Traditional sciences like physics, chemistry and biology rely on the research process to gather empirical evidence for theories. Social sciences like psychology and sociology rely on it too. So, what are the steps to the research process? How is research in psychology carried out? We will start with an overview of the research process.

THE RESEARCH PROCESS: AN OVERVIEW OF THE EIGHT STAGES

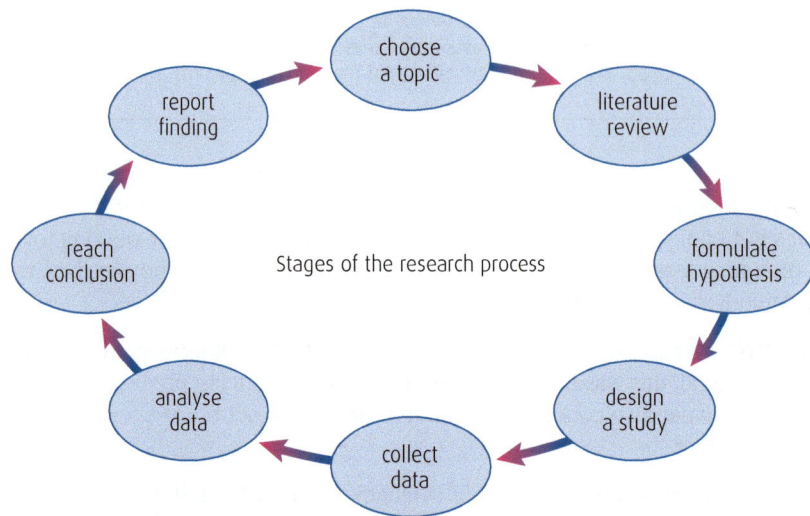

Stages of the research process

(cycle diagram: choose a topic → literature review → formulate hypothesis → design a study → collect data → analyse data → reach conclusion → report finding → choose a topic)

Stage 1: Choose a topic

What do you want to study? What fascinates and motivates you? At this first stage, you might **choose a topic** to start your preliminary investigations. Is there funding for research in this area, or is there expertise available? Should you choose a topic thoroughly explored already or something new? Some of the best research is radical, creative and original.

You may have a very specific research question in mind or be drawn to a broad area of research. If you want to be paid for doing research, go for a research topic that's fashionable or well-funded. Your research will be more likely to have an impact if it's practical and useful to society. However, you might be constrained in your choice of topic due to practical, political or academic reasons.

Stage 2: Conduct a literature review

Early on in your research, it's important to **conduct a literature review**. Wide-ranging background research will help you avoid reinventing the wheel.

Read up on previous research on your chosen topic. The literature review also allows you to build on the work of other people and explore existing theories and concepts from your research area.

Someone else will probably have done relevant research on your chosen topic. The sooner you do the literature review, the better, as it can be very helpful. At all stages, remain focused on your aims. Otherwise, you might get lost in the topic, the library and the internet.

Stage 3: Formulate a hypothesis

What issue will you address? What research question will you explore? You can move towards **formulating a hypothesis** by defining the terms in your research question. When selecting the research question you will address, it's best to focus on one specific aspect of the topic. Once the area of interest is clear, you can formulate a hypothesis by turning your most central research question into predictive statements.

MORE ABOUT THE HYPOTHESIS

A hypothesis is a **statement of prediction** that expresses the relationship between one set of events (for example, changes in an independent variable) and another set of events (for example, changes in a dependent variable). 'When it rains, plants grow' is a hypothesis about there being a relationship between rainy conditions (rain being the independent variable) and plants' growth (growth being the dependent variable).

Independent variable (IV): An IV is assumed to be a causal variable. IVs are presumed to alter and vary before dependent variables and may cause an influence on dependent variables.

Dependent variable (DV): A DV is assumed to be an effect variable. A DV alters or changes in response to causal variables. DVs are not independent, but rather dependent on the influence of prior factors. DVs are sometimes known as response variables.

Extraneous variable (EV): An EV is assumed to be a factor, an influence or a source of variation that's outside the scope of the research study and its hypotheses. Extraneous variables can include factors that have not been controlled or standardised in the conditions for the research. For example, weather, noise, time of day, mood, participant variables and individual differences.

Confounding variable (CV): A CV is assumed to be an awkward variable that messes up your research. It may be an extraneous variable that has masked or hidden the cause-and-effect relationship that was under investigation in your research. For example, if your research involved seeing a band at T in the Park, **mist** would be a confounding variable.

Example:

Hypotheses:

Caffeine (IV) keeps you awake for longer during sleep onset (DV).
Hours spent revising (IV) directly improves exam grades (DV).
Ingesting a slice of cake (IV) improves your mood (DV).

Types of hypotheses

Hypotheses can be directional (one-tailed: specifying one direction of effect) or non-directional (two-tailed: open to two directions of effect). A two-tailed hypothesis is less specific about the predicted direction of effect than a one-tailed hypothesis.

Experimental Hypothesis: An experimental hypothesis makes a statement about one variable affecting another.

Example:

One- and two-tailed hypotheses:

Glucose drinks improve swimming times. This is one-tailed.
Glucose drinks change swimming times. This is two-tailed.

Null Hypothesis: This is the statement of no effect. So, for the previous example, 'glucose drinks have no effect on swimming times' would be a suitable null hypothesis.

THINGS TO DO AND THINK ABOUT

Social science gathers empirical evidence to come to valid conclusions. It does this by using deduction to disprove null hypotheses and it uses induction from patterns in observed data to support or refute experimental hypotheses. In practice, this means you set up a hypothesis and a null hypothesis that cannot be true simultaneously. By the end of your research, one of the hypotheses might be able to be rejected.

ONLINE

For an analysis of types of experiment (lab, field and natural) head to www.brightredbooks.net

DON'T FORGET

A one-tailed hypothesis specifies the direction of the effect, while a two-tailed hypothesis does not.

DON'T FORGET

Remember to clearly define variables, as research hypotheses need to be testable.

VIDEO LINK

Watch an introduction to using research methods at www.brightredbooks.net

ONLINE

If you're unfamiliar with literature reviews, find out more at www.brightredbooks.net

ONLINE TEST

Test yourself on the stages of the research process at www.brightredbooks.net

THE RESEARCH PROCESS AND RESULTS ANALYSIS

Let's now look at the final five stages of the research process.

STAGE 4: DESIGN A STUDY

When designing a research study, you'll choose at least one **method of data collection**. Methods include **experiments**, **surveys**, **interviews**, **case studies** and **observational studies**. It may be possible to choose a number of methods to collect data, and a mixed-method approach allows **triangulation** of the results.

Primary and secondary research

Will your research study be classed as **primary** research or **secondary** research?

Primary research is fresh, first-hand data collection. Are you going to collect new data that's not been collected before? If so, this makes your research, primary research.

Secondary research analyses data that others have collected and presented before. Are you going to rely on existing data that's already been collected and published? If so, your research will be 'desk-style' secondary research.

Designing a study involves more than specifying plans for research methods. You'll also need to specify the variables to be measured, set up the research conditions, organise the questions to be asked, design a procedure, select a sample and choose a way of allocating participants to groups.

STAGE 5: COLLECT DATA

This is the most important part of empirical research. Make sure all the necessary materials and resources are ready before running any investigation. Some of the research materials might need to be specially designed. Good research investigations tend to abide by a voluntary Code of Ethics.

To collect data, the research procedure is run, data recorded and the design followed. Observations and data measurements are made from the sample or the participants' responses. Responses are recorded under the various conditions of the study. Measurements are collected together and collated into tables. Results tables should focus around the specific variables of the aims of the research and be linked to the hypothesis.

Collecting quantitative and qualitative Data

Quantitative research collects numerical data. Methods such as structured observation, closed questions in surveys and laboratory experiments collect quantitative data by making numerical measurements.

Qualitative research produces textual data. It can result from many different methodologies, including open questions in surveys, transcripts of interviews, case notes from a case-study description or just textual accounts of events recorded during a period of observation.

STAGE 6: ANALYSE DATA

This stage of the research process involves analysing the data collected during the investigation. All the data is examined and summarised. Descriptive statistics can be used to create summary tables of raw data. Well-labelled graphs and charts can be constructed to illustrate any emerging trends in the analysis. Does the evidence from the investigation support or refute the hypothesis?

contd

DON'T FORGET

You can allocate participants to groups randomly to avoid investigator bias in sampling.

DON'T FORGET

You can employ counterbalancing of conditions to reduce order effects.

No child participants! Remember that for the Higher Psychology Research Assignment, the SQA **does not allow** you to use children (anyone under 16 years old) as research participants.

ONLINE

Find the Codes of Ethics produced by the British Psychological Society at www.brightredbooks.net

DON'T FORGET

Data collection should remain ethical at all times!

Descriptive statistics

Raw data can take up a lot of space in tables and charts, so statisticians came up with short-hand ways of describing vast columns of numbers and measurements. They invented descriptive statistics for summarising data.

Descriptive statistics that can be used for data analysis including measures of central tendency (mean, median and mode) and measures of dispersion (for example, the range, standard deviation).

Measures of central tendency: measures tending to describe the middle of the data

Mean: The mean measures the average of all the data in a data set. The mean is calculated by adding all the data up and dividing by the number of data points in the data set.

Median: The median represents the middle-ranking number. All the data is ranked from smallest to largest. Then, the middle-ranking number is accepted as the median. However, if there's an even number of ranks, then the average of the two middle-ranking numbers is accepted as the median.

Mode: This is the most commonly occurring data value within the data set. Note that some data sets require more than one mode to describe them. Other data sets have no clear mode, as no value occurs more than once.

Measures of dispersion: measures describing the spread of the data

Range: The range is the full extent of the dispersion between the maximum value in the data set and the minimum value.

Standard deviation: This is the square root of the statistic known as the variance. It can be referred to in research. Thankfully, it's not currently part of the Higher Psychology course!

STAGE 7: REACH CONCLUSIONS

At the end of analysing the data, it may be possible to make some conclusions from the research. This stage involves returning to the original aims and hypotheses of the research. Have the aims been achieved?

STAGE 8: REPORT FINDINGS

The stage of reporting findings involves clearly presenting the aims, method, results, findings and conclusions of the research investigation. To raise the profile of the research, research findings can be reported and presented in research journals, to the press, at university seminars and to conferences around the world. This is one of the most important steps in social science.

THINGS TO DO AND THINK ABOUT

Calculate measures of **central tendency** and a measure of **dispersion** for this data:

People's estimates of the speed of **Car A:**   (km/h) 34, 56, 44, 32, 32, 21, 37, 53

People's estimates of the speed of **Car B:**   (km/h) 67, 78, 57, 24, 24, 64, 74, 74, 48, 23

1. Calculate the **mean, median** and **mode** for Car A.
2. Calculate the **mean, median** and **mode** for Car B.
3. Calculate the **ranges** of the estimates for Car A and for Car B.
4. Which car has the **biggest range** of estimates?
5. Which car did people estimate was going faster? Explain your answer by comparing at least two measures of **central tendency**.

ETHICAL ISSUES AND THE BRITISH PSYCHOLOGICAL SOCIETY

What principles are there to guide ethical practice in psychological research? How have the ethical codes of practice in place today improved research in psychology? Is research better and safer now? What was research like before voluntary ethical codes of practice were published by the British Psychological Society? Let's consider the impact of ethical codes on psychology.

ONLINE

Refer to the British Psychological Society website for the latest Code of Ethics to follow. You can find the link at www.brightredbooks.net

GENERAL ETHICAL ISSUES TO BE CONSIDERED

The SQA encourages all Higher Psychology students to abide by the British Psychological Society's current Code of Ethics. The main ethical principle is to remove any risk of harm to each participant. Here's a list of general ethical principles that should be considered before conducting human participant research.

Informed participation

Before getting consent, participants must be fully **informed** of the aims, purpose and procedure for any investigation. This can be achieved by providing an information sheet known as a 'briefing'. Getting consent from participants is only one half of **informed consent**. Full information about all aspects of the study should be provided in a briefing before asking people if they wish to take part.

Consent

Consent means agreeing to become a participant. While there may be financial incentives to participate, a person must never participate against their will. At the outset, each participant **must agree** to take part. Evidence of agreement can be collected on a signed consent form.

Right to withdrawal

Before, during or after giving consent, a participant **may change their mind** about being involved in the research and this should be respected at all stages. Data and involvement can be withdrawn. There should be no strings or ties making removal of their participation difficult. They must be made aware of their **right to withdraw** at any stage.

Confidentiality and anonymity

Data protection is an important part of psychological research nowadays. Any personal information must be stored confidentially and securely. If used in a report, distributed or published, data should be made **anonymous** by removing all names. Personal information should be kept **confidential**. Results for individual participants should only be discussed in general terms. Specific identities should be protected.

Protection from harm

Psychological research procedures should **cause no harm**, either physically or mentally, beyond that of everyday life. Any harm associated with the research should be considered and **risks removed** before asking participants to take part in the research. Participants should be reminded that any hurtful, difficult or personal questions need not be answered.

Debriefing

At the end of the research procedure, a full explanation of the aims, method and implications of the research should be offered to each participant. This debriefing respects the increased curiosity of the participants at the end of a study.

Debriefing should explain why the research was conducted in the way it was and about how the data will be used. Using a 'debriefing statement' helps provide reassurance for all those involved. Any harmful consequences of the research should also be looked out for at this stage. The debriefing statement should assure participants their individual data will not be discussed in isolation.

contd

Deception

Avoid deception as much as possible. Lies, deceit and misinformation are to be avoided as part of psychological research. Deception in psychological research today might destroy the reputation that the scientific community has regained since famous unethical studies such as Milgram (1963).

In some cases, a level of specific information may be withheld until the end of a study if no harm can be foreseen. However, it's important there's no misinformation. Milgram **falsely** described the purpose of the experiments to the participants as being an investigation into 'punishment and learning'. This acted as cover story. Misinformation was also used in Asch's lines study when he told his participants the experiments were on 'visual perception'. Using misinformation for this purpose is now considered unethical.

Observation

It's usually unethical to observe someone in private and there are laws restricting what can be recorded or watched without their consent. This means most observation in psychological research is disclosed observation (overt observation). The only circumstance where undisclosed observation (covert observation) would be acceptable is in public places where people would reasonably expect to be observed. However, they may still object to being part of the research and ask for their data to be removed from it.

Shared responsibility

All those involved in research share a joint responsibility for pursuing the research ethically. If bad practice is noticed, it should be dealt with. There's a shared responsibility to adhere to ethical principles, and doing nothing in response to colleagues breaching ethical codes of practice is unacceptable.

Competence

Psychological research may involve skilled procedures, sensitive psychological assessments, difficult statistical calculations and even surgical interventions! These practical skills might take years to acquire, include risk of harm if carried out incorrectly and only be acceptable when carried out by qualified people. Before planning research there's the issue of 'competence of the team' to consider.

Mental health advice

Over the course of your research, mental health issues may arise in participants. For ethical reasons, hand out no mental health advice. Your advice may be wrong, lack evidence, be harmful or cause damage to the participants. Even with many hours of psychology training, researchers should stick to research.

If health issues do arise, refer people to a GP or your research supervisor. Learn to use the catch-all phrase: 'Seek professional health'. Do not use your **researcher** role to pretend you're a clinical psychologist.

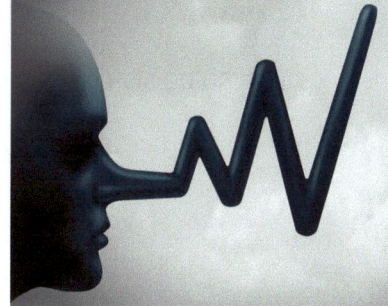

THINGS TO DO AND THINK ABOUT

Ethical Analysis!

Use the four steps below to analyse the ethics of an unethical study:

1. Imagine a really interesting **unethical** study, for example, Milgram's obedience study (1963).

2. Quickly list the reasons the research is unethical (for example, no informed consent, harmful, etc.).

3. Now, accurately list which ethical principles of the BPS Code it breaches.

4. For each principle, explain what procedural steps were unethical and suggest ways the research could be improved ethically.

DON'T FORGET

In Scotland, you need seven years of university training to become a Clinical Psychologist.

VIDEO LINK

Ethical principles are explained in the video entitled 'Ethics in psychology tutorial' at www.brightredbooks.net

ONLINE TEST

Test yourself on ethical issues and the British Psychological Society at www.brightredbooks.net

RESEARCH METHODS: CASE STUDIES

Psychologists might focus in on one or two examples (or cases) to exemplify an area of study.

KEY FEATURES OF THE CASE-STUDY METHOD

Case studies work as illustrative examples to shed light on a poorly understood topic or area. They are in-depth, descriptive, textual accounts of one individual case or a single example. The aim is exploratory and doesn't act as scientific 'proof'. However, case studies can be used to dispute a theory.

Example:

The Black Swan and the 'No Black Swans' Theory
To say there are no black swans is a theory. If someone brings you a single example of a black swan, then the 'no black swans' theory becomes untenable and the theory must be modified. This is refutation by the case study method. However, standing alone, case-study examples do **not** allow generalisation of the wider population. For example, if there's one case of a black swan, we can't conclude that all swans are black.

DON'T FORGET

Remember to revise Freud's case studies 'Little Hans' and 'Anna O'.

DON'T FORGET

A phobia is an intrusive fear that is out of proportion to the danger present.

FAMOUS PSYCHOANALYTIC CASE STUDIES

Famous psychoanalytic case studies include 'Little Hans' by Freud (1909) and 'Anna O' by Freud and Breuer (1895). Freud used these to help explain and support his theories of the unconscious.

Little Hans – Freud (1909) 'Hans really was a little Oedipus'

The case study of Little Hans is known from notes made by Freud in correspondence with the child's father. Little Hans was referred to Freud for medical treatment for a **phobia of horses**. Freud used a longitudinal case-study method to analyse the boy's condition over a period of five years. Freud's case notes list formative experiences with horses that might have caused the phobia and influenced Little Han's personality development.

Little Hans was a small boy born in Vienna in 1903. At aged four and a half, Little Hans witnessed a horse-biting injury and later in that year saw a horse accident involving a carriage falling over in the street. The case notes report the boy developed a phobia of horses at aged five.

Freud claimed the boy experienced traumatic anxiety during the phallic stage of psychosexual development. Little Hans' mother discouraged Hans from playing with his penis by threatening castration. Freud explained that Little Hans was stuck at the phallic stage as a result and suffering an Oedipus complex. Little Hans recalled a dream of being married to his mother and being scared of his father. Freud interpreted this as a repressed desire to get rid of his father and to sleep with his mother.

This led to an unresolved neurotic conflict associated with his father, concerning castration anxiety, which, through symptom substitution, resulted in a phobic anxiety of horses and Little Hans' fascination with his penis. Freud also explained Little Hans' jealousy of his sister as being caused by jealousy for his mother's attention. Other dreams about giraffes and plumbers were also interpreted as caused by an Oedipus complex.

Strengths: Freud hypothesised that conflicts in the early years of childhood were important in forming the developing personality. Freud's case study of Little Hans sketched out a plausible route of causation between neurotic symptoms and early traumatic experiences.

Weaknesses: A single case study cannot be used alone to support a theory. Many other interpretations of the horse phobia are possible. Other factors may have caused it. The case notes are an unreliable data source, with letters written post-event from memory and the boy's own father giving personal interpretations. Freud saw Little Hans only twice; once for a birthday and once for a therapy session.

VIDEO LINK

Find a cut-out animation on the Little Hans case study at www.brightredbooks.net

contd

A FAMOUS EXAMPLE OF A BEHAVIOURIST CASE STUDY: LITTLE ALBERT, WATSON & RAYNER (1920)

To fully explain the case-study method, as used in psychology, it's worth learning about the notorious case study 'Little Albert' by Watson and Rayner (1920) on the conditioning of a phobia in an infant.

Watson and Rayner (1920) wanted to see if they could create a phobia in a 5-year-old infant. Could a phobia be classically conditioned? Would a child learn a phobia by association? Could a phobia be associated with, and triggered by, a neutral stimulus that originally caused no emotional response?

Watson and Rayner (1920) chose a stolid, unemotional child to test the classical conditioning theory previously researched in dogs by Pavlov. This case study would involve a sample size of one: an 11-month-old infant. The important point about this study was that it was classical conditioning in a human participant. The infant's fear response would be triggered and associated with a neutral stimulus (NS).

First, the investigators found out what scared the infant. Very few things seemed to scare Little Albert. But loud noises did. They beat a hammer on a metal bar to make a loud clanging noise behind him. The loud noise was chosen as the unconditioned stimulus and was used to evoke the fear reflex.

In the terms that Pavlov used, Watson and Rayner used the loud noise as the unconditional stimulus (UCS) and they recognised Little Albert's startled response as the unconditional fear response (UCR).

Initially, Little Albert was presented with a white rat that caused no fear response. Then he tried to touch the rat. Immediately, the metal bar was hit to make the loud noise and the infant started violently. Then he tried to touch the rat once more. The bar was struck again and he whimpered and was startled again. After seven days, Little Albert was brought to the lab again. Eventually, the NS became a conditioned stimulus (CS). There were at least seven joint pairings of rat and noise.

Initially, the rat had been an NS. However, now – when the rat was presented alone – the child whimpered and cried, withdrew his hand from touching the rat and tried to crawl away.

Watson and Rayner (1920) investigated whether there was transfer and generalisation of the conditioned response to association with similar appearing stimuli. Little Albert showed the conditioned fear in response to a white rabbit but not a dog. He cried in response to a fur coat and to a Santa Claus mask.

Watson and Rayner (1920) concluded human emotions can be conditioned. Generalisation of early conditioned responses can act to form differences and complexities in our personalities. Behaviourists suggest that early classical conditioning might explain the different reactions of people to the same set of stimuli and events.

THINGS TO DO AND THINK ABOUT

Analysis of the case-study method.

Give yourself 10 minutes to do each of these questions. Use examples from the case studies above to help you expand and develop your answers appropriately.

1. Evaluate Freud's use of Little Hans as a case study. Include two strengths and two weaknesses.

2. Why is the case study method still important to psychology?

3. Analyse the theory of classical conditioning in relation to the case study of Little Albert.

4. Explain how Anna O's neurotic symptoms were treated using the psychoanalytic approach.

5. What are the disadvantages of using the case-study method in psychology?

DON'T FORGET

Remember Little Albert! Can human phobias be conditioned?

VIDEO LINK

Watch the old black and white film showing Watson and Rayner in 1920 at www.brightredbooks.net

ONLINE

Read the original paper about Little Albert at www.brightredbooks.net

ONLINE TEST

Test yourself on research methods at www.brightredbooks.net

STAR STUDY: FREUD AND BREUER (1895): THE CASE STUDY OF ANNA O

This star study is one of Freud's famous case studies. You can read about Anna O below. This case study is summarised as the focus of attention for revision of the case-study method in general. The Anna O case study can also be referred to when writing about evidence for or against the psychoanalytic approach.

PSYCHOANALYSIS, ANNA O AND THE TALKING CURE

Anna O – Freud and Breuer (1895) '... hysterical patients suffer from reminiscences.'

Anna O is the name given to Freud and Breuer's (1895) case study of a 21-year-old woman who Dr Breuer treated and Dr Freud interpreted in his writings while developing his theories of psychoanalysis.

Anna O was diagnosed by Breuer as 'hysterical' and showed symptoms of psychosomatic paralysis of the limbs, neurotic eye motions, vision disruption, moments of absence, linguistic delirium, hydrophobia when drinking and a bedbound lethargy.

In letters to Freud, Anna O was described as an intelligent polyglot (knowing many languages), yet often limiting herself to English rather than German and suffering from melancholia. According to Breuer, Anna O had periods of quiet absence when she constructed fresh fantasies which she would mutter and relate to Breuer in therapy. Breuer used hypnotism to help her retrieve the unconscious meaning of her daydreams. These fantasises were interpreted as sad recollections of her time at her Dad's bed nursing him through sickness. This caring episode of her life ended with her father dying from tuberculosis.

Freud theorised that if a hysterical symptom was traced back to its first occurrence, then in each case, during therapy – if the symptom was talked about – once expressed, it would subside.

At least three instances of the removal of hysterical symptoms were described in this case study. These included drink aversion, visual disturbance and left-arm paralysis. These are described here, in turn.

Anna O's **drink aversion** was treated by psychotherapy. In therapy, they identified the source of the first occurrence of drink aversion being linked to a time when a friend's dog had licked a drinking glass offered to Anna O. After talking about this incident to Breuer, Anna O's drink aversion subsided.

Anna O's **visual disturbance** (macropsia) was identified as being linked to her unstoppable crying at night which made her unable to read her watch clearly. Once the source of her macropsia was talked through, the visual symptoms subsided.

At times, Anna O suffered from a rigid, **left-arm paralysis**. Breuer traced this back to a dead arm sensation she got while caring for her father at his bedside. Once Anna O had a frightening dream: she dreamt her hands had death-like snakeheads on them. When she talked about this dream in therapy, the left-arm paralysis subsided.

Anna O felt her talking therapy acted like 'chimney sweeping' and after relating her daydreams, her mental health improved. She called this the talking cure.

EVALUATION OF THE ANNA O CASE STUDY

STRENGTHS	WEAKNESSES
This case study clearly illustrates the theoretical basis of psychoanalysis. Freud explained psychoanalysis using the case study of Anna O.	Breuer is thought to have been intimately attached to Anna O, so Breuer's case study can therefore be considered unscientific, biased and less than objective.
The Anna O case study reveals Freud's belief that by identifying the original source of the neurotic symptom, talking through its origins should alleviate the anxiety associated with its traumatic beginnings. Catharsis is the process of letting off steam and talking through the meaning of repressed traumatic memories for events 'trapped' in the unconscious mind. Relating and interpreting dreams might perform this function in therapy and support psychoanalysis.	Freud makes the mistake of generalising all neurotic patients from the Anna O case study. The Anna O case study presents the talking therapy as a universal cure. Not all neurotic symptoms can be this easily relieved and 'cured' by talking.

EVALUATION OF THE CASE STUDY METHOD IN GENERAL

STRENGTHS	WEAKNESSES
Case studies can be rich in detail. They are usually qualitative in nature and full of meaning and depth. Case studies can be used to illustrate a point and communicate a theory effectively.	Longitudinal case studies can be time-consuming to produce and construct. Case studies are not as quick to complete as a simple survey.
Multiple sources of data collection can be relied on to form a case study. The result is richly descriptive. A case study might employ many interpretations, many viewpoints and many types of data.	Case studies are more subjective to write than reproducing the transcript of a single, face-to-face interview. The investigator can get too close to the case to maintain an objectively accurate and dispassionate account of the case study.
Case studies are good at describing unique, surprising, rare or challenging individuals who fail to be explained by existing theories. They can be used to refute the universality of an existing theory.	Each case study is unique. Case studies cannot be easily compared. The sample size remains small with the case-study method as they take too long to compile. This prevents science from using them for the induction of patterns of data. It's unwise to generalise the whole population from one single case or example.

THINGS TO DO AND THINK ABOUT

Analyse the importance of the case-study method in psychology

Exam-markers often think that 'proved' is a bad word to use when writing answers for psychology questions. As you answer the following revision questions, think about why 'proved' is too strong a word for the social sciences.

1. Explain why a single case study cannot **'prove'** a theory. (4 marks)

2. What other explanations could account for Anna O's symptom relief? (4 marks)

3. Write a **balanced evaluation** of the case study of Anna O. (6 marks)

4. What ethical issues would emerge if you were to write a case study on one of your friends? (6 marks)

DON'T FORGET

Anna joked that Freud and Breuer's psychoanalytic talking therapy acted like 'chimney sweeping'.

ONLINE

Consider who Anna O really was by following the link at www.brightredbooks.net You might find that Bertha Pappenheim went on to become a successful activist for women's rights!

VIDEO LINK

Listen to Freud speaking to the BBC towards the end of his life at www.brightredbooks.net

ONLINE TEST

Test yourself on research methods at www.brightredbooks.net

RESEARCH METHODS: LABORATORY EXPERIMENTS

There are three types of experiment to examine here: lab, field and natural experiments. They are all sub-types of experiment, but they differ in terms of three important aspects: setting, level of standardisation and experimental manipulation.

Most social science methods involve making observations and recording data in some way, so what is special about experiments? What is the key difference between an experiment and an observational study?

DON'T FORGET

The IV is the focus of the experiment as it is the hypothesised causal variable.

WHAT IS AN EXPERIMENT?

The defining feature of an experiment is that it is an attempt to *formally* conduct a direct **test of cause and effect**. The fundamental point of all experiments is that they are designed to have different conditions of (at least) one specific variable, known as the **independent variable** (IV) to see an effect. Hypotheses are setup, in advance, to make predictions about the possible effects of specific conditions of the IV on at least one variable, known as the **dependent variable** (DV).

In a simple one-factor difference experiment, the *independent variable* is the hypothesised causal factor that may or may not have an effect on the dependent variable. The *dependent variable* is measured as it is assumed to be the hypothesised response variable. The dependent variable may or may not alter in response to the theoretical causal factor, the independent variable.

DON'T FORGET

It is the IV that is directly manipulated for the experiment to test the effect. The DV is the response (or effect) variable that is measured across the different conditions of the experiment.

An experiment should have at least two hypotheses; the experimental hypothesis and the null hypothesis. An experimental hypothesis claims a linkage between an independent variable and a dependent variable, while the null hypothesis in an experiment claims no effect or linkage between the variables, even under condition testing.

Once the experimental conditions are tested (i.e. the procedure is carried out), a conclusion is made about which hypothesis can be refuted.

DON'T FORGET

The DV is the effect factor in the experimental hypothesis. The effect always comes after the cause.

LABORATORY EXPERIMENTS

In the perfect, idealised **laboratory experiment**, the experimenter strives to keep all the experimental conditions standardised as the same, except for one key factor, the independent variable. However, this is not always possible, in practice as many extraneous variables can influence the test of cause and effect. For this reason, experiments are often carried out in a laboratory setting, where conditions might be more easily controlled, kept constant and monitored.

DON'T FORGET

The DV is assumed to be the effect variable. This, in theory, should respond to variation in the IV across the different conditions of the experiment. If it doesn't vary, there may be support for the null hypothesis, i.e. the statement of 'no effect'.

Example:

Pavlov's classical conditioning experiment.
A famous **example** of a laboratory experiment is Pavlov's (1927) test of learning by association in dogs. Pavlov conducted his research as a scientific **laboratory experiment**, as it was carried out under controlled conditions on dogs living in a research facility in Russia. In the lab, Pavlov measured and recorded the salivation response in dogs (the DV) in response to a sequence of conditions (the IV). If the dogs had undergone repeated pairings of a neutral stimulus (a bell) with food, the bell soon became a sufficient condition to trigger the salivation response, even in the absence of food. Pavlov's learning by association is now known as **classical conditioning**.

contd

Analysis of Laboratory Experiments – high control, low ecological validity, high reactivity

Laboratory experiments tend to have the highest level of control over field and natural experiments that are open to more extraneous and confounding variables. However, in behavioural terms, laboratory conditions can feel quite false, artificial and low in ecological validity. This is because lab conditions can suffer from low mundane realism.

As demonstrated by Milgram (1963), laboratory experiments are prone to high levels of participant reactivity. This is because demand characteristics are high in laboratory experiments, with people expecting to obey the experimenter as part of the scientific procedure for an experiment. This demand factor can distort people's behaviour in a laboratory experiment considerably.

Evaluation of Laboratory Experiments

Here is a table to help you evaluate laboratory experiments as a method of research:

METHOD OF RESEARCH: Laboratory Experiments	
Advantages	**Disadvantages**
Advantage: Laboratory experiments let strong conclusions be made about cause and effect hypotheses. This is possible because they involve direct testing of the cause and effect linkage between an independent variable and a dependent variable. Laboratory experiments allow the removal of more extraneous variables and confounding variables dues to the higher level of control in the laboratory than in field experiments or natural experiments.	Disadvantage: Social science focuses on people not objects. While objects usually behave predictably in the laboratory, often, people do not. In laboratories, participants show behavioural reactivity, response bias and individual differences even under standardised conditions.
Advantage: Experiments test the close association between two hypothetically linked variables by repeatedly refuting the null hypothesis. The reliability and validity of experimental results can be increased by repeating an experimental procedure. As long as the conditions of a laboratory experiment are accurately described, the methods should be reproducible and the experimental results can be repeatedly verified and re-tested.	Disadvantage: Whilst lab experiments can be setup in controlled and standardised environments, this can lead to results from only contrived laboratory situations. The standard laboratory situation is known to be artificial, with low levels of ecological validity and poor mundane realism.

DON'T FORGET

What is an experiment? A good way to describe a laboratory experiment is to call it a **formal test of cause and effect**.

THINGS TO DO AND THINK ABOUT

How to analyse types of experiments:

One way to analyse experiments is to compare the experimental method to other non-experimental methods.

- In **non**-experimental methods, such as correlation analysis or questionnaires **no** manipulation of conditions occurs. That is, no formal factor is being tested and there is only watching and recording of responses at different times. Any causal relationship can only be an assumption.

- However, in **lab** and **field** experimental methods, the causal factor (the IV) is directly manipulated to allow observation of a change in the effect (the DV, the response variable; the dependent variable).

ONLINE TEST

To test yourself on this topic, go to our Digital Zone at www.brightredbooks.net/subjects

RESEARCH METHODS: FIELD AND NATURAL EXPERIMENTS

Field experiments are external tests of cause and effect that are not carried out in a laboratory situation. Field experiments have more realism and relevance than laboratory experiments, as they can be applied more directly to everyday situations. The setting of a field experiment is certainly less contrived and artificial than when an experiment is carried out in a laboratory.

DON'T FORGET

Field experiments are conducted in the external world outside the laboratory.

DON'T FORGET

Experimental design in field experiments is the same as for lab experiments, but the whole procedure has moved to a specific location of field interest. The experimenter still manipulates the IV.

DON'T FORGET

Field experiments usually contain more extraneous variables than laboratory experiments.

FIELD SETTING

Field experiments may be carried out in the everyday environment of the participants. For example, a field experiment might be conducted in the street, on the bus, in the workplace or within a public setting. Although field experiments are usually carried out in a realistic setting, the experimenter will still manipulate the experimental conditions of the IV and will measure the dependent variable to see the cause and effect relation in a realistic location.

Field experiments differ from lab experiments in their choice of setting. Rather than aiming for standardisation and control, field experiments aim to increase the mundane realism and ecological validity of the results. They therefore have more chance of encountering confounding variables and certainly include more extraneous variables than laboratory experiments.

Example:

Hofling et al (1966) Obedience Study of Nurses in hospital
A good example of a field experiment is the hospital study by Hofling et al (1966). This was a field experiment on nurses in the hospital setting. The experimenters measured the obedience of nurses to a doctor's telephoned orders, despite the order being unjust and against hospital procedures. They found 21 out of 22 nurses obeyed the order. The results from this obedience experiment can be seen to be directly applicable to health care because of the choice to carry out the study on location in hospital as a field experiment.

Evaluation of Field Experiments

Here is a table that helps you evaluate field experiments as a method of research:

METHOD OF RESEARCH: FIELD EXPERIMENTS	
Advantages	**Disadvantages**
Advantage: Field experiments have increased ecological validity over artificially constructed laboratory scenarios. Therefore, results from field experiments can be more readily trusted to apply to everyday life.	Disadvantage: Field experiments suffer from low control of extraneous and confounding variables. These are irrelevant or intrusive variables that might be easily removed in a laboratory situation. Field results may therefore be caused by many uncontrolled factors.
Advantage: If participants do not know they are part of an experiment, they show more realistic responses in their behaviour. There is less participant reactivity and more mundane realism. This improves the validity of the findings and further increases the applicability of the results.	Disadvantage: Field experiments can be unethical, especially if participants are not approached for informed consent. How do you know you aren't part of a field experiment right now? Refer to the British Psychological Society Code of Ethics.
Advantage: Field experiments can follow up and verify the results of laboratory experiments to increase their reliability and validity. Field testing has become an important part of applying most theoretical advances in science outside the laboratory.	Disadvantage: Field experiments require greater research time and researcher access to field environments. Gaining access and setting up experimental conditions may create real risks for participants and researchers.

NATURAL EXPERIMENTS

Natural experiments are not really controlled experiments. They can, however, be just as useful to reveal linkage and association between cause and effect. Natural experiments rely on the everyday variation of natural conditions to show how one variable links with another. There is no direct manipulation of the independent variable.

contd

Take note that a natural experiment is not exactly an experiment, in the sense that the IV is varied by the experimenter. Rather, the experimental conditions in a natural experiment vary in the course of natural events and a cause and effect relationship is sought afterword from the natural variation.

Natural, Quasi-experiments

For example, looking at the linkage between the four seasons and general happiness levels might lead a researcher to use a natural experiment as a method. They could compare moods in summer, spring, autumn and winter. The season would not be directly manipulated, rather it would be recorded as it occurred. This makes the natural experiment into a quasi-experimental method.

Some experiments cannot be carried out because they are dangerous, risky, unethical or plainly daft to do. That is where a natural experiment can be most revealing. If the natural variation of events throws up some unusual or surprising effects, these can be studied using a natural experiment. Naturally occurring conditions can be compared with other conditions to simulate the manipulation of the independent variable in a lab or a field experiment. One example of a natural experiment is explained in Lockley & Foster (2012) who analyses the data from two sources for causal linkage and associated variation. This example is explained here:

Example:

Lockley & Foster Foster (2012) Fatal Truck accidents and Sleepiness
In Lockley & Foster's (2012) introductory book on sleep, fatal truck accident rates are presented throughout the day and night are analysed for linkage with the daily pattern of reported sleepiness and alcohol-affected driving. Using a quasi-experimental method, Lockley & Foster (2012) concludes there is a causal link between a peak in fatal accident rates between 4-6am in the morning and a maximum in the reported cognitive decline as a result of sleepiness and alcohol intoxication.

Analysis of Natural Experiments – high ecological validity, low control, ethical

While the conclusions from natural experiments can be ethical, compelling and plausible, as the data tends to have high ecological validity, there is a low level of experimenter control. This means other factors cannot be eliminated from conclusions. Yet, direct laboratory experiments or field experiments can be dangerous or unethical, so natural experiments become the preferred choice.

DON'T FORGET

Another name for a natural experiment is the quasi-experimental method.

Evaluation of Natural Experiments

Here is a table that evaluates natural experiments as a method of research:

METHOD OF RESEARCH: NATURAL EXPERIMENTS	
Advantages	**Disadvantages**
Advantage: Natural experiments allow the investigation of unethical, risky or dangerous topics using a quasi-experimental method. This analyses the natural variation of events that would occur anyway, even if the experiment was never carried out.	Disadvantage: Natural experiments tend to use correlation data or try to find associations post-hoc. There is no direct manipulation of cause to see an effect. Rather, data is interpreted after the variation in events.
Advantage: Some experiments may never be feasible in the field or repeatable in the laboratory. However, if they occur naturally, why not explore factors and causes? So, when a series of unfortunate events occur, natural experiments allow learning causes for these events.	Disadvantage: There are low levels of control of extraneous variables in natural experiments. Other factors may be at work, rather than the hypothesised cause. How do we know there are no confounding variables in a natural experiment?
Advantage: Natural experiments are not contrived or artificial. They have high ecological validity, as there is no manipulation of conditions by the experimenter and the procedures follow the natural course of events.	Disadvantage: Hindsight leads to overgeneralization of causes in natural experiments. This leads to post hoc fallacies. For example, 'it was raining when the plague came, therefore, rain causes the plague'. Just because a factor often precedes an event, it is not necessarily the cause.

THINGS TO DO AND THINK ABOUT

Analysis of Field Experiments

While the field experiment has more realism than the laboratory experiment, it loses standardisation of other environmental variables that can be easily controlled in the laboratory. There is more chance of other factors being at work and affecting the results.

Participants may not know they are part of an experiment, as they would normally be in the field setting anyway. On the one hand, this increases the credibility of the participant's responses, thus increasing the ecological validity of the results. However, on the other hand, it can be considered unethical to directly experiment on people without their consent.

ONLINE TEST

To test yourself on research thinking, go to www.brightredbooks.net/subjects

RESEARCH METHODS: OBSERVATION

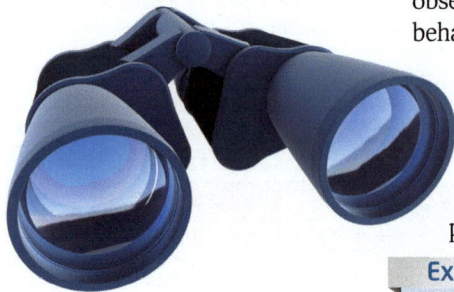

OBSERVATION – KEY FEATURES

What is observation? In most cases of observation, the method of data collection consists of focusing on – and watching – a particular aspect of behaviour, and recording events as data. Data can be recorded either by hand, video or by inter-observer agreement.

There are various types of observation to consider, including overt or covert observation; structured or unstructured observation; and participant or non-participant observation. These are explained below.

One famous example of observation being used is in ethology. Natural history series, like Sir David Attenborough's *The Secret Life of Birds*, rely heavily on observation. The observational method lies at the heart of the success of the ethological approach. In biology and the media, the observational method reveals the behaviour of animals in their natural environment. Can psychology apply the observational method to human life?

TYPES OF OBSERVATION: OVERT VERSUS COVERT OBSERVATION

One of the basic distinctions in types of observation is whether the observational study is disclosed or undisclosed. Do the participants know they are being observed? If they do, it's disclosed, if not, it's undisclosed.

Overt observation

If the participants know in advance that they will be observed, then this is overt, or disclosed, observation. A drawback of this type of observation is that participants may change their behaviour to be more socially desirable (this is sometimes known as the Hawthorne effect).

Covert observation: undisclosed observation

If the participants don't know they're being observed, the observation is covert or undisclosed. Covert observation is undercover and, therefore, more likely to observe realistic behaviour. However, it's often unethical. For example, observing people in their private life when they're unaware they're being observed can be illegal.

Example:

Covert observation: Bandura, Ross and Ross (1961)
Bandura, Ross and Ross (1961) conducted one of the most famous observational studies in psychology. They used covert observation of children in their 'Bobo doll' study to see if children imitated adult behaviour. Unaware they were being watched, the children were observed after being shown films of role models expressing aggression towards toys. Using covert, structured observation to record their results, Bandura, Ross and Ross (1961) found support for their role-modelling theory of vicarious learning.

TYPES OF OBSERVATION: STRUCTURED VERSUS UNSTRUCTURED OBSERVATION

Does the observational method collect quantitative or qualitative data? This depends on whether the observation is **structured** with categories of events to observe over a specific time period, or whether it's **unstructured**, allowing free-form note-taking and qualitative observations.

Structured observation

Structured observation collects quantitative data. It has predefined categories of behaviour (or events) to count. A frequency tally is often used to assist

contd

observers in counting, and the categories of events that the study is focusing on are laid out in advance, in a checklist or observational schedule, to help collect quantitative data.

Example:

Structured observation: Piliavin, Rodin and Piliavin (1969)
Piliavin, Rodin and Piliavin (1969) used a structured observational technique in social psychology to count (and time) the number of acts of kindness (altruistic helping behaviours) they observed under different conditions on the New York underground. If a person collapsed or appeared to be blind, help came more quickly than when a person appeared drunk. This was a quantitative study using a structured observational method in a field experiment.

Unstructured observation

Unstructured observation collects qualitative data. It leaves what to record more up to the observer at the time. Textual observations, casual pictorial notes, verbal recordings and 'jottings down' of interesting happenings can form the data of a qualitative unstructured observation. Here, there are no predefined categories of events to be tallied up or counted.

ONLINE TEST

Test yourself on the observation method at www.brightredbooks.net

TYPES OF OBSERVATION: PARTICIPANT VERSUS NON-PARTICIPANT OBSERVATION

Is the observer part of the group or not?

Participant observation: when you 'fly with the crows'

In participant observation, the observer becomes part of the group. The objective is to experience what it's like to 'fly with the crows' (be part of the group). Participant observers enter the situation being researched and record their experience. As participants, the researchers may have to take on a role for a while to gain access to the group. While in the group, there's the issue of whether they should remain covert or 'out' themselves and declare their research objectives.

Non-participant observation: when you become 'a fly on the wall'

In non-participant observation, the observer is external to the group and doesn't participate in the situation, making little attempt to get involved with those being observed. The observer sits as a 'fly on the wall' and observes –like an external inspector. If the observation is overt, it suffers from the Hawthorne effect.

Example:

Participant observation: Rosenhan (1973)
Rosenhan (1973) published a famous **participant observation** study in a paper titled 'On being sane in insane places'. Along with his colleagues, Rosenhan took part in a participant observation study of psychiatric wards in 1973. His researchers feigned psychotic symptoms to get admitted to hospital, then observed and recorded notes on how they were diagnosed and treated. He found they were stuck with the 'schizophrenia in remission' label, even if they behaved without psychotic symptoms for weeks.
This study relied on covert and structured techniques of observation. This is an important study as the results still challenge the validity of mental health diagnosis today.

THINGS TO DO AND THINK ABOUT

Practise these questions and prompts on the **observation** method:

1. What are the disadvantages of **overt** and **covert** observation? (4 marks)

2. What is meant by **structured** observation and **unstructured** observation? (4 marks)

3. Explain the differences between **participant** and **non-participant** observation. (4 marks)

4. **Evaluate** the observation method. Include **two strengths** and **two weaknesses**. (8 marks)

RESEARCH METHODS: QUESTIONNAIRES AND INTERVIEWS

One of the key features of questionnaires and interviews is that they rely on the self-report method. This, in turn, relies on self-knowledge which may not be complete or even accurate. Questionnaires and interviews can use closed or open questions, thus allowing the production of both quantitative and qualitative data.

DON'T FORGET

A psychological investigation can involve more than one method of collecting research data.

QUESTIONNAIRES AND INTERVIEWS – KEY FEATURES

Questionnaires and interviews tend to be quicker than longitudinal case studies. Questionnaires can be sent out to a wide sample group of people. Interviews tend to be conducted with fewer people and focus on a smaller sample of individuals. Interviews take more time than a survey and may need to be face-to-face. Nowadays, questionnaires and interviews can be carried out over the phone or online using websites with specialist software.

Example:

Freud's interview with The Rat Man – Freud (1909)
An example of the interview technique being used in psychology is Freud's therapy meeting with his client, the 'Rat Man' who suffered from rat delusions. In his case notes, Freud transcribed parts of the therapeutic interview conversations.

TYPES OF INTERVIEW

Interviews can be structured, unstructured or semi-structured. Structured interviews have all the questions planned in advance. These can be compared, compiled and codified easily.

Unstructured interviews are more flexible, unplanned, free-form and they flow from topic to topic without restriction. They gravitate to the most interesting topic at the time.

Semi-structured interviews are partly structured and partly unplanned. They aim to capture the advantages of both types of interview. They have some structure but can be responsive to emerging topics too.

TYPES OF QUESTIONNAIRE

Questionnaires come in many shapes and forms. In long questionnaires, gated questions can be incorporated, so only relevant questions are asked. Open questions can be used with free-form answering. Closed questions can offer a range of options to choose, perhaps in a multi-choice format.

Example:

An example of a questionnaire being used in psychology is Adorno's Type A personality inventory. In its method of data collection, the F-scale inventory was a questionnaire created to find who was anti-democratic and highly prejudiced (Type A).

Thurstone Scales

Another type of questionnaire is the Thurstone scale. Thurstone scales comprise YES/NO-answer questions that can be added up to form an overall scale score, depending on the direction of the statement.

contd

Example:

Thurstone Scale – the YES/NO scale
Here's an example of a six-item Thurstone scale to assess whether you have been revising hard for psychology. It consists of six statements to agree with.

I've organised my psychology notes this year	YES / NO
I've kept up with attendance in class	YES / NO
I've asked questions when I've been stuck	YES / NO
I've made revision flashcards for each topic	YES / NO
I've revised the key studies and can analyse them	YES / NO
I can evaluate each research method	YES / NO

You can work out your 'revision' score out of six.

Likert Scales

Another type of survey is the Likert scale. Likert scales provide a range of numbers on which to express your agreement with statements.

Example:

Likert Scale
Here's an example of a three-item Likert scale that asks for your agreement on Psychology revision.

I've self-marked a few past papers	Agree 1 2 3 4 Disagree
I've practiced answering timed revision questions	Agree 1 2 3 4 Disagree
I've revised every topic for the Higher Psychology exam	Agree 1 2 3 4 Disagree

How high do you score on this exam revision scale?

DON'T FORGET

Note! Some websites help you run questionnaires. They might be free to use at the start, however, they charge you for accessing your results and data analysis at the end.

ONLINE

Have a look at surveymonkey.com to see what surveying products they can offer

VIDEO LINK

Learn how to create and format a Likert Scale using the video at www.brightredbooks.net

EVALUATION OF QUESTIONNAIRES AND INTERVIEWS

STRENGTHS	WEAKNESSES
Questionnaires can reach a wide range of people. This allows conclusions to be made and generalisations are possible, based on patterns and trends in the data. Questionnaires allow statistics, trends and patterns to be described by using the survey sample as representative of the wider population.	Qualitative responses to open questions are hard to codify. Open-answer questions are difficult to process objectively when it comes to collating and reporting the results because of the myriad possible responses. Face-to-face interviews are time-consuming to arrange and may involve significant travel and planning to conduct.
Questions can be selected to be highly relevant to the research topic. For example, if you're researching late-night eating behaviours, you can ask directly about late-night eating habits. The questions selected for inclusion in the questionnaire can be bang on topic.	People may lie as both questionnaires and interviews rely on self-report. People tend to give socially acceptable answers rather than the truth. This tendency is known as social desirability response bias. For example, if the question was 'How often do you drink alcohol?', there's a tendency to answer 'Never!'
Interviews are very responsive. Unstructured interviews can be used to explore surprising topics and interesting revelations made by the interviewee during the research. Whatever crops up in conversation can be pursued and investigated in an unstructured interview. Interview transcripts can be rich in meaning and uniquely descriptive.	There is a low postal return rate with, typically, less than 10% returned by post. The response rate is slightly improved in email and internet surveys. Perhaps this is because there is less effort to respond. Added incentives, such as prizes or rewards, can be added to the survey to increase the response rate.
In face-to-face interviews, you have access to body language cues to confirm or deny the veracity of the interview content. Misunderstood questions can be clarified. Hesitations, deviations or obfuscations can reveal unreliable answers, and lies might be detected from leakage or contradiction in the body language.	

THINGS TO DO AND THINK ABOUT

Make up a questionnaire on a topic of your choice. This could be related to health care, education, crime, growth and development, or a current issue in society.

Ask direct questions to access the data you feel you need. If you're writing a Likert scale, write statements that people can agree or disagree with.

Try including some open questions and some closed questions. If you ever use the questionnaire you create here, refer to the British Psychological Society's Code of Ethics first. Avoid personal questions and include a consent form and a briefing sheet.

ONLINE TEST

Test yourself on research methods at www.brightredbooks.net

SAMPLING TECHNIQUES

This section discusses sampling techniques used to select a data sample from a target population or group. There are six sampling techniques listed here with, each with an evaluation of their usage in research.

INTRODUCTION TO SAMPLING TECHNIQUES

Psychological research relies on a wide range of sampling techniques. The most commonly employed is opportunity sampling, while the most famous and misunderstood is random sampling. Both sampling techniques have serious advantages and disadvantages, which are discussed later. But, first, what is a sample and what's a sampling technique?

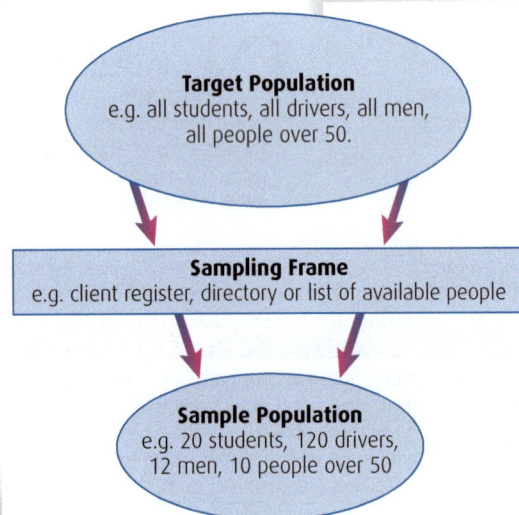

WHAT IS A SAMPLE?

A sample is a small-scale subset of a target population that has been selected for research.

Target Population
e.g. all students, all drivers, all men, all people over 50.

Sampling Frame
e.g. client register, directory or list of available people

Sample Population
e.g. 20 students, 120 drivers, 12 men, 10 people over 50

Sampling techniques determine which measurements will be included in a data set. The target population is the idealised whole group that could be selected for research. It's theoretical in nature. Sampling methods are ways of determining who'll be included in research and what data points will be included in a research study. In general, the sample population is constructed from the sample frame using a **sampling technique**.

Often, a sample is constructed from a list of possible cases from the target population which is known as the **sample frame**. However, sample frames can be inaccurate and have many individuals missing from the list. For example, a school register that misses someone out.

SAMPLING METHODS

There are six sampling methods to learn about here are: opportunity sampling, random sampling, self-selected sampling, systematic sampling, quota sampling and stratified sampling.

Opportunity sampling

Opportunity sampling involves no effort to make the sample representative of the target population other than asking the most convenient people available to take part. Opportunity sampling is, therefore, also known as convenience sampling. It uses anybody who happens to be around at the time of the research and may be very economical with time and money.

Evaluation: Although it's the most quick and convenient method of sampling, the resulting opportunity sample may be skewed and biased in composition. It's unlikely to be representative of the whole target population, possibly reducing the ability to confidently generalise the target population from the sample population.

Random sampling

For a truly **random sample**, there must be an equal chance of selection given to every member of the target population. In practice this is hard to achieve and rarely used. Random selection from a sample frame may be organised by using computer-generated random numbers, throwing a dice, tossing a coin, putting all the names in a hat or using a tombola.

Evaluation: Random sampling helps remove experimenter bias from the sample. However, it doesn't guarantee a sample with good coverage and representation of the target population. Larger random samples should become more representative with size.

contd

Approaching individuals after random selection to do research might become tiresome or awkward if they, ultimately, refuse to take part.

Self-selected sampling

Self-selected sampling allows those who wish to take part in the research to do so; it can be thought of as volunteer sampling. The sample will consist of individuals who want to be part of the research. They'll volunteer, usually by personal choice.

Evaluation: Self-selected sampling may not turn out to represent the whole target population. Volunteer samples tend to be full of active, keen, enthusiastic and co-operative people. Self-selected sampling can be convenient if volunteers are easily available. Waiting for imaginary volunteers to turn up in response to a couple of posters can be time-consuming and fruitless. Self-selection removes experimenter bias but introduces participant bias.

Systematic sampling

Systematic sampling uses a system to remove experimenter and participant bias. Any unbiased and arbitrary 'system' can be applied to select a sample from a sampling frame, such as every fifth or every tenth person from a list. Sticking to the rigour of the arbitrary system ensures the researchers do not skew the construction of their sample; selection is left to the sampling method.

Evaluation: This sampling technique avoids experimenter bias. However, there might be some hidden organisation in the sample frame that introduces an unrecognised bias into the sample. For example, a system of sampling every fourth person from a list of partners that is organised by gender, 'female/male' might inadvertently result in a list of females only.

Quota Sampling

Quota Sampling is all about the **size** of the sample rather than its composition. This technique picks a

sample size up to a specified number (a quota) to fulfil the sample requirements. For example, consider a study that approached a sample of 20 students, 120 drivers and 12 men. Here the quotas were 20, 120 and 12.

Evaluation: Quota sampling ensures a certain size for the sample, encouraging representation of the specified group up to its quota in the sample. However, it only ensures the size of the sample and not its composition. By itself, quota sampling is open to experimenter bias and does not guarantee generality of the sample.

Stratified Sampling

Stratified sampling models the strata of sub-groups in the target population within the sample population. This means dividing the target population into sub-groups and then representing these sub-groups proportionally in the sample population. Stratification attributes that might be used to represent the target population include age characteristics, gender proportions and area of residence.

Evaluation: This sampling technique is one of the most likely to create a representative sample. Including important attributes of the target population in the sample increases its representativeness. A stratified sample tends to allow generalisation of the target from the sample population. This is a direct result of **stratifying** the sample to reflect most of the important features of the target population. However, deciding which stratifications to represent may be hard to determine. Key features of the target population may be forgotten.

Sample Evaluation – There are **three** main issues to consider when evaluating a sample:
- Is the sample **representative**?
- Is the sample population skewed or **biased** in any way?
- Does the sample allow **generalisation**?

THINGS TO DO AND THINK ABOUT

Make a revision table that evaluates each of the sampling techniques above – opportunity sampling, systematic sampling, stratified sampling, quota sampling, random sampling and self-selected sampling.

The table started here already includes opportunity sampling. Fill in the descriptions, advantages and disadvantages of the remaining five sampling methods.

SAMPLING TECHNIQUE	DESCRIPTION OF TECHNIQUE	ADVANTAGES	DISADVANTAGES
Opportunity Sampling	Opportunity sampling is known as convenience sampling. It's based on ease of availability. The researcher simply selects anyone available (for example, nearby) to participate.	Opportunity sampling is very convenient. It's likely to be successful. It can be quick and easy to arrange.	However, opportunity sampling may result in a biased sample as only a certain type of person might be available or approached.

ONLINE

For an advanced paper on sampling techniques, download the Sampling Techniques PDF at www.brightredbooks.net The article is detailed, but it covers each technique.

THE RESEARCH ASSIGNMENT

HOW TO START THE RESEARCH ASSIGNMENT

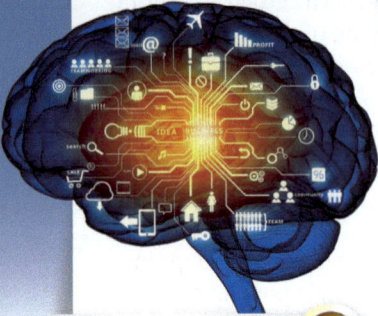

THE STRUCTURE OF THE RESEARCH ASSIGNMENT

The sections of the report

The purpose of the research assignment in Higher Psychology is to give you the opportunity to show higher analytical skills and practical data collection and interpretation skills. It's worth 40 marks out of the total 120 marks for the Higher Psychology course. That means the research assignment is worth around 33% of your course.

Your report should start with a title and finish with appendices. Overall, the report should have the following **sections** for 40 marks:

- Introduction (10 marks)
- Method (10 marks)
- Results (6 marks)
- Discussion & evaluation (8 marks) & (4 marks)
- References (or bibliography) & appropriate presentation and **style** (2 marks)
- Appendices (with raw results data, calculations and materials)

NB: The **style** mark (1 mark) is awarded if you use the appropriate voice, register, writing style and format for a scientific report throughout your report. Your report should include everything needed for another researcher to repeat the procedure of your investigation.

Writing the 2000 to 2500-word report for the Higher Psychology Research Assignment should allow you to demonstrate your skills in conducting ethical research and communicating findings on psychological research topics.

GETTING STARTED

Conducting research is incremental and builds on the work of others. It does not start from scratch. Other researchers might have asked similar questions before. What theories exist already? What research has been done that's related to your chosen topic? There's usually previous research to consider and this must be referred to and taken into account in your research report.

The research process

The primary research you conduct for your Higher Psychology research assignment should be focused, considered, testable, repeatable and clearly reported. So, it's a good idea to follow the eight stages of the research process when producing your research assignment:

- Stage 1 – Choose a topic
- Stage 2 – Review the literature
- Stage 3 – Formulate hypotheses
- Stage 4 – Design a research study
- Stage 5 – Collect data
- Stage 6 – Analyse data
- Stage 7 – Make conclusions
- Stage 8 – Report findings

You can work individually or as a group. If working with a group, you can share the task of collecting data and compile a group raw data table together. However, in **all other** respects, the report is your own responsibility. It is a **single author report** with no shared text.

TOPICS AND BRIEFS

Follow one of the SQA's briefs for the research assignment, or design your own assignment in one of the topics for the exam. The research design must be simple enough to complete in a few weeks and easy to write up within the suggested scientific format

contd

DON'T FORGET

You will lose marks if your report is 10% longer than the maximum limit of 2500 (in other words, a penalty will be applied if the report is over 2750 words long).

DON'T FORGET

Good news! The word count does **not** include words in the title, appendices, references, tables or charts.

DON'T FORGET

Previous research provides much of the insight and terminology that's needed to write the introduction and discussion of your research report.

DON'T FORGET

The early stages of the planning the research assignment are just as important as completing the final report.

DON'T FORGET

Watch out for issues of plagiarism and avoid similar looking reports!

and within 2500 words. So, keep your investigation simple. A comparison of two groups' averages, a correlation between two co-variables or a before and after, repeated-measures study would be perfectly appropriate.

Here are some suggested topics for your research assignment.

Memory

Example:

TITLE: The effects of adding pictures to the free recall of a 20-word list
1. A replication of Murdock's (1962) serial position effect in memory with an interference task.
2. A replication of Loftus and Palmer's (1974) study (using a crash test dummy video clip) on leading questions in eye-witness testimony.
3. A test of visual memory recall by comparing recall for words alone with words plus images.
4. An investigation into the effect of music on performance in a memory recall task.
5. An analysis of the effect of organisation during encoding on memory recall.

Sleep

Example:

TITLE: Do electronic devices reduce total sleep time in adolescents?
1. An analysis of the correlation between sleepiness and cognitive performance.
2. An investigation into the link between average total sleep time per day and spelling ability.
3. A survey for scoring sleep hygiene and investigating its linkage to daytime sleepiness.
4. An investigation of Roffwarg et al (1966) to see whether age and total sleep time are negatively correlated.

Reducing prejudice

Example:

TITLE: Does completing a super-ordinate colouring-in activity with an out-group member reduce prejudice and discrimination?
1. An analysis of age-related changes in prejudice using Adorno's (1950) F-scale measurement.
2. An investigation into whether watching the 'Blue-Eyes – Brown-Eyes' documentary reduces prejudice.
3. A modification of Tajfel's minimal groups classroom experiments on rewarding out-groups.

Conformity and obedience

Example:

TITLE: Gender differences in conformity to interpersonal relationship rules
1. An ethical adaptation of the 'beans in the jar' experiment on conformity to previous estimates by Jenness (1932) – just remove the deception and any anxious discussions.
2. A test of age or gender differences in conformity to a group norm (or a majority activity).
3. An ethical field study replication of the effect of uniforms on obedience as per Bickman (1974).

➕ DON'T FORGET

Whatever you choose for investigating, it must be practical and ethical.

➕ DON'T FORGET

Remember to openly declare the aim of your study at the start to remove any deception.

➕ DON'T FORGET

Avoid unethical group discussions that cause conformity anxiety.

➡ ONLINE

Can we learn from the mistakes of the past? Unethical studies should **never** be repeated or replicated, for example, The Stanford Prison experiment run by Philip Zimbardo. Learn more by watching the clip at www.brightredbooks.net

💭 THINGS TO DO AND THINK ABOUT

Here's a quick pro forma for **planning** your research assignment. If you specify the aspects in the box below at the planning stage, you will have done most of the design for your research. Fill in these fields as you plan your research assignment. Not all options are included here, but the most common design choices are. Circle/select an option or write your own choice:

QUICK RESEARCH ASSIGNMENT: PLANNING PRO-FORMA
- TOPIC AREA: (Select) Memory / Conformity / Prejudice / Obedience / Sleep / Other
- RESEARCH QUESTION: (Write) Does factor X (the IV) affect variable Y (the DV)?
- RELEVANT THEORY: (Write) The Multi-Store Model / Compliance / Type A Theory / Other
- PREVIOUS RESEARCH: (Find) Atkinson and Shiffrin (1968) / Jenness (1932) / Adorno (1950) / Other
- HYPOTHESIS: (Write) It is hypothesised that factor X (the IV) will change variable Y (the DV).
- RESEARCH METHOD: (Select) Laboratory Experiment / Questionnaire / Observation / Other
- RESEARCH DESIGN: (Select) Independent Groups / Repeated Measures / Correlation / Other
- SAMPLE TECHNIQUE: (Select) Opportunity Sampling / Self-selected Sample / Other
- PROCEDURE: (Write) How the standardised procedure will collect data, step by step.

THE INTRODUCTION

At the outset of writing your research assignment, adopt a professional and credible scientific writing style. The research assignment is not a reflective log, nor is it a colloquial story of your woes and troubles during the year! That would be an informal, subjective account. Rather, it is objective and emulates a scientific journal paper. Even if you feel awful about writing this, stay balanced, objective, detached and impartial in your writing.

HOW TO WRITE THE INTRODUCTION SECTION

The introduction to the research assignment is worth 10 marks. It should summarise and review the relevant literature you found during the literature review stage of the research process. It should end with a clear aim statement and a research hypothesis.

For your introduction section, you need to include research results from classic and contemporary research that links directly with your investigation. Use the introduction section to explain relevant terminology, introduce background theory and outline empirical findings from classic and contemporary studies linked to your research.

Once you have read over your topic and reviewed the research in a book, journal or online, you can summarise the most relevant results from each study in a series of brief, punchy paragraphs before you introduce your aims.

Classic and contemporary research review

A summary of the concepts from your background research and your preliminary readings should be included in the introduction.

Here is a sample paragraph showing how a student might introduce background **theory and concepts** relevant to their assignment. In this example, the topic of their research is conformity and the student is introducing Kelman's (1958) tripartite model of conformity as a concept. This example paragraph might gain a mark for introducing relevant concepts but there is no research mentioned.

> **Example:**
>
> Background theory paragraph (2 marks)
>
> According to Kelman (1958), three types of motive for conformity can be distinguished at least theoretically. In this tripartite view, compliance is the first term for conformity at the behavioural level without acceptance of the internal beliefs. The second level of conformity is identification with the group. Identification is motivated by presence of the group and by wanting to retain belonging with the group. Once identification with group membership is removed, the normative conforming behaviour will diminish. Internalisation is the most lasting type of conformity and involves fully accepting the beliefs and values of the majority of the group. Internalised conformity is likely to persist beyond membership or presence of the group.

To access the research assignment marks for an informed introduction, be sure to include classic and contemporary relevant research on the topic of your investigation. This must include methodology and empirical data (that is, findings). Explain the relevant concepts and terminology needed to understand your research aims. Warning! If you do **not** include relevant research, the maximum mark you can expect to get for the Introduction section is half marks.

How to include relevant research

To include relevant research in your introduction, start with the name of the relevant research, for example, Mori and Arai (2010) if the topic is conformity. Then provide the aim of the research in a clear sentence. Briefly summarise the method, the results and

DON'T FORGET

Include the most relevant handful of studies you can find.

DON'T FORGET

You must include both **research evidence** and relevant psychological **concepts** to get full marks.

DON'T FORGET

One **relevant research study**, explained well and written clearly into your introduction, is likely to attract around two marks.

contd

then the conclusion. Remember, at the end of the paragraph, **tie the research back to the aim of your research assignment**. This should keep your introduction relevant.

You will most likely need to include around three relevant pieces of research written into short, snappy paragraphs that elucidate the theoretical and research background to your investigation. These must link with your variables and the hypothetical relationship under investigation.

Aims and hypotheses (2 marks)

There are two further marks available at the end of the introduction for specifying the aim (1 mark) and the hypothesis (1 mark) of your investigation. These can be highlighted in two separate sub-sections towards the end of your introduction.

Operationalisation involves defining the variables in clearly measurable terms. For example, height can be measured, operationally, in centimetres or inches. Intelligence can be measured in terms of an IQ test score. To continue with examples, obedience might be measured in operational terms of voltage level reached – but don't try that one!

Here's an example of an aim statement and a hypothesis statement from a research assignment. Remember, it's important to operationalise the research variables for the investigation (that is, operationalise the IV and DV within the hypotheses).

Example:

Aim and hypothesis

Aim: The aim of this questionnaire study was to see if the gender of the defendant would be associated with a difference in the respondents' chosen length of sentence deemed appropriate for the same crime reported.

Hypothesis: The gender of the defendant will be associated with a difference in the length of sentence suggested by the respondents as appropriate for the same crime reported.

FORMAT AND STYLE OF WRITING

Include the formal language and traditional sections of a typical science report to get full marks. Remember, your style marks depend on how you follow this conventional format. Do not use personal pronouns. 'I' or 'We' can be replaced with 'The researcher(s) …'

There is a mark for choosing an objective and appropriately academic writing style. Stay away from the word 'proves' at all costs! Instead, try using 'This shows evidence for …' or 'This supports …' in its place. For ethical reasons, remove ALL names of tutors, centres, institutions, locations and participants in the final version of your research assignment so that confidentiality of participants is maintained. This might involve correction fluid!

THINGS TO DO AND THINK ABOUT

Start writing your research investigation introduction

- Open a file called 'Research Assignment' and start writing your introduction. Don't delay!

- Remember, a good introduction should be clear and explanatory for the naive reader and refer to both classic and contemporary research evidence to satisfy the academic reader.

- Write a version of your introduction well in advance of your research.

- Ensure your introduction is clear, yet evidence-based.

- Get a second opinion on your introduction from a naive friend. More crucially, get feedback from a well-informed academic. Demanding scrutiny at this early stage will improve the quality of your introduction and possibly your whole report.

- Make changes to the introduction in response to any constructive feedback.

DON'T FORGET

Don't forget to TIE BACK all your research examples! What do they show?

DON'T FORGET

Operationalisation: The effectiveness of memory recall can be **operationalised** as a dependent variable in terms of *the number of words recalled from a 20-word list*.

DON'T FORGET

The introduction section should end with an aim statement followed by a hypothesis statement.

DON'T FORGET

Depersonalise your assignment. Use the third person, past tense.

DON'T FORGET

Aim for an academic-journal style at all times when writing your research assignment.

ONLINE

Use Google Scholar or an Athens login to access online contemporary journal papers on your research assignment topic.

VIDEO LINK

If you're unsure how to conduct a literature review, watch the video on this at www.brightredbooks.net

THE METHOD 1

As soon as you've carried out the research procedure, you can start writing the **method** section of your assignment. Some people find the method section a good place to start writing the report.

STRUCTURE FOR THE WHOLE RESEARCH ASSIGNMENT

The research assignment is a 2000–2500-word report with the following sections:

Title and Contents

- Introduction
- Aims and Hypotheses
- **Method**

- Results
- Discussion
- Evaluation

- Conclusion
- References

Appendices – including Raw Data and Materials

The **Method** section consists of *five* sub-sections – Design / Variables / Sampling / Materials / Procedure – plus an important section afterwards on 'Ethics':

The purpose of the **method** section is to describe the method, design, variables, sampling technique, materials and data collection process. Each of these should be included in a sub-section stating the reason for the choice of method or technique. Explain the benefits of the chosen design and procedure over and above other possible options.

THE METHOD SECTION

DON'T FORGET

It's worth declaring whether your investigation was experimental, non-experimental or an analysis of a correlation.

The method section should declare whether the research conducted used a questionnaire, an interview, a case-study method or an experimental method. Alternatively, was correlation or observation used? You should justify why you chose your method of data collection.

Here's an example of the start of an introduction for a research assignment that uses correlation and adopts a non-experimental method.

Example:

Explain the method (1 mark)

This psychological investigation into total sleep time and life satisfaction was not a test of cause and effect. Rather this study adopted the non-experimental method of self-reporting questionnaires for data collection on this topic. Two questionnaires were combined and administered in tandem to investigate a hypothetical correlation between two co-variables. The two co-variables being investigated were 'total sleep time over two weeks' and 'life satisfaction'. The questionnaire was in two parts; it produced an estimated total sleep time and a life satisfaction score for each participant. The two scores derived from the items in the questionnaire came to represent the two variables being measured and analysed for correlation.

DESIGN

Have a sub-section to explain the design. If an experimental method was chosen, then explain the arrangement of groups, conditions and samples. Was a counterbalanced order of presentation used? How were the groups allocated to different conditions? Was it a repeated-measures design or an independent-measures design? What benefits did this design bring to the investigation? What problems were avoided?

Here's an example of a student explaining a correlational design.

contd

> **Example:**
>
> Explain the design (1 mark):
>
> *As this study was a non-experimental, correlation analysis, it was neither repeated measures nor independent groups design. Rather, the design of the study was to analyse the correlation between paired measures from each participant. The correlation was ultimately analysed visually (in a scattergram) and statistically, using a correlation co-efficient to describe the degree and direction of association.*

VARIABLES

Explain how all the major research variables were measured and controlled in your investigation. If it was experimental, spend time explaining how the IV was manipulated and how the DV was operationally measured. Mention how any extraneous variables were eliminated, standardised or controlled between conditions.

Here's an example of a student explaining the measurement of the variables in their assignment.

> **Example:**
>
> Explain the variables (1 mark)
>
> *The two sleep variables measured in this investigation were 'total sleep time' and 'life satisfaction'. The first variable, mean daily sleep time, was calculated from a sample of 14 days' total sleep time, as reported by the participants in response to items 2, 3 and 4 in the first part of the questionnaire (see Appendix 8). The second variable, life satisfaction, was measured for each participant by summing their own responses to items 5, 6, 7, 8 and 9 in part two of the questionnaire. As all the items in the second part of the questionnaire contributed to measuring life satisfaction, each participant's total for items 5, 6, 7, 8 and 9 resulted in a measure of their total life satisfaction. This summated total, for each participant, was used as the direct, self-reported measure of 'life satisfaction'.*

SAMPLING METHOD

Explain the sample method used. Why was this method of sampling chosen? Given the time constraints, resources and availability of people, what method made sense? Were there any benefits to using this method of sampling?

Here's a student trying to explain their sampling method.

> **Example:**
>
> Explain the sample method (1 mark)
>
> *Twenty participants were selected by opportunity sampling. While this method of sampling might be prone to interviewer bias, this was the most convenient approach to sampling, given the restricted time available and the likelihood of completing the task on time.*

THINGS TO DO AND THINK ABOUT

Check your report and materials for ethical practice!

Maintaining anonymity and confidentiality may involve applying correction tape onto the materials submitted to the SQA. Be prepared to remove participants' details, tutors' contacts and centres' names for full ethics marks.

DON'T FORGET

Remove **all** contact and centre information from your report and materials – other than your own name, centre and candidate number, of course, on the cover.

RESEARCH

THE METHOD 2

PARTICIPANTS

Include a basic description of the general characteristics of your sample without revealing any identifying personal details. To maintain anonymity and protect participant confidentiality, never mention any specific school, centre, institution or organisation that your sample participants came from. If you do, you will lose marks.

Here's a student explaining the characteristics of their sample, without giving individual details.

Example:

Explain the participants (1 mark)

All participants were 16 years old or over. Each of the twenty participants was interviewed individually at a local college and asked to fill in the questionnaire. The average age of the sample was approximately 43 years old, ranging from 16 years to 65 years.

MATERIALS

Explain which materials were used to conduct the research. Include enough description and exemplification to allow another researcher to pick up your assignment and repeat the procedure. Include clear referencing to copies of (or description of) these materials in appendices attached at the end of your assignment.

Here's an example of a section describing the materials for the investigation.

Example:

Explain the materials (1 mark)

Several materials were used in conducting this research. The materials were presented to the participants in a 'research pack'. The research pack materials included a briefing statement (see Appendix One) to ensure participants were aware of the aims and purposes of the investigation. A consent form (see Appendix Two for a blank copy of the consent form) was used to confirm participants were comfortable volunteering to take part. An instruction sheet (see Appendix Three) was given to each participant to standardise the procedure. The questionnaire (see Appendix Four for a blank copy of the questionnaire) was included in the research pack. Finally, a debriefing statement (see Appendix Five) was constructed to fully debrief participants after they had filled in all the items in the questionnaire.

PROCEDURE

In the 'Procedure' sub-section of the method, you should include a fully written and explained, step-by-step account of each action carried out in the research methodology of the assignment. What actions and procedures did the investigators and participants go through to collect the data measurements? Describe the procedure you followed to the point that someone else could repeat the same steps to replicate your investigation.

Here's another student describing a completely different investigation. We can see the **procedure** section for their investigation. You can use the examples above and below to see how the report should be written. Please note, the student examples included in this chapter are deliberately **not** linked. They are examples from *different* reports with various aims and hypotheses. This is done on purpose to discourage 'mindless' copying.

DON'T FORGET

Have you included everything needed in your materials section for someone to repeat your research?

ONLINE

To see how assignments are marked, visit the SQA Understanding Standards website for Higher Psychology via the link at www.brightredbooks.net. This essential site has worked examples of candidate projects and commentaries.

DON'T FORGET

Have you explained the steps taken in running the research to the level they could be repeated by another researcher? Use appendices to explain any complicated procedures.

DON'T FORGET

Write your **own** unique report – don't copy these examples directly.

DON'T FORGET

A 'bullet-point list' might **not** be considered a **'full explanation'** in your research assignment or in the Higher Psychology exam.

Explain the procedure (1 mark)

*For both conditions of the experiment, the participants were randomly allocated into two groups (Groups A and B) of ten people. Once the participants had read the briefing sheet (see Appendix Three) and signed the Consent Form (see Appendix Four) the investigators then followed the standardised instructions and read the participant instructions (see Appendix Six) out loud to the group. If they agreed to continue, each participant was provided with the questionnaire, appropriate to the allocated group. Group A was given the copy of the questionnaire with a photograph of a **male** defendant, while Group B was given a copy of the same questionnaire with a photograph of a **female** defendant. Once the participants had completed the questionnaire on the suitability of sentence length, they were asked to read the debriefing statement (see Appendix Seven). Scoring of the questionnaire is explained in Appendix Eight.*

ETHICAL CONSIDERATIONS

This is one of the most important sections of your research assignment. There are special ethics marks awarded for showing how good ethical practice was followed in your investigation. What specific ethical issues arose in your investigation and how were they handled in your procedure? How was each issue dealt with appropriately? Explain at least four ethical issues that arose, with how they were addressed.

Here's an example of a student describing their ethical concerns.

Example:

Explain ethical issues (4 marks)

One ethical concern that emerged in this practical investigation was data protection. To ensure confidentiality and anonymity of the participants, certain practical procedures were adopted. Consent forms were stored separately from the raw data collected. 1. Firstly the data was made anonymous by removing (or not collecting) names of the participants. 2. Variable measurements were stored in a raw data table in a random order and were labelled with new number identifiers rather than being linked to the order of individuals or personal identities. 3. Participant results and consent forms were stored in two separate locked drawers. 4. All identifying characteristics of the sample of twenty people that volunteered have been removed from this research report.

A second ethical concern that emerged when planning this investigation was the possibility of anxiety caused by the procedure of being involved in psychological research, with the participants perhaps worried about the meaning of their results. Some participants may have felt the procedure was a test of their ability or competence. To address this concern in the research materials, emphasis was placed on reassuring participants in the briefing and in the de-briefing that this was not an intelligence test. Individual data would not be singled out for scrutiny in any discussion and only group trends would be analysed. Individual scores would not be the focus of the report. Each participant was thanked for their participation in advance with no pressure to continue or perform well.

DON'T FORGET

If there was an emerging ethical issue during your research, what did you do to ensure it was dealt with? How did you show ethical consideration?

ONLINE

Find the latest set of marking instructions for the research assignment at www.brightredbooks.net.

THINGS TO DO AND THINK ABOUT

Have you included everything required in the method section?

Refer to the latest set of SQA marking instructions for the research assignment. The marking instructions will be available before you submit the assignment. These outline the sections and sub-sections required for your 2000–2500-word research report. If it helps, have the marking scheme open while you write up your report. Note the emphasis on ethical practice (4 marks).

THE RESULTS

To get to grips with the results section, think of presenting your results in three ways: words, tables and charts. In each case, you're presenting the same results, but in a different format: textually, numerically and visually. This is the three-part shape of the results section.

THE TEXT

In the **first part** of your results section, there should be a full textual description of your results. You should describe where your raw data is collected in the report (usually in an Appendix) and what the data means in terms of measurements and variables. Your text should refer to each table and chart in turn.

THE STATISTICS

The **second part** of the results section is a summary statistical data table which must include measures of central tendency and dispersion to represent the main findings on each main variable, grouping and condition.

Here's an example of a student referring to each of their results using summary statistics to help describe them.

Example:

Analyse your results with statistics (4 marks)

The results of this independent groups design experiment with two conditions. The raw data can be found in Appendix Ten. The raw data has been summarised using measures of central tendency such as the mean for each group. A summary table of statistics describing the two groups in this investigation can be found below. As can be seen in the table, the mean for the first condition (with images) was 12.5 items while the mean for the second condition (without images) was 8.3 items. The range for the first condition was 9, while the range for the second condition was 7 items.

Table 1: Table of Summary Statistics for the Raw Data from this investigation. Two conditions are included here: memory recall for words with images versus memory recall for words alone.

SUMMARY STATISTIC	CONDITION OF MEMORY EXPERIMENT	
	Words with images	Words without images
Mean accuracy of memory recall (mean number of words recalled out of twenty)	12.5	8.3
Range of results for group (maximum accuracy minus minimum accuracy)	9	7

The means for the two groups allows direct comparison of the centre of the data for both groups and allows any difference in the average results to be seen. The difference between the means for these two groups was 4.2 items more for the first group (with images).

Note that if the assignment is investigation of a correlation, the emphasis changes to clearly presenting a table of paired data listing the associated measures from the two co-variables. If your research assignment involves a correlation, include a correlation coefficient (for example, Spearman's or Pearson's correlation coefficient) plus a table of your two co-variables.

Accurately worked-out measures of central tendency and measures of dispersion that are lucidly used to explain findings will attract marks.

THE CHARTS

The **third part** of your results section is a summary chart or graph. It will usually be a bar chart if you have means resulting from different groups or conditions. A bar chart can clearly illustrate similarity or difference between the measures of central tendency for your groups and conditions. If your investigation is a correlational analysis, include a scattergram.

Here's an example of part of the results section for a *Memory* experiment that compares words alone with words with pictures for ease of memory recall. The hypothesis was that images improve memory recall.

Example:

Analyse your results with charts (1 mark)

In Group A, who experienced the memory test condition of 'words without images' the mean recall for the group was 7.8 items, while in Group B, who experienced the memory test condition of 'pictorial images along with the words', the mean recall was 14.8 items. There is a difference of 7 items, on average, between the two groups recall level.

From the statistical calculations of the means for the two groups above results above, it appears that there is support for the experimental hypothesis of this investigation. The presence of images alongside words in this experiment did seem to improve memory recall in a memory-recall task for a list of 20 items.

The difference between the two conditions can be seen in the chart below. This is a bar chart of the mean recall accuracy for both groups, words with images and words without images.

Graph showing the mean recall accuracy for the two conditions of the memory experiment; words with images and words without images

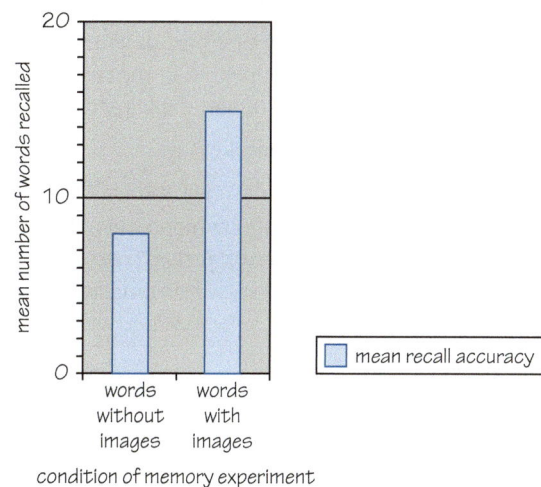

To get maximum marks for the results section, remember to choose an appropriate chart and include axis labels. Provide the reader with a legend and a chart title. You must also refer in the text to the chart (for example, 'See Graph One which shows ...'). Point out any key results or major differences between conditions in your text.

The preliminary hypothesis link

Link the results section back to the original hypothesis in a clear hypothesis statement. Do the results, at first sight, confirm or refute the main hypothesis of your investigation?

Here's an example of a student linking their results back to their original hypothesis.

Example:

State whether the results support the hypothesis (1 mark)

These results appear to support the experimental hypothesis that an organised list of words will be remembered better than a disorganised list of words. The results for the semantically organised list of words had a mean recall of 12.2 while the semantically disorganised list of words had a mean recall of 7.1.

These statistical results will now be discussed in terms of reliability and validity.

THINGS TO DO AND THINK ABOUT

How do you write a successful results section?

Refer to the latest research assignment marking scheme published by the SQA to guide you as to what is needed in your results section.

DON'T FORGET
Include the variable names and the units used to measure the variables in all charts and tables.

DON'T FORGET
Your results section should end with a clear statement on the original hypothesis of your investigation.

DON'T FORGET
Even if you're unhappy with the small amount of poor quality data you collected, you can still get full marks if you write up an assignment that is critical, analytical, explanatory and incisive.

ONLINE TEST
Test yourself on the Research Assignment at www.brightredbooks.net

THE DISCUSSION

The discussion section is your chance to show applied skills in analysing the importance of the data you have just presented in the results section.

THE DISCUSSION SECTION

Make a preliminary statement on how the statistical findings support or go against the main hypothesis of your research. Then, before coming to any conclusion about the results, it's worth considering the validity and reliability of the findings in the following sections.

Refer to the main research hypothesis

In the first part of your discussion, explain any support for the research hypothesis that has appeared in the results. This is an important part of the discussion. Here's an example of a student explaining that the results confirm their experimental hypothesis.

Example:

Is the hypothesis confirmed or refuted? (1 mark)

At first inspection, the results have made progress toward clarifying the aim of the investigation. There seems to be support for the experimental hypothesis that a list of 20 words organised into semantic categories will be recalled better than a list of 20 disorganised words.

Explain the statistical analysis

In the first part of the discussion, explain how the main statistical analysis shows support or goes against the hypothesis. Be sure to refer to the data analysis and summary statistics that most clearly show the investigation gave evidence for (or against) the hypothesis. Here, the student is referring to statistical analysis of the two different conditions in an independent groups design laboratory experiment on memory.

Example:

Refer to the results analysis (1 mark)

Statistical analysis of the results from the investigation revealed that the control group trying to recall the disorganised list of words recalled a mean of 7.8 items, while the group trying to recall the organised list of words recalled a mean of 12.2 items. This represents a difference of 4.4 items between the groups and is big enough a difference to suggest support for the theory that an organised list of words will be better recalled than a disorganised list.

Explain extraneous variables and sources of error

Look for extraneous variables, sources of error and variation in the results. In turn, explain each of these extraneous variables with suggestions for how to remove them in further research. Take an applied, problem-solving approach. Here, a student is discussing certain extraneous variables that were not removed from an investigation.

DON'T FORGET

List extraneous variables and how they could be removed in further research.

Example:

Refer to extraneous variables (2 marks)

Certain extraneous variables were built into the experimental situation and not controlled or standardised. One uncontrolled situation variable that may have affected participant responses was variation in the levels of background noise between the two groups. In the first condition, as it was lunchtime, there was a high level of intrusive noise during the experimental procedure. In the second condition, after school, there was very little noise that could be considered intrusive. This might have acted to assist in raising performance in the second condition over the first. If this experiment was to be run again, it would benefit from a quiet room being booked for both conditions to control distracting noises in the experimental situation.

contd

Make links to previous research and theories (1 mark)

How valid and reliable are your findings? How are they relevant to the aim of your research? Can a statement be made to support the research hypothesis? Can you link your results to the psychological theories and previous research findings mentioned at the outset of your assignment in your introduction section?

Analyse cause and effect associations (1 mark)

Pull out cause and effect relations in your discussion. Analyse factors that seemed important in your research. What appeared to have a big effect? What did not? Suggest how to improve the research and areas for further research.

Consider implications and make suggestions for further research (1 mark)

Why is your research important to society? Make clear the implications of your findings. Should more research be done? How should further research be better or different? Link your findings to a real-world application of your results. How could your research be used to improve society?

> **DON'T FORGET**
>
> You can use the discussion section to link your results to existing theories and concepts.

> **DON'T FORGET**
>
> Stay balanced and detached in your discussion.

EVALUATION SECTION (4 MARKS)

In the evaluation section, you can refer to the many extraneous variables not controlled in this experiment. These weaknesses in your investigation may have affected the validity of the measures and the reliability of the findings. You should suggest a practical way to remove these issues.

Remember to balance your evaluation and to analyse the problems with the research. Always try to suggest an applied solution.

Here is an example of an evaluation point.

Example:

Evaluation point

One factor not controlled was the timings for presentation of the stimuli to be remembered in the memory recall task. In the first condition, the words on the screen were presented to participants at a rate of 1 second per word. In the second condition, the timings were more erratic and closer to 3 seconds per word. Thus, the encoding period was not standardised and it varied between the two groups. As this may have affected the ability to recall the words, in future experiments it would be advisable to control the timings of stimuli onscreen to a standard interval.

Draw the investigation to a conclusion (1 mark)

For the final part of your discussion section, finish with a conclusion. Your conclusion can be a single paragraph in a sub-section called 'Conclusion' which refers back to both the statistical data and the main hypothesis of your research.

THINGS TO DO AND THINK ABOUT

Use your Appendices as attachments.

What goes in an Appendix? Appendices are used to include examples of all the materials, scales, raw data, statistical calculations, analysis tables, scoring systems and any detailing of complex steps in your investigation. This can increase your mark considerably and reduce your word count. It is worth noting **appendices are not included in the word limit** of 2000–2500 words.

> **DON'T FORGET**
>
> Remember to include a 'References' section or a bibliography of sources after the conclusion of your report.

THE HIGHER PSYCHOLOGY EXAM

THE HIGHER EXAM, THE RESEARCH ASSIGNMENT AND HIGHER SKILLS

Your overall Higher Psychology course grade is calculated out of 120. The exam component of the course counts for 80 marks out of the total 120 marks available. Your course grade will be derived from the addition of the mark you get for the final exam and the mark you get for your research assignment (which is worth 40 marks).

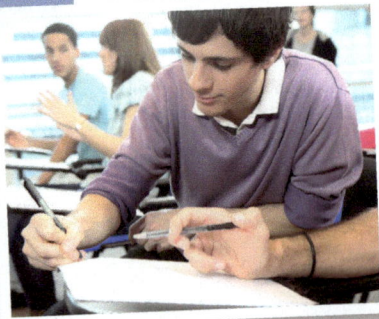

OVERVIEW

In the Higher Psychology exam, you will need to show evidence of Higher skills. Applying, analysing and evaluating are Level 6 skills that take you beyond National 5. This means you must be analysing and evaluating in response to the correct **action words** in the exam.

To get a high grade, you need to apply your knowledge of theories and concepts to research situations with careful analysis of the important factors at work. Use clear, everyday examples and develop your explanations way beyond simple description.

Remember that, in addition to the exam, your research assignment is a 2000–2500-word report that needs to be completed around April. You should show Level 6 skills in this report too. Your research assignment is sent off by your presenting centre to the SQA for marking.

DON'T FORGET

Take a water bottle into exams. You're allowed to rehydrate your brain!

THE HIGHER PSYCHOLOGY EXAM

There are two sections to the Higher Psychology exam. In both of the sections, there can be between two and five questions that combine to make a total of 20 marks per section. The Individual Psychology section is worth 40 marks and the Social Psychology section is also worth 40 marks.

THE INDIVIDUAL SECTION (20 MARKS)

In the Individual section of the exam, there will be mandatory topic questions and optional topic questions.

The mandatory topic in the Individual section is *Sleep, Dreams and Sleep Disorders*. Mandatory topic questions can be quite **specific** to the mandatory topic content in the SQA Higher Psychology course assessment document.

DON'T FORGET

Revise like an Olympian! Practising exam papers speeds up your exam performance.

THE SOCIAL SECTION (20 MARKS)

In the Social section of the exam, there will be mandatory topic questions on *Conformity and Obedience* and optional topic questions.

REVISION TECHNIQUES FOR THE HIGHER PSYCHOLOGY EXAM

When preparing for the exam, consider the following exam revision techniques:

- Use mind-maps for revision followed by completing an example question paper.
- Use flashcards to remember terminology and research findings.
- Use posters on your wall at home for summarising a topic in detail.
- Type up revision sheets from your notes.
- Tick off topics and research concepts once you can explain and apply them.
- Highlight keywords in an old psychology textbook.
- Read original journal papers online and collect evaluative points.
- Get a study buddy to help you discuss and analyse research.
- Organise your psychology notes and folders logically.

SKILLS TO SHOW IN RESPONSE TO DIFFERENT ACTION (COMMAND) WORDS

Example question: **Analyse** Milgram's (1963) research on obedience.

ANALYSE: Pick apart the main factors affecting a situation. Break concepts down into their constituent components. Reveal cause and effect links. Compare with other research evidence for its importance and relevance.

Example question: **Apply** Milgram's (1963) research to an everyday example of obedience.

APPLY: Use detailed knowledge of concepts and theories to explain a situation. Apply psychological theory to everyday behaviour, perhaps, by using examples.

Example question: **Describe** Milgram's (1963) research on obedience.

DESCRIBE: Detail the main attributes of a theory, concepts or a piece of research evidence.

Example question: **Evaluate** Milgram's (1963) research on obedience.

EVALUATE: Evaluation includes judging the quality, importance or value of whatever is being evaluated. Strengths and weaknesses can be explained to form a conclusion. Outlining problems and then making suggestions for solutions or improvements might gain extra marks.

Example question: **Explain** Milgram's (1963) research on obedience.

EXPLAIN: Clearly outline how a concept or theory works to reveal the nature of a topic. Examples can be used to illustrate, develop or support your explanation. Remember to recap and tie your explanation back to the question, after using an example.

Example question: **Justify** Milgram's (1963) research on obedience.

JUSTIFY: Support a choice or conclusion with an explanation of why the choice was made. Refer to any evidence used in the reasoning.

ONLINE

Use the past papers and marking instructions for Higher Psychology on the SQA website for exam practice. Find the link at www.brightredbooks.net/subjects

THINGS TO DO AND THINK ABOUT

Time for some exam practice!

Try our sample paper on the next page. Start the clock and aim to complete it in the time alloted. When you've completed the paper, think of ten ways to improve your exam performance by 1%. In theory, if each technique gave you a 1% advantage, your mark could improve by 10%! That could be enough to raise your grade.

HIGHER PSYCHOLOGY – SAMPLE EXAM

To improve your chances of exam success, practice sitting this sample exam. You can try your hand at this paper with notes shut, phones off and a clock. Give yourself 2 hours 40 minutes.

DON'T FORGET

The specimen question paper here *only* includes the options covered by this book.

DON'T FORGET

You might try using past paper questions available online from the SQA website.

THE COURSE EXAM – A SPECIMEN QUESTION PAPER FOR HIGHER PSYCHOLOGY

These pages present a sample paper for the Higher Psychology course that includes the individual topic option of **Memory** and the social topic option of **Prejudice**.

NATIONAL QUALIFICATIONS – SAMPLE PAPER

Higher Psychology – Specimen External Exam Question Paper

H

TOTAL MARKS: 80
Duration: 2 hours 40 minutes

SECTION 1 – INDIVIDUAL BEHAVIOUR = 40 marks

In the 'individual behaviour' section complete Question 1 and Question 2. Then continue onto the social psychology section below.

INDIVIDUAL BEHAVIOUR – SLEEP AND DREAMS – Complete Question 1

QUESTION 1

1 (a) Explain how sleep maintains psychological processes   (5 marks)

1 (b) Analyse Freud's theory of dreaming   (15 marks)

QUESTION 2

2 (a) Explain coding in short-term memory   (4 marks)

2 (b) Analyse the multi-store model of memory   (8 marks)

2 (c) Read the following scenario about Omar:

> On the phone, Omar's father asks him to vacuum the stairs, feed the cat, put the bin out and turn the oven off. During this long phone-call, a delivery arrives at the door requiring a signature.

Using two theories of forgetting, explain why Omar might not remember to turn the oven off.   (8 marks)

SECTION 2 – SOCIAL BEHAVIOUR = 40 marks

In the Social Behaviour section, complete Question 1 and Question 2

SOCIAL BEHAVIOUR – QUESTION 1 – Conformity and Obedience

1 (a) Analyse the methodology of Milgram's (1963)
        classic study on obedience to authority   (6 marks).

1 (b) Read the following scenario about Debbie:

> Debbie joins a yoga class and really enjoys it. On her first day, most of the class members are carrying a yoga mat. Even though they are not required for the class, Debbie decides to buy a yoga mat and take it to class.

        Explain conformity factors that might have affected
        Debbie's decision to take a yoga mat to class   (6 marks).

1 (c) Explain different types of conformity and why people
        might show cultural differences in conformity   (8 marks).

SOCIAL BEHAVIOUR – Reducing Prejudice

2 (a) Read the following scenario about Chrissie:

> Chrissie is a wheelchair user and a Para-Olympian swimmer. Chrissie leads a busy and active life. However, when she went to a meeting at the bank with her brother concerning her finances, the banker excluded her from the conversation by talking to Chrissie's brother instead.

        Explain the types of discrimination shown towards Chrissie in the
        scenario above   (4 marks).

2 (b) Evaluate the authoritarian personality theory
        of prejudice   (6 marks).

2 (c) Explain how prejudice can be reduced by affirmative action and
        the media   (10 marks)

DON'T FORGET

Can you explain a point? Use the phrase 'which means' to show explanation skills.

DON'T FORGET

If you answer a practice paper section by section, try to stick to 2 minutes per mark rule.

THINGS TO DO AND THINK ABOUT

Use other sample papers and past papers to try your hand at an exam under closed book exam conditions. This means keeping the books shut and the phones off. Include words like 'because' and 'therefore' as these show explanation skills.

Useful *explanatory* and *analytical* phrases you might use in your answers:

'This leads to...'   '...because...'   'Compare this with...'   'This supports...'

'Factors include...'   'However...'   'Therefore...'   'Against this...'   'This increases...'

'This research shows...'   'On the other hand...'   '...whereas...'   'This lowers...'

REFERENCES (SELECTED & A-Z)

Aboud FE & Levy SR (2000) Interventions to reduce prejudice and discrimination in children and adolescents. In Oskamp S (Ed.) *Reducing prejudice and discrimination* pp 269–293 Mahwah, NJ: Lawrence Erlbaum Associates

Abrams D, Wetherell M, Cochrane S, Hogg MA &Turner JC (1990) Knowing what to think by knowing who you are: Self-categorisation and the nature of norm formation. *British Journal of Social Psychology* 29 pp 97–119

Adorno TW, Frenkel-Brunswik E, Levinson DJ & Sanford RN (1950) *The authoritarian personality*. New York: Harper and Row

Allen VL & Levine JM (1971) Social pressure and personal preference. *Journal of Experimental Social Psychology* 7 pp 122–124

Allport GW (1954) *The nature of prejudice*. Cambridge, Mass: Addison-Wesley Publications.

Arai M & Mori K (2013) A Questionnaire Analysis of the Asch Experiment without Using Confederates. *Scientific Research: Psychology* 4 (11) pp 888–890

Aronson E & Bridgeman D (1979) Jigsaw groups and the desegregated classroom: In pursuit of common goals *Personality and Social Psychology Bulletin* 5 pp 438–446

Aronson E (2004) *The social animal*. New York: Worth Publishers

Asch SE (1946) Forming impressions of personality. *Journal of Abnormal and Social Psychology* 41 pp 258–290

Asch SE (1951) Effects of group pressure upon the modification and distortion of judgment. *Groups, leadership and men*. Pittsburgh: Carnegie Press

Asch SE (1952) *Social Psychology*. Englewood Cliffs, NJ: Prentice Hall

Asch SE (1955) Opinions and Social Pressure. *Scientific American* Nov.193 (5) pp 31–35

Aserinsky E & Kleitman N (1953) Regularly occurring periods of eye motility, and concomitant phenomena, during sleep. *Science* 118 pp 273–274

Atkinson RC & Shiffrin RM (1968) *Human memory: A proposed system and its control processes*. In Spence 98 KW Spence JT *The psychology of learning and motivation (Volume 2)* pp. 89–195 New York: Academic Press

Axmacher N, Haupt S, Fernandez G, Elger CE & Fell J (2008) The role of sleep in declarative memory consolidation – direct evidence by intra-cranial EEG. *Cerebral Cortex* 18 pp 500–507

Baddeley AD (1966a) Short-term memory for word sequences as a function of acoustic, semantic and formal similarity. *Quarterly Journal of Experimental Psychology* 18 pp 362–365

Baddeley, AD (1966b) The influence of acoustic and semantic similarity on long-term memory for word sequences. *Quarterly Journal of Experimental Psychology* 18 (4) pp 302–309

Baddeley AD (1997) *Human Memory, Theory and Practice* 2nd edition. Hove: Psychology Press

Baddeley AD (2000) The episodic buffer: a new component of working memory? *Trends in Cognitive Sciences* 4 pp 417–423

Baddeley AD & Hitch GJ (1974) Working memory. *The Psychology of Learning and Motivation* 8 pp 47–89

Bahrick HP, Bahrick PO & Wittinger RP (1975) Fifty years of memory for names and faces: a cross-sectional approach. *Journal of Experimental Psychology: General* 104 pp 54–75

Bandura A, Ross D & Ross SA (1961) Transmission of aggression through imitation of aggressive models. *Journal of Abnormal and Social Psychology* 63 pp 575–582

Baron RS, VanDello J & Brunsman B (1996) The forgotten variable in conformity research: The impact of task importance on social influence. *Journal of Personality and Social Psychology* 71 pp 915–927

Bartlett FC (1932) *Remembering: A Study in Experimental and Social Psychology*. Cambridge: Cambridge University Press

Bear MF, Connors BW & Paradiso MA (2001) *Neuroscience: Exploring the Brain*, Second Edition. Baltimore: Lippincott Williams and Wilkins

Bickman L (1974) The Social Power of a Uniform. *Journal of Applied Social Psychology* 4 pp 47–61

Bond R & Smith PB (1996) Culture and Conformity: A Meta-Analysis of Studies Using Asch's (1952, 1956) Line Judgment Task. *Psychological Bulletin, American Psychological Association Inc.* 119 (I) pp 111–137

Born J & Wilhelm I (2012) System consolidation of memory during sleep. *Psychological Research*. 76 (2) pp 192–203

Bornstein RF & Kennedy TD (1994) Interpersonal dependency and academic performance. *Journal of Personality Disorders* 8 pp 240–248

Bousfield WA (1953) The occurrence of clustering in the recall of randomly arranged associates. *Journal of General Psychology* 49 pp 229–240

Bower GH, Clark MC, Lesgold AM & Winzenz D (1969) Hierarchical Retrieval Schemes in Recall of Categorized Word Lists. *Journal of Verbal Learning and Verbal Behaviour* 8 pp 323–343

Bradford E (2011) 'Tidal wave of sleep disorders'. BBC News, Scotland: Health Correspondent, BBC News Online. 6 October 2011

Breuer J & Freud S (1895) *On the Psychical Mechanism of Hysterical Phenomena: Preliminary Communication*. In The Standard Edition of the Complete Psychological Works of Sigmund Freud. Vol. 2, *Studies on Hysteria*. (1955) Translation: Strachey J. Volumes 1–17. London: Hogarth

Breuer J & Freud S (1895) *Studies in Hysteria*. London: Penguin

Brodmann K (1909) Vergleichende Lokalisationslehre der Großhirnrinde in ihren Prinzipien dargestellt auf Grund des Zellenbaues, Barth, Leipzig. Translation in: Garey LJ (1994) *Brodmann's Localisation in the Cerebral Cortex: The Principles of Comparative Localisation in the Cerebral Cortex Based on Cytoarchitectonics*. London: Smith Gordon

Buzan T (1974) *Use Your Head*. BBC Active, Pearson Education Group, Essex

Carskadon MA, Wolfson AR & Acebo C (1982) Adolescent sleep patterns, circadian timing, and sleepiness at a transition to early school days. *Sleep* 21 pp 871–881

Chandra S (1973) The effects of group pressure in perception: A cross-cultural conformity study. *International Journal of Psychology* 8 pp 37–39

Collins AM & Quillian MR (1969) Retrieval time from semantic memory. *Journal of Verbal Learning and Verbal Behavior* 8 pp 240–247

Conrad R (1964) Acoustic confusions in immediate memory. *British Journal of Psychology* 55 pp 75–84

Corkin S, Amaral DG, Gonzalez RG, Johnson KA & Hyman BT (1997) H. M.'s medial temporal lobe lesion: Findings from magnetic resonance imaging. *The Journal of Neuroscience* 17 pp 3964–3979

Craik FIM & Lockhart RS (1972) Levels of processing: A framework for memory research. *Journal of Verbal Learning & Verbal Behavior* 11 (6) pp 671–684

Craik FIM & Tulving E (1975) Depth of processing and the retention of words in episodic memory. *Journal of Experimental Psychology: General* 104 pp 268–294

Crick F & Mitchison G (1983) The function of dream sleep. *Nature* 304 pp 111–114

Crick F & Mitchison G (1986) REM-sleep and neural nets. *Journal of Mind and Behavior* 7 pp 229–250

Crowne DP and Marlowe D (1964) *The Approval Motive*. York: Wiley

Crutchfield RS (1955) Conformity and Character. *American Psychologist* 10 pp 191–198

Czeisler CA, Johnson MP, Duffy JF, Brown EN, Ronda JM & Kronauer RE (1990) Exposure to bright light and darkness to treat physiologic maladaptation to night work. *New English Journal of Medicine* 322 pp 1253–1259

Darwin CR (1859) *The origin of species by means of natural selection, or the preservation of favoured races in the struggle for life*. London: John Murray

Dement W & Kleitman N (1957) The relation of eye movements during sleep to dream activity: An objective method for the study of dreaming. *Journal of Experimental Psychology* 53 (5) pp 339–346

Deutsch M & Gerard HB (1955) A study of normative and informational social influences upon individual judgment. *Journal of Abnormal and Social Psychology* 51 pp 629–36

Dollard J, Doob LW, Miller NE, Mowrer OH & Sears RR (1939) *Frustration and Aggression*. New Haven: Yale University Press

Doms M (1983) The minority influence effect: an alternative approach *Current issues in European social psychology*. Cambridge, Cambridge University Press

Eagly AH (1987) *Sex differences in Social Behaviour: A social role interpretation*. Hillsdale, NJ: Earlbaum

Eagly AH & Carli LL (1981) Sex of researchers and sex-typed communications as determinants of sex differences in influenceability: A meta-analysis of social influence studies. *Psychological Bulletin* 90 (1)

Ebbinghaus H. (1885) *Memory: A contribution to experimental psychology*. Translation: Ruger HA, Bussenius CE New York: Dover (1964)

Espie CA, Kyle SD, Williams C, Ong JC, Douglas NJ, Hames P, Brown JS (2012) A randomized, placebo-controlled trial of online cognitive behavioral therapy for chronic insomnia disorder delivered via an automated media-rich web application. *Sleep* 35 pp 769–81

Espie CA, MacMahon KM, Kelly HL, Broomfield NM, Douglas NJ, Engleman HM, McKinstry B, Morin CM, Walker A & Wilson P (2007) Randomised clinical effectiveness trial of nurse-administered small group CBT for persistent insomnia in general practice. *Sleep* 30 pp 574–584

Espie CA, Inglis SJ, Tessier S & Harvey L (2001) The clinical effectiveness of cognitive behaviour therapy for chronic insomnia: Implementation and evaluation of a sleep clinic in general medical practice. *Behavioural Research Therapy* 39 pp 45–60

Farrand P, Hussain F & Hennessy E (2002) The efficacy of the 'mind map' study technique. *Medical Education* 36 pp 426–431

Fein S & Spencer SJ (1997) Prejudice as Self-image Maintenance: Affirming the Self Through Derogating Others. *Journal of Personality and Social Psychology* 73 (1) pp 31–44

Festinger L (1957) *A Theory of Cognitive Dissonance*. Stanford, CA: Stanford University Press

Fiske ST & Taylor SE (1991) *Social Cognition* 2nd edition. New York: McGraw-Hill

Frankl V (2006) *Man's Search for Meaning*. Boston: Beacon Press

French JRP & Raven B (1959) *The bases of social power*. In: Cartwright D & Zander A *Group dynamics*. New York: Harper & Row

Freud S (1900) *Die Traumdeutung*. Translation by Crick J./Robertson R (Ed.). In *The Interpretation of Dreams*. Oxford University Press (2000)

Freud S (1901) *Zur Psychopathogie zur Altagslebens*. Translation by A. A. Brill: *The Psychopathology of Everyday Life*, London: Fisher Unwin (1914)

Freud S (1909) Analysis of a Phobia in a Five-Year Old Boy ('Little Hans'). In: The Standard Edition of the Complete Psychological Works of Sigmund Freud. Case Histories. Translation: Strachey J. Volumes 1–24. London: Hogarth (1955)

Freud S (1923) *Das Ich und Das Es* Translation by Riviere J: *The Ego and the Id*. Hogarth Press and Institute of Psycho-analysis, London (1927)

Geiselman RE, Fisher RP, MacKinnon DP & Holland HL (1985) Eyewitness memory enhancement in the police interview: Cognitive retrieval mnemonics versus hypnosis. *Journal of Applied Psychology* 70 [2] pp 401–412

Glanzer M & Cunitz AR (1966) Two storage mechanisms in free recall. Journal of Verbal Learning and Verbal Behavior 5(4) pp 351–360

Glucksberg S & King LJ (1967) Motivated forgetting mediated by implicit verbal chaining: A laboratory analog of repression. *Science* 158 pp 517–519

Green DJ & Gillette R (1982) Circadian rhythm of firing rate recorded from single cells in the rat suprachiasmatic slice. *Brain Research* 245 pp 283–8

Hall CS & Van De Castle RL (1966) *The content analysis of dreams*. New York: Appleton-Century-Crofts

Haney C, Banks WC & Zimbardo PG (1973) A study of prisoners and guards in a simulated prison. *Naval Research Review* 30 pp 4–17

Hebb DO (1949) *The Organization of Behavior: A Neuropsychological Theory*. New York: John Wiley & Sons.

Hobson JA (1995) *Sleep*. New York: WH Freeman & Company

Hobson JA & McCarley RW (1977) "The brain as a dream state generator: an activation / synthesis hypothesis of the dream process." *American Journal of Psychiatry* 134 pp 1335–1348

Hobson JA (2002) *Dreaming-an introduction to the science of sleep*. New York: Oxford University Press

contd

Hofling CK, Brotzman E, Dalrymple S, Graves N & Bierce C (1966) An experimental study of nurse-physician relations. *Journal of Nervous and Mental Disease 143*, pp 171–180

Horne JA (1988) *Why we sleep: the functions of sleep in humans and other mammals.* Oxford: Oxford University Press

Huber R, Ghilardi MF, Massimini M & Tononi G (2004) Local sleep and learning. *Nature* 430 pp 78–81

Jacobs J (1887) Experiments in Prehension. *Mind* 12 pp 75–79

Jenness A (1932) The role of discussion in changing opinion regarding a matter of fact. *The Journal of Abnormal and Social Psychology* 27 pp 279–296

Johns MW (1991) A new method for measuring daytime sleepiness. *Sleep* 14 pp 540–545

Jones E & Nisbett R (1971) *The actor and the observer: Divergent perceptions of the causes of behavior.* New York: General Learning Press

Kelman HC (1958) Compliance, identification, and internalization: Three processes of attitude change. *Journal of Conflict Resolution* 2 (1) pp 51–60

King ML (1963) In Hansen DD (2003) *The Dream: Martin Luther King Jr. and the Speech that Inspired a Nation.* New York, NY: Harper Collins

Kohlberg L (1969) *Stage and sequence: The cognitive-developmental approach to socialisation.* In Goslin D A, Handbook of socialisation theory and research. Chicago: Rand McNally.

Krueger JM, Walter J & Levin C (1985) Factor S and related somnogens: an immune theory for slow-wave sleep. In McGinty D et al (eds) *Brain Mechanisms of Sleep.* Raven Press pp 253–276

LaBerge S (1980) Lucid dreaming: An exploratory study of consciousness during sleep. *Doctoral dissertation* Stanford University

Lashley KS (1929) *Brain mechanisms and intelligence: A quantitative study of injuries to the brain.* Chicago, IL: University of Chicago Press

Levinger G & Clark J (1961) Emotional factors in the forgetting of word associations. *Journal of Abnormal Social Psychology* 62 pp 99–105

Lockley SW & Foster RG (2012) *Sleep: a Very Short Introduction.* Oxford: OUP

Loftus EF & Palmer JC (1974) Reconstruction of Automobile Destruction: An Example of the Interaction between Language and Memory. *Journal of Verbal Learning and Verbal Behaviour* 13 pp 585–589

Loomis RJ & Spilka B (1972) Social desirability and conformity in a group test situation. *Psychological Reports* 30 pp 199–203

Loomis A, Newton Harvey E & Hobart GA (1937) Cerebral States during sleep, as studied by human brain potentials. *Journal of Experimental Psychology* 21 (2) pp 127–144

Maguire EA, Gadian DG, Johnsrude IS, Good CD, Ashburner J, Frackowiak RS & Frith CD (2000) Navigation-related structural change in the hippocampi of taxi drivers. *Proceedings of the National Academy of Sciences, USA* 97 (8) pp 4398–4403

Meddis R (1975) On the function of sleep. *Animal Behaviour* 23 (3) pp 676–691

Milgram S (1963) Behavioural Study of Obedience. *Journal of Abnormal and Social Psychology* 67 (4) pp 371–378

Milgram S (1974) *Obedience to Authority: An Experimental View.* London: Tavistock Publications

Miller DT & Ross M (1975) Self-Serving Biases in the Attribution of Causality: Fact or Fiction? *Psychological Bulletin* 82 (2) pp 213–225

Miller GA (1956) *The Magical Number Seven, Plus or Minus Two: Some Limits on our Capacity for Processing Information.* Psychological Review 63 pp 81–97

Mishkin M & Appenzeller T (1987) The anatomy of memory. *Scientific American.* 256 pp 80–89

Mori K and Arai M (2010) No need to fake it: Reproduction of the Asch experiment without confederates. *International Journal of Psychology* 45 pp 390–397

Morris D (1977) *Manwatching: A field guide to human behaviour.* London: Book Club Associates

Murdock BB & Walker KD (1969) Modality effects in free recall. *Journal of Verbal Leaning and Verbal Behavior* 8 pp 665–676

Nisbett RE & Wilson TD (1977) Telling more than we can know: Verbal reports on mental processes. *Psychological Review* 84 (3) pp 231–259

O'Keefe JA (1979) Place units in the hippocampus of the freely moving rat. *Experimental Neurology* 51 pp 78–109

Olton DS & Samuelson RJ (1976) Remembrance of places passed: Spatial memory in rats. *Journal of Experimental Psychology: Animal Behavior Processes* 2 (2) pp 97–116

Oskamp S (2000) Multiple paths to reducing prejudice and discrimination. In Oskamp S (Ed.) *Reducing prejudice and discrimination* pp 1–19 Mahwah, NJ: Erlbaum

Oswald I (1966) *Sleep.* London: Pelican

Paivio A (1969) Mental Imagery in Associative Learning and Memory *Psychological Review* 76 pp 241–263

Pavlov IP (1927) *Conditioned reflexes: An investigation of the physiological activity of the cerebral cortex.* Translation of Military Academy Lectures given in Petrograd (1924) New York: Dover Publications (1960)

Payne JD & Nadel L (2004) Sleep, dreams, and memory consolidation: the role of the stress hormone cortisol. *Learning & Memory* 11 (6) pp 671–8

Penfield W (1958) *The excitable cortex in conscious man.* Liverpool: Liverpool University Press

Perrin S & Spencer C (1981) Independence or Conformity in the Asch experiment as a reflection of cultural and situational factors. *British Journal of Social Psychology* 20 pp 205–209

Peterson LR & Peterson MJ (1959) Short-term retention of individual verbal items. *Journal of Experimental Psychology* 58 pp 193–198

Piaget J & Cook M (1953) *The origin of intelligence in the child.* London: Routledge

Piliavin IM, Rodin J and Piliavin JA (1969) Good Samaritanism: an Underground Phenomenon? *Journal of Personality and Social Psychology* 13 (4) pp 289–99

Plato's Republic (380BC) Translation: Waterfield R (1994) *Plato: Republic. Translated, with notes and an introduction.* Oxford: Oxford World's Classics

Plihal W & Born J (1997) Effects of early and late nocturnal sleep on declarative and procedural memory. *Journal of Cognitive Neuroscience* 9 (4) pp 534–47

Rank SG & Jacobson CK (1977) Hospital Nurses' Compliance with Medication Overdose Orders: A Failure to Replicate. *Journal of Health and Social Behavior* 18 pp 188–93

Rauscher FH, Shaw GL & Ky KN (1993) Music and spatial task performance. *Nature* 365 p 611

Rechtschaffen A & Kales A (1968) *A manual of standardized terminology, techniques and scoring system of sleep stages in human subjects.* Los Angeles: Brain Information Service / Brain Research Institute, University of California

Richard E, Nisbett RE & Wilson TD (1977) The Halo Effect: Evidence for Unconscious Alteration of Judgments. *Journal of Personality and Social Psychology* 35 (4) pp 250–256

Roffwarg HP, Muzio JN & Dement WC (1966) Ontogenetic Development of the Human Sleep-Dream Cycle. *Science* pp 604–619

Rosen RC, Lewin DS, Goldberg L & Woolfolk RL (2000) Psychophysiological insomnia: combined effects of pharmacotherapy and relaxation-based treatments. *Sleep Medicine* 1 pp 279–88

Rosenberg MJ & Hovland CI (1960) *Cognitive, Affective and Behavioral Components of Attitudes.* In Rosenberg MJ & Hovland CI (eds.) *Attitude Organization and Change: An Analysis of Consistency Among Attitude Components.* New Haven: Yale University Press

Rosenhan DL (1973) On being sane in insane places. *Science* 179 pp 250–258

Rosenthal R & Jacobson L (1968) *Pygmalion in the Classroom.* New York: Holt, Rinehart & Winston

Ross L (1977) The intuitive psychologist and his shortcomings: Distortions in the attribution process. *Advances in experimental social psychology* 10 pp 173–220

Salas RE & Gamaldo CE (2008) Adverse effects of sleep deprivation in the ICU. *Critical Care Clinician* 3 pp 461–476

Sassin JF, Parker DC, Mace JW, Gotlin RW, Johnson LC & Rossman LG (1969) Human growth hormone release: relation to slow-wave sleep and sleep-waking cycles. *Science* 165 (3892) pp 513–515

Savard J, Laroche L, Simard S, Ivers H & Morin CM (2003) Chronic insomnia and immune functioning. *Psychosomatic Medicine* 65 (2) pp 211–221

Scoville WB & Milner B (1957) Loss of Recent Memory after Bilateral Hippocampal Lesions. *Journal of Neurology, Neurosurgery and Psychiatry* 20 (11) pp 11–21

Shallice T & Warrington EK (1970) Independent functioning of verbal memory stores: a neuropsychological study. *Quarterly Journal of Experimental Psychology* 22 (2) pp 261–273

Sherif M (1935) A study of some social factors in perception. *Archives of Psychology* 27 (187)

Sherif M (1948) *An Outline of Social Psychology.* New York: Harper & Row

Sherif M (1958) Superordinate goals in the reduction of intergroup conflict. *American Journal of Sociology* 63 pp 349–356

Sherif M (1966) In Common Predicament. *Social Psychology of Intergroup Conflict and Cooperation* pp 24–61. Boston: Houghton Mifflin Company

Sherif M, Harvey OJ, White BJ, Hood WR & Sherif Norman CW (1961) *Intergroup conflict and cooperation: The Robbers Cave experiment* University of Oklahoma Book Exchange

Smith P, Bond MH & Kagitcibasi C (2006) *Understanding social psychology across cultures. Living and working in a changing world.* Thousand Oaks: Sage

Snowman J & Biehler RF (2000) *Psychology applied to teaching.* Boston: Houghton Mifflin

Solms M (2000) Dreaming and REM sleep are controlled by different brain mechanisms. *Behavioral and Brain Sciences* 23 (6) pp 843–850

Sperling G (1960) The information available in brief visual presentations. *Psychological Monographs* 74 pp 1–29

Sperling G (1963) A model for visual memory tasks. *Human Factors* 5 pp 19–31

Squire LR (1987) *Memory and Brain.* New York: Oxford University Press

Stang DJ (1972) *Conformity, ability and self-esteem.* Representative Research in Social Psychology, Department of Psychology, University of North Carolina

Stickgold R (1998) Sleep: off-line memory reprocessing. *Trends in Cognitive Science* 2 (12) pp 484–492

Tajfel H & Turner JC (1979) An integrative theory of intergroup conflict. In W. G. Austin WG & Worchel S (Eds.) *The Social Psychology of Intergroup Relations.* Monterey, CA: Brooks-Cole

Tajfel H (1970) Experiments in intergroup discrimination. *Scientific American* 223 pp 96–102

Tajfel H (1978) The achievement of inter-group differentiation. In Tajfel H (Ed) *Differentiation between social groups* pp 77–100 London: Academic Press

Taylor SE (1981) The interface of cognitive and social psychology. In Harvey JH (Ed.) *Cognition, social behavior, and the environment.* Hillsdale, NJ: Lawrence Erlbaum Associates

Tinbergen N (1953) *Social Behaviour in Animals: With Special Reference to Vertebrates.* Methuen & Co.

Tobler I (2005) Phylogeny of sleep regulation. In: Kryger MH, Roth T, Dement WC (Eds) *Principles and Practice of Sleep Medicine* pp 77–90 Philadelphia: Elsevier Saunders

Turner JC (1982) Towards a cognitive redefinition of the social group. In H. Tajfel (Ed.), *Social identity and intergroup relations* pp 15–40 Cambridge: Cambridge University Press

Tversky A & Kahneman D (1974) Judgement Under Uncertainty: Heuristic and Biases. *Science* 185 (4157) pp 1124–1131

Van Cauter E & Plat L (1996) Physiology of growth hormone secretion during sleep *The Journal of Pediatrics* 128 (5) S32–S37

Van Der Werf YD, Menno EA, Schoonheim M, Sanz-Arigita EJ, Vis JC, Wim De Rijke & Van Someren EJW (2009) Sleep benefits subsequent hippocampal functioning. *Nature Neuroscience* 2 pp 122–123

Von Restorff H (1933) Über die Wirkung von Bereichsbildungen im Spurenfeld. *Psychologische Forschung* 18 pp 229–342

Walker MP, Stickgold R, Alsop D, Gaab N, Schlaug G (2005) Sleep-dependent motor memory plasticity in the human brain. *Neuroscience* 133 pp 911–17

Watson JB & Rayner R (1920) Conditioned Emotional Reactions *Journal of Experimental Psychology* 3 pp 1–14

Wearing D (2005) *Forever today: a memoir of love and amnesia.* Corgi Books

Webb WB (1975) *Sleep: The Gentle Tyrant.* Englewood Cliffs, New Jersey: Prentice-Hall

World Health Organisation (2016) ICD-10: *International statistical classification of diseases and related health problems* 10th revision, fifth edition

Yerkes RM & Dodson JD (1908) The relation of strength of stimulus to rapidity of habit-formation *Journal of Comparative Neurology and Psychology* 18 pp 459–482

Zammit G, Wang-Weigand S, Rosenthal M & Peng X (2009) Effect of ramelteon on middle-of-the-night balance in older adults with chronic insomnia *Journal of Clinical Sleep Medicine* 15 pp 34–40

Zepelin H, Siegel JM, Tobler I (2005) Mammalian sleep. In: Kryger MH, Roth T, Dement WC (Eds) *Principles and Practice of Sleep Medicine* pp 91–100 Philadelphia: Elsevier Saunders

INDEX